THE HACIENDA

THE
HACIENDA

A Memoir

Lisa St Aubin de Terán

LITTLE, BROWN AND COMPANY

Boston New York Toronto London

First U.S. Edition

ISBN 0-316-81634-5
Library of Congress Catalog Card Number 97-76350

10 9 8 7 6 5 4 3 2 1

MV-NY

Printed in the United States of America

For Iseult

1

OVER AND OVER again before I ever went there, I heard the name 'La Hacienda'. It was a place where sugar-cane grew in unimaginable abundance and avocado pears that dwarfed all others. It was a place without any clear dimensions: a frontierless tract of land steeped in history. When I asked where it was, I was always told it was in the Andes, never anywhere specific, just 'en los Andes', as though this mythical *hacienda* were the heart, the living core of a great mountain range. When I asked how big it was, the better to visualise it, the answer was that it stretched for as far as the eye could see and then further. When I asked who lived there, I was told first of the past; it was where the Teráns used to live, and then of the present: it was the domain of *la gente*, the people. Little by little, I discovered that 'the people' in question were tithed peasants of the estate and that they too had lived there for centuries.

And I learnt that the lost man I had married in London was the last of a dynasty of Teráns whose lands dated back to the Capitan Pobladores: the first settlers from Spain who arrived in Venezuela via Santo Domingo on the second voyage of

Christopher Columbus. Everything else I was told thereafter was woven in a tapestry of myth and history. Characters from the past were discussed and criticised with the same familiarity as the cousins who had just left the breakfast table. Time, it seemed, had warped on the *hacienda* and spun its web over all its sons and daughters. It spun its web over me.

Long before I went there, my imagination was fired by the idea of its terrestrial paradise. My husband spoke very little, and when he did it was mostly of the past, not the immediate past but the heyday of the Teráns when they peopled the Andes, trailing their military honours across their plantations. It was as though through sheer nostalgia he could force himself back generations to a time when life had a sense of purpose and his family were worshipped like gods.

My mother came from the Channel Islands, my father from South America. By my first birthday their relationship had ended and a sour silence hung over it. I rarely saw my father. I lived with my three half-sisters and our mother, who was borne down by whatever irreversible trauma the last of her four marriages had brought her. Secretly, as I grew up in south London, wrapped in the alienation of being half-foreign, introverted and unnaturally shy, I longed to be somewhere where I felt I belonged: to not be different. It became my ambition to go to the Andes, to live there off unspeakably hot chilli peppers and tropical fruits.

Until the age of ten, I proposed to become a doctor and to place my services at the disposal of the former Republic of Gran Colombia. After a complicated operation for peritonitis and a subsequent treatment, which involved being lifted in and out of salt baths for several weeks with some of the usually hidden workings of my insides visible as rubber tubes oozed noxious waste round them, I discovered that I was far too squeamish to study medicine. I chose, from my hospital bed, to be an archaeologist instead. During the year that it took me to recover from this bout, I read all I could about South American history the better to prepare myself for eventual field trips to the Andes.

In my early teens, my father sometimes took me on trips to America, Canada and once, when I was sixteen, to the Caribbean and to Georgetown, Guyana where my paternal grandmother lived. He complained that my shyness often crossed the border into rudeness with my failure to acknowledge his fellow diplomats and academics when they chanced to recognise me in London.

When I first met Don Jaime Terán on an insalubrious street in south London, it was a mixture of my father's admonitions and my own yearning for the Andes that made me reply to Don Jaime's abrupt introduction of 'South America' with my own 'Yes.' The next eight months of our courtship rarely strayed into the realm of words. With the help of a dictionary, he asked me, repeatedly and loudly, to marry him. He followed me to school and back, waiting outside on a park bench while I prepared for my Cambridge University entrance exams. He proposed marriage to me at bus stops and in supermarket queues. He became, together with his two comrades Otto and Elias, accepted by my family and friends. Although his proposals embarrassed me, he never really pestered or bothered me, he just followed me: an exotic, handsome shadow wherever I went. He carried an aura of sadness around with him which I found intriguing. His friends deferred to him and pampered him as though he were a rare tropical plant.

I became enmeshed in this situation without ever questioning it. My curiosity was reserved for books. I read incessantly.

The English are notorious for their political apathy and I was no exception. The fact that Jaime and his friends were political exiles and discussed politics in heated debates scarcely penetrated the poetry I was consuming or the Latin or the Latin American geography. I had decided to be a poet. I made up my mind at the age of twelve. I knew that poets were penniless, so I decided to earn my living by archaeology. I had tunnel vision. Whenever I gave my Venezuelan guard the slip, I spent my hours at the National Gallery. It wasn't easy to get away from Jaime, and I didn't often try.

He said he would die if I didn't marry him. He said it was my destiny. I was sixteen and I didn't know then that it was an old cliché, as though, somewhere, there is a little *latino* lexicon of courtship which is learnt by heart in adolescence and then regurgitated to girl after girl.

After eight months, with the help of an interpreter, I married Jaime at the Lambeth Registry Office. He hadn't brought a wedding ring, so my mother, Joanna, gave me one of hers. After the wedding, Jaime and I went to see *Zabriskie Point* at the cinema. My mother, although she was enchanted by Jaime and his chivalric ways, had tried to dissuade me from marrying on general principle: her ample experience of marriage had not been good. I was stubborn. I had decided to do it in a public-spirited way: it seemed to mean a lot to him and it didn't mean much to me. Then I continued to prepare for my exams while the conclave of Venezuelans plotted to decamp to Italy.

Most of the Venezuelans I met in London had been to the *hacienda* and spoke of it as pilgrims do of a shrine. All fruits and flowers were paltry by comparison to its production. No orange tasted as sweet or peeled as easily as the Californian grafts back there. No mango, be it from Fortnum & Mason or Brixton market was ever half as good. Even birds, it seemed, flew less gracefully over English skies than the bluebirds that circled the *hacienda*. It was galling to live in a constant state of negative comparison, surrounded by the second rate. I refused to accept the innate superiority of all things Andean, but I wanted to see for myself this garden of Eden.

Sometimes, there would be as many as twenty Venezuelans staying at my mother's suburban flat. Sometimes it would just be Jaime and me. From the beginning, and for many months, Otto disliked me intensely. He was irked by my ignorance, by my passivity and my Englishness. He was a man on the run for his life; he had been one of the leaders of a guerrilla war in Latin America, then, in his uneasy exile, he conducted another guerrilla war with me. For a year after I mastered Spanish, I kept my counsel and feigned not to understand. Had I read and daydreamed a little less intensely, I would have learnt far more than the nuggets I gleaned from eavesdropping occasionally between tomes.

Gradually I pieced together a scenario of clandestinity, of false documents and myriad illegalities. What emerged, though, was never more than that to me: a scenario. It was a fantasy revealed and sanded down by daily contact into something infinitely duller than the books I read. While Otto nagged me constantly to be less conspicuous, to abandon the Edwardian fancy dress so dear to my heart, to hide and fear as they did in their precarious position, I blundered on without an ounce of courage, immunised to danger by being inanely unaware.

During the next two years I drifted in the wake of the Venezuelan runaways between Paris, Bologna and Milan. I learnt next to nothing about Venezuela beyond the lore and

legend of the Andes, the Teráns and the *hacienda*. Four hundred years of inbreeding had rendered the family a full crop of
eccentricities which were listed and recounted like touch-
stones for the comfort of its sons. Otto and Jaime were
distantly related, as were most of the other exiled Andeans we
met along the way. Only Elias was untouched by the many
taints of the clan, and he too was amused by its carrying on.
The Teráns died young, struck down where they stood by
congenital heart disease. One lived in total darkness; another
lived on his balcony; another was enamoured of a dog called
Jacqueline; another drove her car in reverse until the engine
burnt out and then bought another and did it again; one was
a miser, another a sadist; one was a tramp, another was cata-
tonic; there were a nymphomaniac, an alchemist, and one had
been building an aeroplane in his back yard for twenty years
out of powered milk tins. Everyone spoke of the Andes with
affection, indulgence and pride. I didn't think that what they
said was true; they were stories. On the day of my marriage,
when Jaime confessed to me that he was a bank robber and a
wanted man, I didn't really believe him either. I found his confession vaguely reassuring. At last we had something in
common: he was a fantasist and so was I.

2

Towards the end of 1971, Elias was deported from Italy. In the interim, there had been much discussion about a return to Latin America. In Venezuela, Jaime had been legally exiled, Otto was wanted dead or alive, but preferably alive for some in-depth questioning, and Elias was wanted, preferably dead. So none of the trio could return home, but all were pining for South America. Otto was an old friend of Salvador Allende's, whose position as president of Chile was daily more precarious. Allende was asking for Otto, and Otto wanted to go to him. In the early spring of 1972, it was decided that we would sail at the earliest date to Santiago in Chile.

The group was a kernel of three men, with myself as a peripheral outsider. It changed when an envoy came to London with the news that Jaime was pardoned. A cousin in the secret police sent word that the news was not a trick; Jaime was free to return to the *hacienda* whenever he wished. And he wished. For the first time since I had known him, he became eloquent. He took on all arguments on the subject, ending with what became his inevitable edict: he wanted to go home, he wanted me to go with him, and he'd rather die than do anything else. Meanwhile, Otto had been drip-feeding me a love of Chile and a desire to go there. He counted on me to change Jaime's mind. I was promoted from camp follower to member of the junta. While Jaime slept, Otto, Elias and I made plans of how we could stay together. They told me the details of their past, the present and their future. I saw their trip to Chile as Byronic. For the first time, I felt an urge to do something rather than read about it.

While I dreamed of the southern Andes, Jaime dreamed of his own. He was like a fish out of water. He attributed his monumental lethargy and his growing melancholy to a home-sickness that was destroying him. Sometimes he spoke of the things we could do on the *hacienda* together, of the improvements we could make. He spoke of *la gente*, the workers who were waiting for him.

I was torn: I was far closer to both Otto and Elias than I was to Jaime. I had married a stranger and a virtual stranger he had remained. I had thought, at first, that he hardly spoke to me because I didn't speak Spanish. It was only after I learnt to speak Spanish that I realised that he just didn't talk. Most of his thoughts were translated by his friends. When he stopped, as was his wont, in the street in London or Paris or Rome, and stared up at the buildings, I was told that he was comparing their height, in his mind's eye to the chimney flue of his sugar furnace. It was the tallest chimney in the Andes. When he stared at motes of dust drifting through a slice of light, I was told he was thinking about the *hacienda*. When he lay for days at a stretch in bed with his eyes half-closed, I was told he was missing his lands.

I failed to persuade Jaime to go to Chile with the others. Instead, he promised that we would go to the *hacienda* for a year, after which, if I wanted to leave, or the others still couldn't join us there, we would find them again and resume our communal peregrination.

Otto warned me not to go. He told me I'd never get back; the year would last for ever and I would die there of loneliness or neglect. He told me that I would never be accepted. He said the family would hate me for not being one of them, for having married Jaime, for stealing him, for being nobody. The malign gossip of the town would swallow me up. I would be starved of books and company; starved of life. 'It'll smother you,' he said. 'And Jaime will change. You should never let him go back there. If you care for him at all, you should stop him from ever going back.'

But I had married Jaime, and he kept telling me that if I cared for him at all, I had to go there, to the *hacienda*. He said he wouldn't go without me and he had to return.

Our last few months in London had been ones of waiting. Jaime had a seemingly endless supply of cousins. One of them, day by day, was going to send us two tickets from Southampton to La Guaira. The strain of the non-arrival of these tickets was such that Jaime took to his bed, sleeping twenty-two hours a day. The tension of his two waking hours was such that I conquered my passivity and arranged for our sea passage myself. I didn't have any cousins, but through friends of my parents I tugged a few strings and we sailed courtesy of Booker and Co., the sugar magnates of Guyana.

I had said goodbye to my mother and sisters, neighbours and friends so often in weekly expectation of our departure that it had begun to feel like a very bad pantomime dragging on past its season. We none of us had much more emotion left to squeeze into a last farewell. My trunks had been packed and repacked until I knew their inventory off by heart. Apart from our cabin luggage, we had two big trunks of books, one of clothes, one of miscellany and one which was packed and donated by my mother and comprised what she felt I would need as a survival kit in the tropical wilderness I was heading for. It contained many medicines, a Tilley lamp, scalpels, knives, firelighters, a hard hat, wellington boots and that mainstay of all English women travellers, a pile of gaberdine squares. Last, but not least, we had two tea chests of Pedigree Chum dog food and a dozen sacks of mixed meal biscuits.

Jaime's grandfather, Don Rodolfo Terán Labastida, had been the only adult male survivor of a massacre carried out against the Terán family in 1905. The lower part of his face had been shot away and then replaced in New York by a platinum jaw. While this platinum jaw was being made and fitted, Don Rodolfo bought himself a beagle puppy which he called Redi. When Don Rodolfo returned to the *hacienda*, he took Redi with him. Once there, in the spirit of the Teráns of old, Redi fornicated across the length and breadth of the state of Trujillo, stirring his pure genes into thousands of mongrels. Thus the beagle became both familiar and prized. By carefully breeding back, cousin to cousin, for fifteen generations, almost full-blooded beagles were running around by the hundred. Jaime assured me that it would be impossible to return to the Andes without an accompanying beagle hound. In the event, we took two, with pedigrees of unrivalled champions and a string of surnames as long as Jaime's own. They were a belated wedding present from my mother together with travelling kennels, export permits, collars and leads.

The sugar magnate's ships didn't sale to La Guaira, so he arranged for us to sail on a Spanish vessel, the *Montserrat*, that did. It sailed from Southampton to Venezuela via Vigo, La Coruña, Tenerife and Trinidad. It seemed, though, that repeated goodbyes were to be the order of the day because three days before we were due to sail, the ship caught fire in her dock and the voyage was postponed for a further three weeks.

Otto had instructed me to take nothing with me that could incriminate anyone else. I was to have no addresses, telephone numbers or photographs other than of my immediate family. Being a compulsive hoarder, I had ignored his warnings and taken a writing box full of such mementoes. As the ship pulled out of sight of Southampton, I had second thoughts about them. I tore them up and scattered them overboard, where they fell into the sea like confetti for the following gulls. It was done less through a fear of the future than a need to break away from the past. I had been told to forget my two years of travelling and to recreate them as an extended honeymoon. Jaime explained to me the countries I was to say we had travelled in. 'Why?' I asked. Then he introduced me to the law of his country. It was a dictatorship that ruled over the nominally democratic government, it ruled over the secret police and the army, the church, social hierarchy and friends. It was called *Qué dirán?* What will they say? What will people say? It was all about not losing face. So I had to pretend that the time since my marriage had been spent on glamorous travel staying at villas and fine hotels, not sleeping on railway stations. Jaime assured me that everything would be fine. I would be treated like a princess. I was reassured. I have always been easily reassured. He also promised me, during the first hours of our voyage, that our sons and daughters would also be treated like royalty too. This was less reassuring: after six months of treatment at the best sub-fertility clinic in London, I had been told I could never have children. I was barren, sterile, and Jaime knew this well. My sterility was said to be a side effect of my childhood TB. In that first moment of my new life, it seemed best to remind him of this. He interrupted me, 'Never tell anyone you were tubercular,' he said. 'If they knew you'd had the tiger on your back, no one would speak to you; remember that.'

As I tore up the ties I had to my known world, I tried to visualise the place I was going to. The *conquistadores* saw the raft-like huts of the Mayan Indians floating on the surface of Lake Maracaibo, a city built on water, and they called it little Venice. The Indians stepped from raft to raft across the lagoon, unsteady on their feet. Now I was sailing there on a raft of deceit.

We travelled first class in a luxury marred only by the presence of our two beagle hounds. The *Montserrat* was part of the Spanish line. It had Spanish staff and Spanish food and Spanish ways. Spaniards are not renowned for their love of dogs. While we had a berth draped in blue satin, Ross and Megan, the dogs, were locked into a sheep crate on the upper deck. There were only five first-class passengers on the ship and the meals were long and lavish. However, after each one, I had to release the sad, sea-sick hounds, swill out their crate, feed and walk them and then scrape up their scattered excrement and tip it into the sea.

It was my first sea voyage and it fulfilled my romantic fantasies. I leant over the deckrail for hours at a time watching the translucent fins of flying fish dip into the Atlantic Ocean. I made friends with a man from the United Nations and a missionary bound for the Orinoco basin. To them, I described what I thought my life as a sugar planter would be, in a place of unequalled natural beauty. They asked me what I'd do if I didn't like it, if it wasn't as I dreamt. I assured them that this could not be. I refused to worry: things had to work out; I had burnt my bridges. At least for a year, I had to stay. It was May, and it was hot. Once the sea-sickness of the first few days eased and we had cleared the Bay of Biscay, I thought of all the flowers of the tropics, of orchids and wild bougainvillaeas, of humming birds and bluebirds, and of myself planting a garden in the foot-hills of the Andes with all the seeds my mother and I had bought and packed. When any doubts occurred, I blocked them out by thinking up all the metaphors for the sea I could imagine. The days passed slowly and yet I felt them pass with some regret, my life was in suspension on board; after the vagaries of the last two years I was enchanted by the sheer luxury. Although, as though to prove the French saying that 'La vie est une tartine de merde', in between my hours of basking, I hitched up my gown and ballasted my dreams clearing up after my two incontinent dogs for the sixteen days of our sailing.

A further guy rope to tug me back from my state of bliss existed and took a first hard pull on my first night on board. I discovered that the Spanish I spoke so fluently was socially unacceptable. I had learnt to speak it from three men, and I spoke like a man and swore like a trooper. In English, I was a linguistic prude. As a child, it had amused me (and irritated everyone else) to adopt the archaic parlance of Jane Austen. By the age of eighteen I had dropped eighteenth century usage, but I never swore. Otto had explained many things to me, but never that women spoke one way, and men another.

The chief steward came to our table accompanied by two more stewards. One arranged my starched napkin in my lap, another served me water. They were all smiles hovering around their special guest, me, the child bride. With great deference, the chief steward asked me what *hors d'oeuvre* I would have and whether I would have cod or brill. I turned to him, believing myself to be as polite as a girl in a first-class dining room can be on her best behaviour, and asked, 'What the fuck is cod?'

The three stewards backed away from our table. Then they regrouped and returned some three minutes later and continued to serve with a chill disdain. I pointed to my order, as I would for the rest of the voyage. The Spanish language had opened the doors of spontaneous communication to me. It had lifted me out of the mostly silent world I had locked myself in. Now I would have to relearn Spanish and learn to recognise and eliminate the obscenities and profanities that I used so freely.

3

As the *Montserrat* sailed within sight of the port of Guaira, Jaime, who was a man given to pacing, began to pace the upper deck compulsively. The lower half of his face was set strangely, as though calcified with tension. When I spoke to him, he stared through me with noble disdain and not a flicker of recognition. Together with my deep and serious reading, I was also an inveterate secret reader of comics and women's magazines. The latter were full of tips about the male menopause and how to cope. Since I had married a man who was more than twice my age, I attributed many of my husband's emotional eccentricities to the all-embracing symptoms of the male menopause. He had so clearly exhibited the first: a sudden passion for a schoolgirl. With two recalcitrant beagles wrapping their leads round other passengers' legs while trying simultaneously to yank me into the sea, I had little time other than to register that my husband didn't seem to know me.

A cousin, who was a general, was supposed to be meeting us. He didn't turn up. I was jostled down the gangplank, hard put to keep my feet for the pulling dogs. It seemed the dogs should have stayed in their travelling kennels. A swarm of

National Guards came to examine their papers. The luggage was unloaded, hurled down from the hold on to the concrete quay. As passengers saw their possessions splintering and spilling, a scene of collective hysteria ensued. Meanwhile, like a ventriloquist's dummy, Jaime tensed and relaxed his partial grimace.

As we left after our short stopover in Trinidad, he had instructed me on how to get through customs and immigration. If he himself were arrested, he told me how to get to Caracas and who to ask for help. He told me to make my way through customs without him because it would be easier and not to let the dogs out of my sight. However, nobody wanted to steal Jaime's liberty that day, they just wanted to steal our luggage, all of it, and they particularly wanted to steal the dogs. The customs hall was divided like a children's playground, striped and checked in coloured chalks as though for some elaborate hopscotch. No passenger was allowed to touch his or her own baggage, it was all moved by porters. Each porter corresponded to a particular zone, a strip of colour. After crossing each colour frontier, the porters had to be paid off. They insisted on being paid before they started too, a bribe to haul a trunk two metres across a dusty floor and another bribe to let go of it. On the quayside, outside, people were wailing, laughing, chattering and squabbling. Inside, they just screeched at each other and gabbled, cursing as the porters held the entire ship's baggage hostage to their avarice and caprice.

The money I had saved, and the money I had been given, was disappearing at the rate of knots. The charges, displayed on a blackboard were approximately two pounds per bag, but they were two pounds every few seconds. The alternative to paying seemed to be not only the confiscation of one's goods (and dogs) but the prospect of never getting out of that mad carousel of a customs hall. As my luggage inched forward across the expensive strips of no man's land to a new colour, I began to suffer from battle fatigue. The few hundred pounds I had scraped together to set myself up in the New World were almost exhausted, even my private hidden stocks of squirrelled dollar bills were finished. I saw no hope of completing the customs stick-up intact, and had no idea what to do at the other end of it should I be lucky enough to get through. Jaime had wandered off somewhere and been gone for what felt like a long time.

Across the hall, he was returning, no longer vacant in his look. Behind him was an older man who looked disturbingly like Jaime, striding and waving his arms. Behind him, was a younger clone. The former was in full military regalia and his arm-waving had some effect in the hall. In less than half an hour he had all our trunks and the kennels loaded on to a pick-up truck and a boy sitting astride them to keep guard.

Some twenty minutes away from the port on the road into Caracas, we stopped at a low ranch with a tin roof and sat on a veranda festooned with puce bougainvillaea and encircled by litter and Pepsi Cola bottles. The cousins had come to the quayside in time, but had somehow failed to see us, and suspecting foul play, they had embarked and had the ship searched. Having come away with nothing more than some flat tins of quince jelly and some excellent brandy, they had eventually caught up with us at customs.

I drank coconut water and ate fried chicken with maize cakes and peppers, smiled and spoke as little as I could. The sixteen days aboard had been insufficient to clean up my vocabulary and lax syntax. The hounds got some water and their Pedigree Chum. Tree-frogs and cicadas competed with the exchange of voices, excited whispers and the tuneless bleeps combined to form a tropical sedative. There was a general air of drowsiness.

My first impressions overlapped, wrapped in the heat. Wherever we went people stared so persistently that I hardly had a chance to see them. The maxi-skirt, then in vogue in London, had not, it seemed, reached Venezuela before I disembarked in mine. My floor-length dress produced not only surprise but hilarity. Girls, in particular, were reduced to helpless giggles. At lunch the waitress in her short cotton frock and plastic slippers was unable to serve us and laughed so hard she had a fit of some kind, which the general attributed to intestinal worms.

The landscape was lush and green and peppered with makeshift shacks made out of breeze blocks or wattle and daub and, sometimes, just sheets of rusty corrugated iron. The cars were American, the driving aggressive and haphazard. The dogs I saw were mangy and rickety and made such an obvious contrast to the plump pampered hounds on the back of our truck that I felt embarrassed to have brought them. We drove through stretches of poverty, and then by the Highway to Caracas.

I knew Caracas had skyscrapers because I knew that in the earthquake of 1968 a section of the city called Los Palos Grandes had crumpled to the ground. I knew that Venezuela was oil rich and corrupt. Los Palos Grandes had been built without foundations. Ninety per cent of what I had heard about Venezuela was about the *hacienda*. I suppose I was expecting everything to fit the descriptions of a sugar plantation. The big, modern, bustling Americanised city of concrete highrises came as a total shock. Where was the jungle? Where were the snakes? The boa constrictors and the mapanares, the monkeys and pumas, where were they among these slick concrete sidewalks? I felt completely disorientated. I began to imagine the *hacienda* as a place of concrete towers wreathed in tropical flowers. I had braced myself to live in the wilds, instead I found myself in a place obsessed by the spending and display of wealth.

Everyone talked all the time at the same time, scarcely listening, just gabbling over, and the talk was all of money and designer names. Not arriving in the latest Caraqueñan fashion (which was several years behind London) made me as grave a disappointment to my hosts as they were to me. Not showing the visible signs of well-tended wealth was my first unforgivable *faux pas*. My hair was long and loosely pinned up by myself, it bore no hairdresser's stamp. Only peasants did their own hair. My nails were unmanicured, my face unmade-up. Despite my high-collared long-sleeved long dress, I appeared scandalously naked.

The men mixed with men, the women with women. Upon arrival, I was handed over to the ladies. Not wishing to add insult to injury, I spoke as little as possible, not wishing to loose a string of oaths into that cream of Caraqueñan society. It was thus assumed that I didn't speak or understand Spanish and what might otherwise have been said in private was said in my hearing. I was plied with orange juice, mandarin juice, pineapple juice and papaya juice, sat down in a big creaking leather armchair and then dissected forensically.

The general consensus of opinion was that I wouldn't last a week out in the wilderness. Somewhere between pity and mirth, my plight was discussed and settled. In Valera, where I was being taken, they would scratch my eyes out on arrival On the *hacienda*, if at night I turned my back, someone would stick a knife in it, as had happened to so many others. I had no natural command, no style, no class, no *cachet*. I was heading for a place of savages, wilder than the Wild West. Jaime would be safe. Jaime was a Terán, but I was obviously a nobody and was bound to perish there together with my adorably pure dogs. Ross and Megan's pedigrees were discussed and it was thought ironic that the hounds were acceptable while I was not. Why hadn't Jaime married a wife with a pedigree, instead of worrying about the dogs? It was typical of the Teráns, it was the Labastida surfacing. And wasn't it a shame to take such fine livestock to behind God's back? Would it be possible to persuade me to leave the dogs in Caracas?

The leather on my chair creaked. It was brand new. Everything around me was new, tended by subdued Indian girls in shifts and plastic flip-flops who shadowed round the room with their eyes permanently glued to the polished marble floor.

'And then she doesn't even speak cristiano? Doesn't speak at all? Do you think she can?' Was I half-witted? And where had I come from (in that terrible dress!)? Who were my family? Who was I? Nobody, obviously nobody.

I wondered if it would be better or worse to speak. To do so would be to show I understood what had been said about me, not to do so was to invite more of the same. It wasn't ever a serious dilemma, it would take years of practice to get a word in edgeways with a gaggle of women. It was a skill I had yet to learn.

We had arranged to spend five days in Caracas. Within an hour of arriving, Jaime announced that the five would be two. I counted the hours while the tally of my faults and misde-meanours unfolded before me: Jaime Terán was the most eligible bachelor in the Andes and had never married in all these years despite who knew what opportunities. And now he'd married this mute child, which was strange really; and if she was half-witted . . . well, it would be tragic, what with the inbreeding over the last few centuries. Goodness knew what would come out, but it probably wouldn't come to that. I probably wouldn't last more than a few weeks, or a month, which was probably best under the circumstances . . .

Mosquitoes hummed incessantly round the room and tree-frogs croaked from a courtyard while the disapproving voices droned on and on . . . 'And no children. Do you think they are really married? Perhaps he picked her up on the ship . . .'

I wanted to leave, to be left alone, not to have my teeth discussed, or my nose or feet. Venezuelans have tiny feet, I have not. It was too much of a jump from the demure non-committal society I had grown up in. Personal remarks were bad enough, but this was personal demolition. I was hurt and cowed. I didn't know then, as I do now, that I had arrived in a society where malign gossip and character assassination are part of the daily diet. It is a technique universally applied to friends and rivals alike. I had come to a place where words were used between friends, about friends and between family about family. Words, however nasty, were friendly, you didn't waste words on enemies. Hatred and silence went hand in hand: two sinister colleagues. Silence was objectionable. It would be the same on the *hacienda*, no one used words to destroy an enemy; if someone really didn't like someone else, they'd just kill them.

The scalding criticism was part of a ritual. Had I been honest and admitted to understanding Spanish, most of the comments would have been spoken behind my back. Had I had the confidence to speak for myself, to bring news and interest into their lives, I would have made a better candidate for adoption into their hermetic society. To a certain extent, they took their cue from my husband, and he was distant to me. Then they took their cue from me and I was afraid to talk, afraid to mention Otto or Elias or any of our other friends, afraid to start dropping don'ts: don't say we were poor, don't say my mother was married four times, don't say I write poetry; don't mention TB, don't tell them anything about Italy, don't slouch, don't . . . It didn't leave much for me to be or do. I had to invent myself and I hadn't done that yet.

Meanwhile, my first taste of Latin America was playing havoc with my insides and I needed a bathroom. I waited at least an hour for some fissure in the talk to ask for one. There was no gap, not even a hairline crack; I would have to speak over like everyone else. Their voices were all louder than mine. I would have to shout over them all and the caged parrots too. I honed down my question, checked it for indecencies, practised it and then called it out. Nobody heard me and my need was great. I yelled,

'Donde está el baño, por favor?'

One of the ladies dropped a cup and the fine porcelain handle landed beside my size seven shoe as though the breakage were my fault too. A bell was rung. A maid slip-slopped in to mop up. Nothing else happened for a few seconds and then as though a record had been put back on at full volume, the conversation resumed exactly where it had broken off. I stood up and called again. This time I was escorted to the appropriate room. Behind me a wave of criticism covered my tracks . . . 'Isn't she tall? Terrible posture, so rude . . .'

Five minutes later, the key that had turned so easily to lock me in, wouldn't let me out. I tried again, waited, retried, and after what I knew to be an inexcusably long time, I panicked. I called out in the hope that one of the servants would hear me. There was no response. It was a big house. I called again, waited, hammered on the door and finally gave up and decided to climb out of the window. It was long, thin and horizontal and it was high up on the wall. It gave on to a balcony full of caged canaries. By standing on the lavatory cistern, I was able to hoist one leg out of the window, and then my head. I was just pulling the seven metres of Swiss voile that made up the skirt of my Edwardian dress when the lady of the house came out on to the balcony to commune with her canaries. Our eyes met, she studied what I was doing without comment and then I climbed down while she returned to the sitting room. I followed her and sat like a lizard that has just crawled out from under a stone until I was collected and dropped at the next household.

My last visit was to an aunt who travelled yearly to Europe, read books, collected antiques, bred orchids and lived in a gentle haven above the city. Publicly she cast her not insubstantial vote in my favour.

Before we left Caracas, we visited yet another cousin who was confined to a clinic for the criminally insane. Apart from the two armed guards in the entrance hall, this clinic looked exactly like a rather smart house. The cousin in question greeted us effusively and then accompanied us to a bar some streets away. He explained that upon being convicted, he had bought the clinic in question, moved it to its present pleasant neighbourhood, staffed it with his friends and shifted some of his favourite cellmates in with him. Since he was the boss, he could come and go as he pleased, and had done for some years. I asked him what he'd been convicted of and he told me, 'I murdered my wife.'

That night we set off for the *hacienda*, Jaime and I, the beagle hounds, our luggage, and another accompanying cousin. It was a ten-hour drive. By the time we reached Valera, news

of our arrival had preceded us to the Andes. Even my climbing out of the lavatory widow had been added to the litany of
criticism that passed from house to house. I had heard Valera
referred to as La Caldera, the cauldron, because it was where
gossip, scandal and sheer malice were said to simmer constantly. We would be staying in Valera for a mere three hours
before making the last short leg of our journey to the *hacienda*
itself.

We were already in the foot-hills of the mountains. On
either side the road was flanked by fields of sugar-cane. The
cousin was at the wheel. As we approached the first straggling
slums on the outskirts of the town, Jaime suggested that we
drive straight through and go directly to the *hacienda*. I crossed
my fingers. The cousin refused.

'Just drive on.'

'I can't.'

'I'll explain it later, just drive on. I want to go home, it's
been four years!'

The cousin refused.

'*Qué dirán?*'

Jaime closed his eyes and let himself be driven like a lamb
to the slaughter to the Plaza Bolivar, the main square, to greet
his kin. It was his world and it embraced him. I put the dogs
on their leads and walked them around the square and then I
waited, leaning up against the truck for him to be done with
his reunions. Some children came out to talk to me, they
were shy but persistent and we whiled away some time. In two
houses, I was called and sat and sipped sugar water with
lemon while Jaime the silent regaled the household with tales
of his travels. I felt something change in me: a spark of character emerged. I determined to manage on the *hacienda*, to
cope on my own, no matter what. I realised what Otto had

been trying to explain to me: on the *hacienda* I would be on my own. I wouldn't be able to count on the man I'd married.

Waiting to go up to the *hacienda*, I began to compose a letter in my head to my mother. I would have to describe the things I saw and did. I would have to edit my life, recounting it by the stepping stones between the lies of omission. She suffered from depression, she worried about me, we had always been very close. She needed me to have a good marriage, to be happy. She had told me not to marry so young, not to marry across culture and language; now I would have to hide from her whatever hardships came my way and string all the good things that came along like beads on a rosary to show to her. I began to gather the beads, to tell them myself for comfort, to have a parallel life that ran more smoothly than my own.

4

CLIMBING UPHILL AWAY from Valera towards the village of Mendoza Fría, the lands of the *hacienda* began unannounced by anything more spectacular than a ragged clump of banana palms which the accompanying cousin pointed out to me. Then the land stretched on either side of the road along the wide valley. To the left the River Momboy ran its course parallel to the road. The fields of sugar-cane and scrub rose gently into hills and then on up into crumpled steeper slopes, wooded and tangled save for swathes of pale pink where the *capín melado* grass crowded its pink tassels on to the small plateaux. There was an entire palette of varying greens culminating in the blue-greens of the horizon.

I asked how much of what I saw was the *hacienda*. The cousin told me, 'If you look up to the crest of the hills for as far as the eye can see, that is the *hacienda*, and then there's a valley on the other side and that is the *hacienda*, and then it runs up to the far range of hills beyond it.'

'And on the other side of the road?'

'That is the *hacienda*.'

'And beyond the hills there?'

The cousin nodded and drove on, climbing steadily along the road overhung with jacaranda trees. After a few minutes, we braked slightly by a dirt road and a small stone bridge, 'That's where Calichano lives.'

'Who's Calichano?'

The driver shrugged and shook his head as though I should have known. We drove on for another five minutes or so in silence. I was trying to memorise the things I was seeing, the sweep of the river, the clusters of huts on the hill, and to find names for the shades of green I kept seeing, differing beyond my vocabulary. To the right there was a high escarpment that blocked out any view beyond the jumble of ferns and grasses and hanging roots that bound the black earth to its bank. To the right, fields of sugar-cane obscured the river. Every time we passed a hut or cottage of any size, my heart leapt to feel some instant recognition and affection for my future home.

I knew that the big house, 'La Casa Grande', had been rented out for some years to a grilled chicken restaurant called 'Los Pollos de Eladio'. Eladio had been given six months' notice to quit, this was his fourth month and so for eight weeks we would be living in the little house, 'La Casa del Trapiche', a cottage by the river near to the sugar factory or *trapiche* itself. Having heard so much about the big house, about its arches and balconies, its cantilevered green marble staircase and its courtyard with its giant avocado tree upon which my deceased father-in-law had grown prize orchids, I was disappointed not to be going there. However, I was pretending not to be, and pretended so successfully that I had persuaded myself that rather than arrive at a beautiful Spanish colonial mansion and a courtyard full of hibiscus, it would be a pleasant adventure to live like a pioneer in a small cottage with a tin roof and a cement floor and the near-by millstream as the only source of running water. Since every house we passed was small and had a tin roof, I was ready for each and all of them. But we drove on, slowing abruptly to turn on to a dirt road on the left, then downhill to the river and the bridge. At the end of the road, was the famous chimney flue, round, red brick and towering over the valley. Beside it a sea of pantiles undulated across the factory building, sloping down to a tin roof the size of a small field. Under this roof and spilling on to the track that ran beside it was the straw-like *vagasse*, the crushed and dessicated sugar-cane used to fuel the furnaces. We bumped along the lesser road at an angle from the bridge until we came to some old planks bridging the millrace, and the house I was to live in was before me.

It had a pillared veranda almost as big as the house. It was ten metres long and three metres wide, the pillars were chewed tree trunks. There was a small barred window at the front. Right in front of the veranda, leaving only a passage a metre wide where the old road, the *camino real*, had once run its cobbles from Valera to Mendoza Fría, there was a gigantic bamboo tree. The clump of bamboo was as long as the house and some thirty metres high. It overshadowed everything else, and was impressive and awe-inspiring. It was the sort of botanical specimen I had longed for. Momentarily, I lost interest in the house, its potential squalor or grandeur, its size and position. The bamboo, the old road and the veranda seemed enough: they justified my journey.

I swung my legs over the steep edge of the veranda and contemplated the Andes as filtered through the colossal bamboo. The hounds were released and then tied to tree pillars beside me. I felt a strange sensation of having come home, of being somewhere I belonged. Ross and Megan had succeeded in half-strangling themselves on their leads and were dangling over the edge of the veranda, choking. I disentangled them and walked them around the house. The big room had once been a general store and had the dilapidated look of something out of the American Deep South. It was made of wattle and daub, roofed in tin; and someone had very hastily whitewashed it inside and out, so recently that the lime smelt fresh. It had two small windows and high rafters pierced with hooks. The floor was of a substance I could not immediately identify: it was compacted dirt. Behind the long room was a much smaller open-roofed space. The building was loosely arranged and had been added to; the general store was the oldest and biggest part, and the additions enclosed a small courtyard. There were two small empty half-derelict store-rooms, a kitchen, which was recognisable by the black smoke ingrained in each of its walls and its low ceiling, and a workshop. The kitchen had no windows, in fact it had nothing at all. The workshop, on the other hand, was as pretty as a country cottage can be, with four large shuttered windows, a proper door, a pantiled roof, brick walls and a jasmine plant cascading over its façade. There was no bathroom. I had been so taken by my place on the veranda I hadn't seen the others leaving. When I looked around I didn't know where they had gone.

The entire valley had begun to shake, echoing and thudding in the most alarming way. The dogs were frightened. The tin roof was rattling up and down. Between thuds there was a clanking-creaking which I eventually located as coming from the sugar factory. I dragged the dogs uphill to where an enormous hydraulic wheel was turning.

I looked down at the cavernous brick pit of the wheel while its iron shafts thumped round. It was too loud to speak and be heard. When we moved away, I heard that this was how the workers were summoned on the estate. Its clanking resounded and vibrated along the valley and could be heard by the foreman in his house on the hill. Releasing the millwheel was a summons, leaving it loose signalled an emergency. In times of disaster, the wheel could gather the entire workforce to the factory.

Within minutes, a man came hurrying along the road to the main bridge. He was tall and very dark. His skin was an ashy charcoal, his hair was tight grizzled curls. As he walked, the tooled leather scabbard that he wore strapped to his waist swung like a sword. He was gaunt with a beaked nose and high, sucked-in cheeks. His mouth was thin and twisted in a smile. His eyes were dark and rheumy. He wore a faded check shirt and baggy canvas trousers, short on the leg. For shoes he wore woven sandals. His gait was uneven, gangly, unvarying in its haste.

When he saw Jaime, he embraced him and held him tightly for some time. The muscles in his face were twitching. He held on as though if he let go he would fall down. As he approached, I thought he was a man of about fifty, gripped by emotion he looked more like sixty. In fact, he was seventy-eight. He was Antonio Moreno, the foreman of the estate. He had worked on the *hacienda* since he was seven years old. His father had been foreman before him, and his grandfather had fought in the War of Independence. Otto had told me he would be the one person I could trust. Antonio told us he had seen the truck, they all had, he hadn't needed to hear the wheel, he was already on his way down. 'And the others, *la gente?*'

They were all there, on the hill across the way, they had all seen our arrival, were all watching. I looked across the landscape and could see nothing but occasional curls of smoke rising out from among the trees in the middle distance. I saw no one.

Antonio welcomed me to the *hacienda*. He walked us back down to the little house. He apologised for it. Jaime had insisted that we needed nothing except for two hammocks. There was no furniture in the house, if we needed anything, we should . . . Jaime cut him short, we needed nothing, we were fine. They unloaded the trunks on to the veranda. Antonio came out and thanked me for returning Jaime to them. He seemed quite distraught. He asked if he should send his wife or daughter down to help. Jaime said no, we wanted to be left alone. We needed to rest. We wanted to be left alone. Antonio left us and then Jaime left to drive his cousin back home. He said, 'Ya vengo.' It meant, 'I'll be back in no time.' I knew it didn't mean anything. Venezuelans have a different concept of time. Jaime had said that under no circumstances was I to go into the workshop, it had been his father's, it was sacred, out of bounds.

The waterwheel had been tied still. I walked the dogs a little way along the *camino real*. Clumps of white lilies grew wild along the bank of the river, their scent filled the air. Beyond the bamboo, there were other trees, guava and mango and a hummock of banana palms that had died in the centre to make a clearing encircled by the translucent hanging leaves of newer palms. It occurred to me that there might be snakes in the dead leaves. I went back to the house. I opened a trunk and took out some books, I opened another and found the Bath Oliver biscuits my mother had packed. The bottle of Pepsi Cola the cousin had left for me had filled with ants. I didn't mind, I didn't like fizzy drinks. I unpacked a repast of Pedigree Chum and bonemeal biscuits for the dogs, arranged their kennels near me, fed, walked and settled them in their mobile homes. Then I sat on a trunk and ate biscuits and read. Within twenty minutes the light began to fade, and two minutes later it had gone, leaving me in the dark. I have never liked the dark. I am afraid of it.

I was surprised to notice that I was not afraid of the dark any more, *per se*. I felt more frustrated at not being able to read, at not being able to go anywhere, and not having anything to drink, and after I had eaten half a tin of dry biscuits, at not having anything to eat. I began to distinguish between the sounds: there was the trickle of the millrace, the whoosh of the river, the constant monotonous whistle of the cicadas, the call of birds, the sound of breeze running through the feathers of the sugar-cane, the rustle of insects in the tall grass, the patter of what I later saw was a gecko who lived in the rafters. There was the snuffly breathing of the dogs in their kennels. There was the whisper of cockroaches scuttling across the floor. There was a squeaking of bats, another squeaking which I later found to be rats. There was the whirr of mosquitoes.

I thought for a while of all the things I would do, starting in the morning in this my new life as a pioneer. I thought of the knife and the hat that I had bought at the Army & Navy Stores for Antonio Moreno and wished that I had brought him more. I thought of my books and looked forward to unpacking them. Far across the river and the road I could hear the throb of Mariachi music drifting down from Los Pollos de Eladio. There was a blur of light around it. At one point, a waft of grilled chicken reached me. Los Pollos de Eladio was even more out of bounds than the workshop. What would happen if I found my way there and got myself half a chicken in chilli sauce? I knew something had happened but I didn't know what. No one in the family spoke to Eladio. There was a feud.

I fell asleep, curled up on top of a trunk and was woken by Jaime returning just before midnight.

'Why,' he asked, 'was I in the dark?'

On looking round the house, I had seen a solitary lightbulb hanging high over a rafter, but I had seen no switch anywhere in the house. In lieu of switches, the bulb had to be screwed into its socket. It was considered miracle enough to have electricity at all without resorting to such nonsense as switches.

I seemed to be the only person who found it strange that my first evening should have been spent alone.

That night I slept in a hammock slung over a beam. In the morning, I felt much older than my eighteen years and stiff and cold in every joint. It had been so hot in the day and hot in the evening, how could it be chilly in the morning? And yet it was, and would be every morning until the sun climbed over the hilltops and warmed the valley again.

In the morning, I rose and washed in the cold millstream. I was thirsty. Then I let the dogs off their leads and spent the next four hours chasing them. When I returned, Antonio Moreno and a boy, Antonio José, his son, were building a bamboo palisade back and front where the courtyard opened out. Jaime, in his shirt-sleeves, was helping them. I had never seen Jaime working before, he was naturally very apathetic. Seeing him hammering and cutting the thick bamboo, I believed that perhaps he had been right and all he needed to do was return to the *hacienda* to function properly. I thought that perhaps if we could get through these first few weeks, it might be possible for Jaime to run the *hacienda* after all. He had been in prison, he had been in exile, and now he had come home. It was bound to take some re-adjustment. I would manage as best I could, all I really needed was something to eat. By mid-afternoon the fence was finished. I suggested that we go and get something to eat. Jaime said he would go. It seemed the curse of lethargy was breaking. He left. Antonio left with his son, and I stayed back and began to plan a garden inside the open prison they had made for me and the two beagle hounds.

5

WHEN I SAY that my first impression of the *hacienda* was one of having found my home, it is true. Yet it was a first impression and it was followed by many others. The place on the veranda where I eventually slung my hammock was my space, it was not a sensation that was echoed anywhere else in the house, most of which filled me with a feeling of alienation, loneliness, and often, despair.

I unpacked the trunks and arranged their contents in the big bare room. The dogs, who had passed their first puppydom and progressed to a delinquent adolescence, systematically gnawed their way through everything I had brought. Only what was left locked back in the trunks or hung over the high rafters escaped their relentless chewing. Books, records, clothes, ornaments and medicines alike fell prey to their teeth. If I let them loose, they ran away. They could run for hours at a stretch. When we bought them, their proud breeder had boasted that a beagle could run for thirty miles non-stop. Each time they absconded, I would catch sight of the white tips of their tails erect above the pink grass of the clearings in the wood.

At first, I chased them, running and scrambling across the vast estate, calling. But I rarely caught them, and it was so exhausting to run in the sun, and so hard to find my way back guided only by the brick flue of the *trapiche*'s furnace that I gave up and left it in the lap of the gods that they would return. Week by week the palisade around the little house was heightened, strengthened, mended and improved, and week by week they found ways to escape from it.

I felt imprisoned by its bamboo stakes and barbed wire. If I opened either of the windows, the dogs jumped out of them. Had they not been a wedding present from my mother, I think I would have just let them go; as it was, they were my link to her. She loved them and would be coming to visit me and them before the year was out.

It began to rain within days of my arrival and then it rained every day. I had only been to the tropics once before, in the middle of the dry season. I knew that it rained in the rainy season, but despite growing up in London, I didn't know that it would be like a daily drowning or that it would last, almost without respite for six months. It reduced my small courtyard to a muddy trench, it dripped through the tin roof and gave the floor a slimy patina. It hammered on the roof so loudly that no other sounds were audible above its drumming. It mildewed the contents of the trunks. It covered my shoes with a nap of green mould every morning. It washed away the seeds I had planted. It filled the stretch of road from the bridge to my house with almost impassable ruts. It swelled the millrace and it flushed innumerable snakes out into the open. And it caused the electricity to fail for days on end, depriving me of the comfort of my one lightbulb.

I was left very much to my own devices, sometimes for several days on end. Every day Antonio Moreno came by to say hello. He stayed for a few minutes, hovering uneasily outside the house, and then went on his way. If Jaime was there, they would go off together and talk by the *trapiche*. Mostly though, Antonio would ask for him and I would tell him he wasn't there. On the third day, Antonio brought his daughter, Coromoto to meet me. She was so shy she hid behind him, covering her dark face with her hands.

'She'll come down every day,' he told me. 'If you need anything, tell her.'

She did come down every day, often dragging a small brother behind her, but she hid at the corner of the workshop wall and refused to come nearer than shouting distance for some weeks. She just stood and watched me with her black eyes wide in wonder at all she saw, frowning in such a way that her already crowded features looked permanently cross. Both Coromoto and her baby brother turned out to be good at catching the escaping beagles. In order to hand them over to me, she had to let me approach her. After which ordeal, having survived unscathed and unbitten, Coromoto came up to the palisade. Eventually her curiosity got the better of her and she began almost to impale herself on the bamboo stakes to lean over and look round the house. Then one day she came in, and she stayed, coming and going regularly, jealous of her post as confidante.

Jaime came back to the *hacienda* less and less and Antonio Moreno tailed off his visits to me accordingly. Coromoto came in his stead. Asking her for the things I needed was not always easy. More than anything else, I wanted food, but I didn't see how I could ask her directly, given the obvious poverty of her clothes and those of the half-naked Goyo, the brother she often dragged in her wake. I thought that the best solution would be to get out, to get off the *hacienda*, if only to do some shopping, and then return. I had virtually no money left; enough maybe to buy hard rations to last a month. A sack of rice, for instance, for me and the dogs. I had brought a dozen tins of tea from Jackson's of Piccadilly. I brewed up water in a used milk tin and then drank from a Russian bowl I had brought with me.

The windowless, lightless kitchen was half a metre lower than the storerooms behind it and filled with rainwater. Since cooking meant making a campfire, I chose to do this on the veranda. Coromoto used to watch me, intrigued. She asked me what I was drinking and I told her, 'Tea.' She looked instantly sad, 'Are you ill, Doña?'

Nothing I could say would convince her that I was not. Tea was used only medicinally on the *hacienda*. It was a cure for dysentery and lesser diarrhoeas. I drank tea every hour. Coromoto ran back and spread the news.

Two hours later Antonio Moreno came hurrying down the hill. He wore a straw hat and there were points on the neighbouring hill at which I could discern the top of his hat coming down the track long before he reached me.

Was I ill, did I need a doctor, should he walk to Mendoza Fría and get help?

I reassured him, and he accepted my explanation. He was a man of the world. Living among the Teráns for nearly eight decades he knew a lot about eccentricity, and if someone wanted to consume vast quantities of medicine for pleasure that was their prerogative.

When I first arrived on the *hacienda*, I felt ashamed. I was ashamed to be so personally inadequate that despite my relatively pampered upbringing I was unable to provide for myself. And I felt ashamed that the person I had married had brought me to a place and left me without any food. It was the absence of food that rankled. Had we both been in the same predicament, I could have forgiven him, but I knew that he must be eating. He was going into town regularly, sleeping over. It seemed like the greatest betrayal. I was not particularly disturbed by what else he might or might not be doing; it was the food. I thanked God for the tea I had brought with me even though, despite living on a sugar plantation, I had to drink it sugarless. I thanked my mother for the Bath Olivers and the shortbread biscuits that she had packed. The tea was lasting, but the biscuits were soon gone. Ross and Megan had managed to open the third and last tin and had demolished the lot before I found them. I chased them for several miles along the edge of the River Momboy with a view to killing them at the time. Antonio brought me down a hand of bananas.

Each time Jaime returned, I tackled him on the subject of food, trying every ploy from tact to hysteria. He seemed scarcely to recognise me, he had no idea what I was talking about. Sometimes I seemed to get through and he would leave, supposedly to bring back supplies. He didn't return, though, and apart from a cheese and ham sandwich I once found in one of his pockets, he never brought anything edible back with him.

The work I was doing was hard. I chased the dogs, I shovelled mud out of the house, I carried big boulders up from the river to use as stepping stones across the courtyard. I partially dammed the millrace so that when I sat under its mini-waterfall to bathe it didn't keep bodily washing me downstream. I was hungry.

Meanwhile, every night, from across the river and across the road, strains of music and a fragrance of grilled chicken continued to lure me. I had seen the end of the big house, La

Casa Grande, that I had heard so much about. It was on two floors. Underneath it there were three wide arches, above a long wooden balcony. On either side of the arches was a wing, each with large shuttered windows. While chasing the dogs, I had been in places on the *hacienda* from where I could look down on the rest of it. It was well named, it was indeed a big house.

After a week, a lady drove up to the *trapiche*, parked her car by the mounds of *vagasse* and picked her way over the pitted path to me. She said her name was Zoraida and she was an old friend of Jaime's. She was clutching two brown paper bags in her hands.

'I brought you these,' she said, holding up a bag of ripe tomatoes, 'and I hope you don't think me silly, but Jaime always liked enamel things like *la gente* use, I brought you some.'

She held up the other bag and opened it to show two scarlet enamel mugs and two matching plates.

I asked her in, but she wouldn't stay, she said she'd come back later when Jaime was there.

'Do you like it here?' she asked as she was leaving.

'It's beautiful.'

'Yes, but . . .'

Then she left, hopscotching over the broken path, caught in the rain. After she left, I kicked myself for not having jumped in her car and gone with her to wherever she was going. The arrival of the tomatoes had temporarily allayed my pangs and my shyness had got the better of me. Things that I could not say to Antonio Moreno and Coromoto, I might have been able to explain to her. For several days following her visit, I walked the dogs up and down the *camino real* along the river bank for fear of missing Zoraida when she returned.

I sliced the tomatoes up with the Wilkinson's pruning knife I had brought (in duplicate) for future grafting of the avocado trees. Then I ate them off a plate *al fresco*, which was more *al* drizzle and they brought back to me the pleasantest memories of Italy.

At the time I arrived on the *hacienda*, my natural response to all difficulties was to cry. During my two years in Italy, I felt that I had matured enormously by the timing of my tears. Where once I had cried spontaneously at every setback, I now waited until I was on my own to weep. I wept for nostalgia over the tomatoes. Then the rain increased and drove me in off the veranda to sit on a trunk and wait for it to cease and there I began to remember more clearly the Italian idyll I was missing so. Things had not, on the whole, gone well in Italy. My life there had been more squalid than anything else. While there, I had constantly contrasted my plight, being married as I was to a Venezuelan grandee, to what life would be like in the lap of luxury on his mythical *hacienda*. Now that I was on the *hacienda*, I was already harking back to Italy.

If it rained any more, I thought, I'd be buried in mud. If I cried any more, I would drown in my tears. Would someone else be acting like me in this predicament? Would someone else be as inept? I was living on a vast plantation that, by marriage, was half mine. I was hungry. I had chewed endless green stringy mangoes and picked the worms out of dozens of hard, thin-fleshed guavas and bloated myself on tea, but it just wasn't going to be enough. Antonio's bananas had helped, but they too were running out and they already made me sick. All this for nothing. I was living opposite a restaurant. It was eight minutes' walk away. I had timed it with the new watch I had bought in Tenerife. I had never used a watch before, and now that time had become meaningless I had one to measure it by. What did I care for the Terán pride when it came down to choosing between it and starvation? I would wait three days, and if in that time no food was forthcoming, I would defy the ban and go to Los Pollos de Eladio and eat.

Otto had warned me many times not to underestimate the importance of pride in the Andes. 'And the Teráns . . .', he would say, shaking his hand as though their pride was so huge it defied description. 'They kill for it out there.' But I was too shy and embarrassed to ask Antonio for food. And Otto had also told me almost every day since I'd met him that I was ridiculous. It was ridiculous to live in darkness on the one side of the River Momboy doubled up in a hammock with hunger cramps, while a restaurant served chicken and chilli to the sound of Mariachi music on the other side. I had two fifty *bolívar* notes left, squirrelled away. Each one was worth over five pounds, which in 1972, in Venezuela, was, I knew, enough to dine out on for many days.

Coromoto came, wet through in her cotton frock. I asked her why she never wore a cardigan. She told me, simply, that she didn't have one. She had two frocks, one in the wash and one on. I gave her a cardigan of mine which floated on her. She was eight years old and stocky but very short. She was afraid to take it and ran away. Later that afternoon she returned with Antonio.

'Tell him,' she said.

Tell him what? I was obsessed by my forthcoming treason. I was going to go to La Casa Grande. How did Coromoto know that? I hadn't told her. I'd asked her once about it and she'd said that they all boycotted the place. They couldn't afford it anyway, but it was a desecration. Doña Antonieta, my mother-in-law had rented it out while Don Jaime was in prison. It was a disgrace. All the Teráns were turning in their graves. No one from the *hacienda* worked there, and they skirted round it in a big detour so as not to see the house defiled. Eladio was a peasant, *un peón*. This last was an interesting verdict, because I was under the impression that Coromoto was also a peasant, *un peón*. She explained, everyone on the *hacienda* was *gente*, people, Eladio was the *peón*. He had no ancestors to vouch for him, he came from nowhere, there was no tradition to hold him up.

'Go on, Doña, tell him.'

I blushed. I was a big blusher.

'The jacket. Tell him.'

'She's to have a jacket,' I told Antonio.

'No, Doña.'

'Yes. I want her to take it.'

Antonio bowed his head. I fetched the jacket and gave it to her. After they left, Coromoto with my mother's hand-knitted cardigan flapping round her knees, I realised I had tasted my first sip of power. I could not be contradicted if I insisted.

6

THREE DAYS PASSED and nothing happened except the dawn broke, as it did every morning at half-past five, and lit up the pockets of rising mist in the hills. At half-past nine, the sun climbed over the crests and steamed the valley. At irregular intervals during the day, the rain abated and it was hot and blindingly bright. The tin roofs heated up to the point where, had I had an egg, I could have fried it on them, then the rain began again, battering down. At seven fifteen, the sun dropped like a reluctant firework behind the hills and bats replaced the birds in the sky.

By day the valley was scented with the cloying sweetness of wild lilies blended with the rich moist smell of tropical under-growth. Overlaying this was the residual fermented sweetness of the piled *vagasse* and a sickly smell, which was also strangely sweet, of decomposing flesh. Circling vultures pin-pointed the sources of the last. One or two could always be seen hovering somewhere along the valley, ready to tear the meat off whatever carcass was on the day's menu. Since there was no rubbish collection anywhere in the neighbourhood, there was always something for the vultures.

By night, the musty smell of mould competed with the heavy fragrance of the *dama de noche*, the night-flowering jasmine that grew all over the end of the workshop.

My resolve to defect, albeit very temporarily, to the despised Pollos de Eladio, was stiffened by the total absence of my husband during the three days of my waiting.

I spent hours deciding what to wear. From my brief sojourn in Valera, I had seen that the average Valerana of any class wore very tight pink slacks, high-heeled sandals, big frilly blouses and voluminous bows around a neck cut low enough to display substantial necklaces of gold ingots and assorted jewels, earrings to match and costly knuckle-dusters. Hair was worn variously dyed and rigorously permed, lacquered and cut in styles that required a daily, *de rigueur*, visit to the hair-dresser's. Make-up was heavy and bright. Hands were always professionally manicured, feet were pedicured and nails glistened in varnished hibiscus colours. Most of the women were short and it was fashionable to be plump. Given this, it was impossible for me to look normal; my dilemma was how to look as unalarming and unridiculous as I could.

I settled on the dress I had been married in: it was the plainest one I owned and it was only three-quarter length instead of trailing on the ground. I put on stockings for the first time since I had arrived, took my hat, and taking advantage of a gap in the rain, I ran along the path in the dark towards the music and the light of Los Pollos de Eladio. When I reached the corner of the *trapiche*, I turned towards the bridge and made straight for the big house, crossing the road and climbing up the hill directly in front of it to the arches.

The light that had seemed so bright from afar was dimmer as I clambered up the hill towards it. The grass was wet, the track uneven and muddy. I told myself it would be unforgivable to turn back. I had to go on. When I finally reached the steps up to the arches, I felt quite drunk with adrenalin. I was disconcerted not to be greeted by the noisy, busy dining halls I had braced myself to face. The first hall led on to another and then another, each arched and empty. However, the smell of frying chicken fat was unmistakable, and the sound of music was beating out from what still sounded like a long way off. I followed it and my nose, through the high hallways, across their tiled terracotta floors, through the series of arches and on to a long wide corridor that opened on to undergrowth on one side and a series of rooms with closed doors on the other. A solitary, uncovered lightbulb half-way along this corridor threw its dim light over the house. I heard voices, loud shouting voices and I called out. The voices stopped, leaving only the cicadas and the croaking of frogs. I called again, 'Oh.'

It was the same thing I had shouted out the first time and it was all I was capable of. I heard whispering and a muffled scuffle, louder whispering and then a door opened and a red-eyed half-dressed, half-drunk young man emerged and glowered at me.

'What do you want?' he demanded. 'What are you doing here?' He put his face quite close to mine and I inhaled a gust of aniseed. Behind him, a girl was rearranging her thin, ragged dress.

'What's she doing here? Who is she? How do you know her? Who is she?' she shrieked at the man. I took a step back and mumbled, 'Los Pollos de Eladio.'

'Who is she? What's she doing here?' the girl insisted. Her face was contorting with rage.

The young man completely ignored me, and turned to placate his girlfriend. 'I swear by my mother and the blessed virgin, I have never seen her before.'

The girl pushed past him and pushed me, forcibly in the ribs, 'Where did you meet him?'

This was not the scenario I had mapped out for the evening, not even remotely. This was supposed to be my evening, my moment of betrayal and it was supposed to be about food and pride. Not wanting to be unduly selfish, I pulled myself up from my habitual slouch and interrupted the jealous flow that was spilling over me.

'Look, it's quite simple. I have come to Los Pollos de Eladio.' It seemed simple to me, but the couple were certainly drunk, and possibly slow-witted and it took some minutes to learn that the music I heard nightly came from their transistor radio. The food that I smelled was their supper. They were custodians for Eladio. Los Pollos de Eladio had actually moved to another location and might or might not be returning soon. They didn't know how soon, they thought perhaps next year. They didn't know how far away the restaurant now was, they thought very far. The question, who was I, remained uppermost in their minds. If I wasn't going to get my chicken, then I wasn't going to tell them. They were both befuddled on rotgut rum and with any luck, by morning, they would imagine they had dreamed my apparition. Since they were ostracised by everyone around them, there would be nobody to tell of my visit. I slunk back to the *trapiche* and stumbled through the night, thankful that the new moon which made my steps so hard to find might also be hiding me from prying eyes. It was ten o'clock.

Coromoto had told me that they were all asleep by an hour or so after sundown. There was no electricity on the *hacienda* beyond the *trapiche* and the big house. *La gente* lived by the sun. And they were like me afraid of the dark. Whereas my fear was a general uneasiness, theirs was very specific. El

Coco, the Bogey Man walked the night. I crept back to my little house, feeling very guilty and very stupid.

I had taken to going to bed early myself, to read and think and mope in the company of the snoring beagles, bats, mosquitoes and a number of tiny mice and much bigger cockroaches. Both hounds barked and bayed as I approached. I hoped, since they barked and bayed at the rustle of every passing frog, that their frenzy would not draw attention to my clandestine outing.

When I got back, I couldn't sleep. I wondered what would happen if Jaime got to know of what I had done. I rocked in my hammock on the veranda and pondered how best to deal with my plight. I decided to deny it, if asked, to say I hadn't been there. I went in and changed my dress, hiding the offending garment at the bottom of a trunk. I did my hair differently and waited. Although my mission had been a failure, I felt better for having been. I had done something, albeit pathetic, but I'd done it instead of drifting passively on whatever current might carry me along. I realised, as never before how absurdly passive I was. The very next day I would ask Coromoto where her family bought their food and that would be that.

The *hacienda* was peppered with mud huts, one or two rooms long with tin roofs and palisades of sticks like my own. Each of these huts had a row of milk tins in front of it, filled with various plants. One windowless room was generally the kitchen and permanently filled with smoke from a brush fire built between three flat stones. The better-off workers had a kitchen table, the poorer families had rough benches and a few logs and stones for the children to sit on. A well-stocked kitchen had three aluminium pots, a coffee can, a hot plate of cast iron, a battery of enamel mugs and bowls and half a dozen spoons. Food was chopped up with a machete. When the men of the house wore out their machetes on the sugar-cane, the old one passed into the kitchen. Water was carried in used kerosene tins from the nearest spring to the house in a long trail, in which even the smallest children took their turn. Morning and afternoon, the water was lugged up and downhill to the kitchens. Brush for the fire was gathered daily, again by the children, and carried back in big bundles. Everyone carried things on their heads. A cloth was wound into a tight ring, placed on the crown and then the heavy tins were hoisted on. Coromoto showed me how it was done. Each household kept three or four chickens and a pig which scrabbled around in the mud and dust (depending on the season) within the palisade.

Coromoto pointed out some of the homesteads visible from the top of the *trapiche*. She told me a string of names each linked to one another, mapping out the *hacienda* by the intricate relationship between each family. There were Zara, her mother, and Antonio, her brother Antonio José, Goyo and Capino, her baby brother, and Ernesto too. Then there were Petra and Natividad, plus Josefa, his wife and Maria, their only daughter and four or five children of Maria's, who was daft, and kept going off and coming back pregnant. 'She's bewitched,' Coromoto confided, 'by Antonio Mejia, but he's in love with his donkey. Every year, he comes back for Maria and takes her off. They live under the bridge down the road. Then he sends her back with a big belly. Luckily most of the children die or poor Natividad could never feed them all. Maria never does any work, she just sits on the path and combs her hair, waiting for her boyfriend.'

Then there was Abigail, 'She's a bitch and we don't talk to her. She's got five sons.' Then there was Eladio. 'He's got air in his brain.'

'How do you get that?' I asked.

'He saw an eagle.'

'And?'

'And he got air in his brain and El Mudo is his son and he doesn't speak but he could, he just won't. He's never spoken.'

'Then how do you know he could speak if he never has?'

'He just could.'

Then there were Abrán and Matilde his mother and the Briceños. Every time Coromoto mentioned the Briceños, she rolled her eyes.

'What's that supposed to mean?'

She'd shrug and refuse to say while implying that if she did choose, there was no end to what she could tell. The list grew and grew, and grew more confusing. I asked her if she could write the names down for me. She shook her head. She couldn't write.

'Well, how many families live here?'

'Thousands.'

She didn't know how many thousands were, she couldn't count. Thousands, in *hacienda*-speak meant more than ten.

The *hacienda*, I learnt, was criss-crossed with feuds. Entire families were not on speaking terms with other families and hadn't been for generations. I tackled Coromoto on the ones she listed as being enemies of her own. She didn't know what they'd done, it was before her time, she just knew never to speak to them, to cross the road if they approached, to cut them dead.

On the morning after my abortive visit to the big house, I waited for Coromoto to come. She usually reached me at about eleven o'clock, which was when she had finished doing her morning chores. She was always punctual. She had shown

great interest in my watch and I had done my best to explain
the use of a clock to her. She seemed to think that it made an
interesting bracelet, but couldn't understand why I should
need to be guided by a piece of metal on my wrist when all
you needed was the sun. Then she showed me how to tell the
time by *tanteo*, by guessing from the sun. It worked to within
fifteen minutes.

Buses and trains had been a lot more difficult to explain.
Coromoto loved to get me trying, and delighted in the stories
that I told. Story-telling was a well-respected art. There was
no television on the *hacienda* and none of the workers could
read or write. Stories were told and handed on, gathering
momentum and detail like barnacles on a ship's hull as they
passed from mouth to mouth. She didn't believe many of my
stories, but she enjoyed hearing them retold; she learnt and
repeated them, spreading news of technology to her family and
friends. She found the notion of trains particularly enchanting.
Since travelling anywhere further than up and down the hill
was considered a pointless exercise, Coromoto could not
understand the necessity for any form of public transport.
Why would anyone want to go away? The only people to
leave the *hacienda* were the boys who were pressganged into
the National Guard. No one in their right minds would choose
to leave. And given that roads were made of tarmac, cobbles or
dust, why would anyone waste good iron and lay it on the
ground? My whole story was palpably a figment of my imagination, but it was one that Coromoto liked to probe. She
made me describe the carriages and the engine, the plush
seats, the luggage racks, the steps and wheels. When I told her
that people travelled on trains for days on end, she tried to
catch me out with all sorts of trick questions. How did they
eat? How did they pee? I told her about the bathrooms and the

buffet cars. The logistics of running water on a train were the part that Coromoto loved best. She had never seen a lavatory or a wash-basin, but she knew what taps were and she knew that they ran on water piped from a stream. The transference of this natural phenomenon to an articulated metal snake filled her with admiration. When I came up with tales like the moving metal and the mobile taps, I carved a little niche for myself in her estimation. I was quite obviously useless at all normal pursuits, but I gained points for fantasy.

The day after my escapade, Coromoto didn't materialise. I waited until five o'clock for her and then took to the hills with the hounds. This time, instead of passing the wicket gates of the muddy yards and huts, I started going in. My presence was greeted with a mixture of reactions that ran from embarrass-ment to suspicion and fear. The workers and their families scuttled back into their huts, grouped in silence until I left again. I discovered later that there is nowhere more formal than the Venezuelan Andes. Nobody speaks to anyone unless they have been properly introduced. The world extends for two days' walk either side of their homes, beyond there is nothing. Columbus's sailors could scarcely have been more afraid of falling off the edge of the world than *la gente* were of venturing beyond the parameters of the land they knew.

In the uplands, known as *el páramo*, was the town of Timotes. Further down there were Valera and Trujillo; these were the places that foreigners came from. During my time on the *hacienda*, I gathered that cities like Mérida, Barquisimeto, Maracaibo and Caracas were also there in the common par-lance, but geographically they were not in their rightful places. The *gente* believed them to all lie somewhere between Timotes and Trujillo, within the net of the state of Trujillo, in the Andean state, and never beyond, because there was no beyond. The road ran through the *hacienda* and the surrounding valley of the Cañada de Mendoza, the *gente* were Mendoceros. Beyond the frontier of Carmania to the north and the village of Mendoza Fría to the south, nothing was considered to be of interest or importance. Theirs was a society sealed against outsiders and proud of it. The only contact with the outside world was the road; and the road was treated like an evil force to be contended with. It was believed to be a source of contamination as dangerous as cholera. The road was avoided.

The further away from the road people lived, the greater their fear and superstition about it. Over the crest of the first hill and in the valley and hill beyond, virtually no one had ever ventured as far as the road. Each household elected one member to travel out for supplies. Once or twice a month, this sacrificial victim would set out with his donkey and brave the horrors of the road in order to barter goods for salt, sugar, sardines, *fideos* (a spaghetti of sorts), chocolate pellets, machetes and kerosene. The tales they told of the twentieth century fomented their families' phobias. Their inexperience with traffic often ended in accidents, confirming everyone's belief that the road was a bad and greedy monster that swallowed up lives and spat them out as a heap of mangled bones.

While I lived in the Casa del Trapiche, the road itself was a deterrent to would-be visitors from the *hacienda*. But the greatest deterrent of all was the fact that I was a stranger and strangers brought nothing but trouble. I was an outsider. Anyone who didn't share the blood of the others in their veins was an outsider. Antonio Moreno was different, he was one of them but also a mediator between the Teráns and *la gente*. He was a man of the world, a rich man who owned a cow and lived in a hut with three rooms. He knew about outsiders, he had married one, his wife Zara came from outside Mendoza Fría. Her neighbours would always criticise her and look askance at Coromoto and her four brothers. They were Antonio Moreno's children, so there could be nothing overt, just an undercurrent of distrust, a whisper of disapproval. Coromoto was wayward and headstrong, she flaunted convention. She pulled rank, hiding behind her father to hang around by the road. She had told me that her neighbours were cross with her for coming daily to consort with me. They warned her away and taunted her.

When she didn't come to see me, I wondered if she had succumbed to her neighbours' pressure and decided to stay away. I also wondered whether I had been spotted visiting Los Pollos de Eladio and been sent to Coventry as a result. I didn't know the ways of the *hacienda* then, I didn't know that they didn't talk to strangers, so I thought the surrounding silence was personal rather than general.

The next night I lay in my hammock and tried to devise ways of breaking through, of raising a greeting at least from *la gente*.

By day I traipsed around the hills, getting lost, finding my way, trying to cull something other than suspicious silence from the huts I visited. Since Coromoto hadn't come to me, I was also trying to find her. It seemed easy from a distance to locate Antonio Moreno's cottage; it was longer than the others, and, like my own, there was a big bamboo near-by. But the valley was planted out with overgrown sugar-cane which obscured everything from view. The tangled paths between the fields were like tunnels cut through the stalks. It was like travelling through a maze. Every path looked identical to the last and I continually lost my way. Above the cane-fields, on terraced slopes, there were groves of low avocado trees. Where the avocados ended, the scrubland began.

It was only after hours of exploration that I located Antonio Moreno's home, which I recognised by the presence of a naked Goyo sitting in the mud shelling black beans from their pods into an enamel bowl. He looked up, saw me and started to scream. A woman came running into the yard. It was Zara. She was shy but friendly, she didn't speak to me but from her soothing of her son, I sensed that I could go in and talk to her. I followed her up two long steps made out of levelled tree trunks to the veranda of her hut. Along the edge were dozens of pots, pails, buckets, rusty saucepans and used milk tins all planted into a garden. There were rosemary and sage, geraniums and petunias, a rose, a hibiscus, an oleander; there were coriander and parsley, poinsettia, tradescantia and swamp palms. Some of the tins had bare sticks stuck in as cuttings, others had already sprouted their first leaves. The overall effect was very pretty. Zara saw me admiring them and giggled. She was prone to giggling nervously in lieu of speech.

My arrival threw her into a fluster of housewifely worries. She dusted the one chair on the veranda and invited me to sit down, she shouted to Goyo to put some clothes on and to make a broom and sweep the porch. She called to another child to shoo the fat-bellied pigs that were snuffling around my boots into their pen. She shooed a cloud of chickens off the porch, she called for brushwood to stoke the fire, she called Coromoto to get up and help, and she kept apologising for the mess, repeating over and over again, 'Doña, perdón.'

'I thought I'd come and say hello,' I told her.

'It's all dirty.'

'I just wanted to say hello.'

'It's the rains, it does this . . . the mess . . . the children, and Coromoto ill . . . COROMOTO!'

Zara was fair-skinned. She had grey-brown eyes with a permanently bewildered expression in them, as though she had just put something down and was looking for it. Her hands were big and raw, her pale upper arms were as well developed as a man's while the rest of her frame was skinny. She was flat-chested. As we spoke, she kept smoothing her dress down and smoothing her lank brown hair, apologising for her appearance, wiping at mud and oil stains on her dress. Her feet were bare, her toes splayed and horny. She bobbed on and off the porch, fanning a fire that I heard her coaxing and then threatening. Each time she returned, she had made some slight adjustment to her appearance; added the woven *cotiza* slippers to her bare feet, swept back her hair anew with a comb, washed her face so hurriedly the sweat and grime had smeared grey streaks down her young face. She was twenty-six years old to Antonio's seventy-eight. She loved him with a passion that had started when she was fourteen and had eloped with him from La Casa Grande where she had been employed as a washer-woman. When I knew her better, she would say, at least once a visit, 'Look at my arms, look at the muscles, I got them from ringing linen for the Teráns.'

Coromoto emerged from the end room looking gaunt and weary. She looked thoroughly miserable and told me she had an attack of worms.

'When I cough, they come out of my nose.'

Zara chided her, I wouldn't want to hear about her illness. I tried to say something sympathetic, but neither Coromoto nor her mother seemed to want that. Illness is treated differently there; it is something to be ashamed of. It merits no sympathy and gets none. Only babies are cosseted when they are ill. Coromoto roused herself and set about helping Goyo to make a broom while Zara brewed up coffee and brought me some.

A bundle of branches from an escoba bush had their stems forced through the empty cylinder of a sardine tin together with a stout stick. Then water was scattered from a standing kerosene tin and the loose dust on the mud floor was raised into a smother, mostly to resettle a few steps further along, some to be tipped over the edge of the porch.

The coffee came, served scalding in an enamel mug so hot the handle burnt my hand. There was about a quarter of a litre, thick and strong. I drank it all except the residue of dark grey sludge at the bottom of the mug. It made me quite light-headed and brought me out in a sweat. Outside the rain had started again. I had tied my dogs up at a stake by a big lemon tree outside the palisade, where they were attempting death by strangulation while Zara's two mongrels hurled themselves at the fence in a frenzy of barking. Zara sent a child to serve them some milk which they promptly tipped down the hill. I watched it spill.

'It doesn't matter,' Zara said. 'I use the milk to make cheese and the whey for the pigs. The children can't drink milk; it's bad for them.'

Zara had a baby on her lap who climbed down at that moment and tottered away.

'Doesn't the baby drink milk?'

Zara giggled and stared at me.

'Milk would kill him.'

'What does he drink then?'

'*Guarapo.*'

'Which is?'

'Sugar boiled with water.'

'He lives off that?'

Zara smiled a broad grin of wide teeth.

'No, Doña, he drinks *guarapo* with *guaca*.'

'What's *guaca*?'

'*Guaca*.'

Every time Zara spoke to one of her children, they replied 'Señora', even the little ones.

The rain beat down with torrential force, drumming on the tin roof and splashing on to the porch. Coromoto, who was so talkative at my house, was almost silent, leaving me to struggle with her mother's embarrassment. Zara kept asking nervously, to no one in particular, 'Will it ever cease to rain?'

From which I thought I ought to end my visit as soon as possible and put her out of her paroxysm of worry. She thanked me for Coromoto's jacket. She told me how tall I was. She asked me if I was pregnant. She told me that I'd have to get pregnant quickly or nobody would talk to me. They were good people, the *gente*, they were just afraid of outsiders. Well, they were mostly good with a few noticeable exceptions. At which pronouncement, Zara made her right hand like the horns of a bull and held it away from her.

'What's that?' I asked. It was the same gesture that some of the huddled homesteaders had made towards me when I tried to approach them.

'It's the evil eye,' Zara told me, shocked that I didn't know it. And she made it again, to ward off whatever evil my ignorance might have visited on her kin. Our talk was shouted over the rain and the choking of my hounds. The makeshift broom stood visibly on the porch beside me. I learnt later that to hide the broom behind a door was a way of getting rid of an unwelcome visitor, so it was a mark of hospitality to leave it in view. Seeing the empty sardine tin, I had an idea. 'Where do you buy sardines?' I asked Zara.

She looked at me as though I was daft.

'Sardines, where do you buy them round here?'

Zara looked at Coromoto and Coromoto looked at Zara and they shrugged.

'At the shop, Doña, at the *bodega.*'

'And where's the shop?'

'At Calichano's'

'I want to buy some sardines,' I told them.

'But you're a lady, you can't eat sardines.'

'I really like them, I always have, I miss them here and I want to go and buy some. I want to go to the *bodega.*'

'But you can't go to the *bodega,*' Zara said. 'You're the Doña. It's a rough place, it's for *la gente.* You couldn't go there, what would people say, *qué dirán?*'

'Do you go to the *bodega?*'

'Oh, no, I haven't been down to the road since before Coromoto was born. I used to go to the *trapiche* to take Antonio his food, but ever since Antonio José could carry the billycans he has been.'

'And Coromoto, does she go?'

'She has been, on errands, she knows where it is.'

'Could she go for me?'

'And buy sardines?'

'Yes, and maybe a few other things. I could pay her to go.'

Zara's eyes flashed, 'She will go because you are the Doña. You are never to pay her anything.'

She turned away from me and glared at her sad sick daughter.

'Do you understand?' she asked Coromoto in an almost savage way that contrasted so with her soft gentle demeanour of before that I started in my chair. Zara turned back to me, calm again.

'Perdóname, Doña,' she said again, repeating it as she had when I first entered, forgive me, forgive me.

'Coromoto will go to you in the morning and run your errand.' The rain, it seemed, was not going to abate. The dizziness from the coffee had passed and I knew that it would be dark in another two hours. I stood up to go.

'You can't leave,' Zara told me. 'It's still raining.'

'That's all right, I don't mind the rain.'

'But you're the Doña, you can't go outside in the rain.'

'You all do.'

'Yes, but that's different, you can't.'

'Why not?'

'Que dirán?'

7

Coromoto turned up the next morning looking bedraggled and unenthusiastic. She had Goyo with her, dressed in a brightly coloured shirt whose two remaining buttons were threatening to burst. They both carried their *cotiza* sandals in brown paper bags.

'Why don't you wear them?' I asked as she squelched barefoot through the mud.

'They'll get wet.'

'Then why bring them?'

'We'll put them on outside the shop.'

I had made a list and had my fifty *bolívar* note ready for her. She was unimpressed by my list and held the offending bit of paper away from her as though it had an unsavoury smell.

'What do I do with that?'

'Give it to the shopkeeper.'

'Why?'

'So he knows what I want.'

The shopkeeper couldn't read either, nobody could on the *hacienda*.

'Just tell me.'

I told her and had hardly got past bread, butter and eggs, when she stopped me short. You didn't buy eggs in shops, you gathered them from hens. She didn't know what bread or butter were but she was sure they wouldn't sell them at the *bodega*. She ran through a list of what they did sell: black beans, rice, coffee, corn, lime, kerosene, tallow, candles, tinder, sardines, *fideos*, fish, sugar, *guaca*, split peas, vegetables and oil, string, machetes, hot plates and cones for straining coffee. I modified my list, which Coromoto carried verbally, setting off for the five-kilometre round trip like a condemned prisoner *en route* for the gallows.

She was gone for hours. While she was away, a man drove up to the house in a battered pick-up truck and parked beside the *trapiche*. He jerked a sack out of the back of the truck and carried it towards me. He shook my hand and introduced himself with a reel of complicated names. We had met, he said, in Valera on my way through. He had brought me a present. He held out the sack, 'It's for you, Doña Lisaveta.'

I took the sack and thanked him. As we were speaking, Jaime returned. He greeted my visitor effusively and with many 'compadres'.

'What is it?' Jaime asked, nodding towards the sack in my hand.

'It's for the *musiua*.'

I was the *musiua*, the European, the name derived from the French Monsieur. Jaime took the sack from my hand and put it on the concrete floor of the veranda. Then he loosed the string around its neck.

'I bet you never guess what's inside,' the *compadre* said. Jaime put his hand in and then blanched, pulling his hand out with a vulture's beak clamped over the wrist. Behind the beak was an enraged vulture. Its head was bare, grey and wrinkled and its long featherless neck was creased into dry folds like an old man's scrotum. Its yellow eyes were furious, its black feathers all ruffled on its wings.

'It's called Napoleon,' the *compadre* told me, laughing. 'A vulture can tear the hide off a cow. Look what it's doing to his hand, it'll break it.'

Between the three of us, we managed to persuade Napoleon to relinquish the wrist, but he held a grudge ever afterwards and was wary of Jaime and, whenever he got the chance, vindictive. The feeling was mutual. Napoleon became my pet, my companion.

The two men left together to walk over the sugar fields, swapping 'Compadres' and camaraderie as they made their way back up the track. I heard my visitor mention my name, and Jaime turned back and called, 'Ya vengo' (I'll be right back).

I turned my attention to Napoleon. One of his wings had been clipped so he couldn't fly more than a few yards. The *compadre* had shown me how to control him by throwing a cloth over his head. 'He'll eat anything that's meat or fish. He's a devil for meat. If you have a cut or a sore, cover it, he'll tear you apart, it's his nature. He's more intelligent than a dog, watch him, he understands. He doesn't talk but you get the feeling he could do if he chose . . . I've reared him since he was a chick, but you can have him now. He'll stop you from feeling lonely, you'll see.'

Coromoto returned, laden. Goyo was a long way behind her, marching over the cobbles of the *camino real* on his short sturdy legs, trailing what looked like a huge piece of shoe leather behind him on a string. The shoe leather had a head and a mouth like an O full of jagged teeth. It was a fish dessicated to a wafer. I had, increasingly often over the twelve days of my doñaship, wondered at what point the dogs' tinned food would stop turning my stomach and begin to look like a possible meal for me. By gnawing green mangoes and drinking tea, I had managed to pass the dog-food test without succumbing to the delights of Pedigree Chum (although the meal biscuits were edible in a plain sort of way). As Goyo abandoned the dried salt fish in the dirt, I thought it looked vastly less appetising than the dogs' food, and, on picking it up, I really couldn't see any way to cook it, let alone eat it. Coromoto had brought back a pile of brown paper bags, each containing one kilo of something. A kilo of rice, a kilo of black beans, a kilo of sugar that was dark brown and in a solid block, a kilo of split peas, a kilo of onions which were small and half-rotten and a kilo of garlic, each tooth of which was as small as a baby's teeth. Last but not least, she brought me the *guaca*. This was the best and dearest. It came in a tin with a picture of a bonneted woman wrapped in a plaid and was Quaker Porridge Oats.

High on the hills, where the Indian corn grows poorly, oats are the only cereal that will grow. Oats and potatoes are the staple diet of the high Andes, and a trickle of oats had crept into the diet there in the foot-hills. The one patent food that was sold happened to be my favourite. Coromoto returned my fifty *bolívar* note, it was too big, they hadn't had change at the *bodega*. I had spent nine *bolívars* in all, which had been tabbed.

'What's that?' Coromoto asked, backing off the veranda. Inside the long room, Napoleon was venting his frustration at having been put in a sack, at having been pulled out of it, at having been moved and at being locked up. Whatever he could pull to the ground, he did.

'It's a vulture.'

Coromoto and Goyo both made the sign against the evil eye.

'It's just a vulture that someone brought me, he's a bit upset, he's . . .'

The children had taken to their heels. They didn't return for two weeks. The vulture is a bird of ill omen, a harbinger of death.

For some days, Napoleon and I bonded. He was miserable and stood in a huddle on the veranda, staring resentfully at me. The two beagle hounds, who had behaved with nothing but maladjustment since their arrival and seemed to share between them no more than a residual brain cell, miraculously respected Napoleon. It was the first bit of sense they had shown. Had they engaged in a tussle, the vulture could easily have killed them both, and for once, the hounds seemed to accept this with grace and fortitude. Cars, trucks, savage dogs, snakes, wasps, poisonous toads, all continued to present a suicidal challenge to the dogs, but they gave Napoleon a wide berth. When we went for walks, they strained ahead, leaving Napoleon to strut behind me, with his wings folded behind his back and his head bowed in thought in true Napoleonic style.

At night, he kept me company, hooding his eyes, turning his head and sleeping beside my hammock. I shared my first tin of sardines with him. He ate his with relish, but mine made me sick. Then I cooked some rice in the tin I had been using to boil up my water and although it cooked badly, after I had sprinkled it with Sainsbury's dried herbs from my trunk it felt like a feast set for a princess. Napoleon declined to share it and found that vultures like Pedigree Chum.

8

I LIVED FROM day to day, curbing my ambitions and aspirations to merely reaching the night. The sensation I had felt in the first days when I tried to shovel the invading mud from out of my new house, of fighting a losing battle, of ploughing the sea, stayed with me. At the end of each day I seemed to have achieved nothing but to be able to say I had been present during its course. Since there was rarely anyone to say this to, and, increasingly, I began to think I was becoming invisible, I was never satisfied with my achievement.

I washed my clothes in the millrace, wrung them and then hung them in the house, either to be pulled down by the dogs or by Napoleon, or to gather mildew spots from the incessant damp. I swept the floors with a broom made up in the way Coromoto had shown me with the sticks and the sardine tin, and I shooed dust and mud from one side of the house to the next. I set and reset seeds to start a garden, but might as well have broadcast them to the wind. I saw innumerable humming birds, parrots, parakeets, and once, the mythical bluebirds I had heard of in London. In all of these apparitions I took pleasure, as I did in the wealth of wild flowers and grasses that grew wild in the black fertile earth. More than anything else, though, I remember being borne down by the loneliness and the rain. Looking back, I wondered how Otto had had the nerve to complain about the rain in England. The rain on the *hacienda* was permanent, it ranged from mist to drizzle to torrents of water. The light was bright, the weather warm and rainbows competed with each other sometimes for a space in the sky. The monotony of the rain was soul-destroying and the damp crept into my bones and into my mind. I mildewed.

For two months whatever lines of communication, however tenuous in the past, there had been between myself and the man I had married, broke down. There were no arguments, fights; there was nothing. It was as though I didn't exist. I had omitted to take a mirror with me to the *hacienda*, but I kept the brass locks on the trunks polished with lemon juice, so as to be able to check my reflection in them from time to time, to persuade myself that I was there, that I wasn't in a surreal dream. Visitors came and went, dropping by to say hello. Occasionally, in their presence, I became a proper living person again, addressed not only by them but by their cousin Jaime. Alone, though, I ceased to be. I didn't realise for years that I was living with a schizophrenic. So much of the new world I had come to was strange to me, marital defection was just another facet of this foreign unmapped land.

The visitors brought improvements. They nosed past Jaime and discovered that we were living without any furniture, pots and pans or plumbing. They chided him. He ignored them in a friendly sort of way, changing the subject, talking sugar and avocado pears. There was a code that his close friends and cousins seemed to know, when Jaime ignored them and wandered bodily off whistling tunelessly like a kettle letting off steam, that they could pull him back to ground as though by a cord by talking about avocado pears. It reprogrammed him and then, as though nothing untoward had occurred, their talk could continue wherever it had broken off before the fruit cipher had been inserted. Again, it took me years to learn that after his return to the *hacienda*, if I wanted to have any verbal communication with Jaime, I had to say 'avocado', *aguacate*, and the word had to occur early in the sentence and it had to be reinforced by repetition. Once I learnt the names of over a dozen varieties of avocado pears, I could substitute them for the generic term. This meant that, eventually, I could appear to be having a reasonably long conversation with my husband in public. I could speak and he would respond. Later, during the years when I was running the *hacienda*, it was necessary, both to appease the *qué diráns* and for the continuance of my regency, that Don Jaime did not appear to be at odds with me.

Tact and strategy are not the gifts of adolescence. On the *hacienda*, age was a merit; it earned respect and admiration. In a place fraught with hazards, where earthquakes, floods, drought, poverty and epidemics were the business of every day, it was a considerable achievement to reach old age. It was part of the tradition of the Andes that age was honoured. Children all greeted their parents formally as Señor and Señora, they asked for their blessing when they entered and left their presence, they obeyed them not only during their childhood, but for life. Since child labour scooped up the children from the age of eight onwards, there was no cult of childhood there. Children were just inadequate adults. I didn't strike *la gente* as an adult, I looked like a child of twelve, a grotesquely tall child and a foreigner to boot. I was, nominally, the Doña of a semi-feudal estate with fifty-two families of vassals, but until such time as I joined their community by a blood tie, I was someone to be disregarded. For the members of the family on neighbouring estates and for the cousins in Valera, I was too young to be taken seriously. Nobody believed I was eighteen. Everyone believed I was a fool, why else had I consented to live in a peasant's hut made out of mud? Why didn't I drive? Why didn't I cruise up and down the Highway to the hairdresser's like a normal woman?

There wasn't really anyone in between. There were *la gente* from our *hacienda* and the workers from the sugar plantations which joined it in either direction and then there was the family, each branch of which lived in luxurious isolation on islands of kitsch, pampered by servants and bolstered by wealth that had never run out and never would. Life at the top was a battle against boredom, and at the other end it was a fight for survival. I didn't fit in anywhere. I didn't want to join the club of the rich. I saw more and more ways in which I could be of use on the *hacienda*, if only in teaching the children to read, the rudiments of better nutrition and providing a better standard of living for *la gente*. Only Zara and Antonio spoke to me though, and Coromoto and Goyo when they finally returned despite the vulture.

Then one afternoon, a drunken, shrunken old man came tottering down the track to my house and asked me to give him some money, which I did. He staggered away having whispered to me in a vapour of rot-gut rum, 'God bless you, Doña, and keep you from ill. You will be like Doña Delia. I'll come back and see you. I'll be there for you.'

He didn't actually return for a year, but when he did he was true to his word. He became the houseman and every night after all the chores were done and the darkness was locked into the sound of cicadas, it was he, Benito Mendoza, who kept me company and told me the history of the *hacienda* courtesy of his eighty-six years of almost constant inebriation.

When Jaime failed to respond to his cousins' suggestions about sanitising the house, some of them took it into their own hands to improve my circumstances. A bathroom was added at the back of the house by the millrace. The plumbing was fairly rudimentary: the lavatory flushed straight into the stream. After more than two months of bathing in the millrace and squatting in the long grass, it was very welcome.

A builder called *el maestro* Ramón Rivas came to do the work. He put in the bathroom, cemented the floor and punched two holes in the kitchen wall for windows. Someone brought a bed, someone else a chair and a small table, someone else a kerosene cooker of the kind used for camping. The pick-up truck we had returned from Caracas in had stayed and then disappeared. For a while, there was no transport; then another similar-looking truck materialised and was parked beside the *trapiche* whenever Don Jaime was in residence.

Mostly, I spent my days in a state of almost total lethargy. Since I no longer feared starvation and didn't have to worry any more about how to procure my food, I seemed to have lost my grasp on reality. I picked the moments out of each day like sea glass from sand. Coromoto's visits, Napoleon's company, the few moments in the day when the hounds were quiet and sweet, a cat and a kitten that I found in the storeroom and fed and cosseted. I savoured the times when the rain stopped and left the vegetation covered in glistening drops like dew, like crystal balls. I gathered endless bunches of wild flowers and herbs, collected leaves. I made lists of pretty insects that I saw and described the plumage of the abundant tropical birds in letters to my mother. I knitted together a blanket of things to tell her about my life on the *hacienda*, dropping all the stitches of all the moments that disturbed me and would disturb her. I wrote about my life as a rural idyll, I pretended to have no regrets, to be a part of the everyday life of the *hacienda* and to live in marital bliss. I exaggerated, I think, looking back now, because I was so very out of my depth.

When, in a sudden volte-face, Jaime came home one day and stepped back into my life as though he had never left it and expressed concern over how I could have lost so much weight overnight, I slipped back into being his wife. For three weeks, I rode out every day with him to bars and restaurants and to visit people's houses. The interlude felt no more real than the preceding loneliness and I was scarcely less apathetic. After three weeks, when he left one morning saying, 'Ya vengo', it didn't really surprise me when he didn't return.

During that interlude, he also picked up the reins of the *hacienda* and brought the men of the *hacienda* back to work. A field of sugar-cane was cut and carried to the *trapiche*, and on the second day the furnaces were lit, the wheel loosed and the cane-crusher set in motion. This was the *molienda*, the crushing and boiling of sugar. The furnaces burnt day and night fuelled by the mountain of *vagasse*. There were fifteen workers in the factory, the *trapicheros*. Within the hierarchy of the *hacienda*, these were the key men. Each was skilled in his work and earned more than the field workers. They worked in shifts, eight hours on and four hours off for the five days of the *molienda*. From five-thirty in the morning until five-thirty in the afternoon, reinforcements of cut cane were delivered to the *trapiche* and then fed through the cast-iron rollers of the cane-crusher. Antonio Moreno was in his element, bustling round and round the factory, overseeing everything and everyone. Trails of small children trudged backwards and forwards over the bridge, carrying billycans of food to their fathers and brothers. None of the *trapicheros* went home either to eat or sleep. They ate from their billycans and slept in the *vagasse*.

The sugar was made into blocks of one kilo and then packed twenty-four blocks at a time in bundles wrapped in cane leaves and tied with string. The sugar was a rich dark brown except for the last few hundred kilos which were nearly black. Antonio was critical of the outcome. Apparently the sugar should have been a light beige with a white nap. The darker the colour, the lower the price.

The cane had been carried to the *trapiche* in an ex-American army Power Wagon, a peeling green monster bound together with chains. It was so battered that whenever it started it seemed like a miracle. *La gente* called it 'La Povva'. During the *molienda*, I got used to seeing La Povva lurching across the bridge and choking up the sharp hill to the cane-crusher. It was driven by a man called Abrán. When the sugar was ready and stacked in La Povva, filling the entire back of the lorry and covered over with canvas against the persistent drizzle, Antonio Moreno drove it into Valera to sell. I was surprised to see him drive. It was as though he stepped out of his timewarp when he took the wheel. He returned, some hours later with a brown paper bag full of money. Everything came in brown paper bags.

The next day, which was a Saturday, the men were paid. When the *hacienda* got into full swing, this weekly routine of paying the workers was a way of keeping track on time. The men were paid at one o'clock on Saturdays and had been for as long as they could remember.

Everyone seemed happy with the *molienda*. During the years when Jaime was away, the sugar had been sold as cane to another estate. In sugar-farming terms, this was shameful. A plantation, to have any pride, had to boil its own sugar. The workers were glad to be back doing what they had grown up to do. A *molienda* brought extra pay, the bigger the harvest, the more money the *trapicheros* earned. I too found the bustle reassuring. It brought the centre of attention to my side of the road, and by visiting the factory and dawdling on the bridge, I could say hello to people, safe in the knowledge that they would say hello to me, however reluctantly. If I went to their compounds, they could hide and keep their silence, but at the *molienda*, if the Doña said 'Good morning', it was traditional to say 'Good morning' back.

When people talked, what they said was interrupted by their spitting out little pools of what looked like black blood. It was actually a chewing tobacco called *chimó*. When I say chewing, it wasn't chewed, as such, it was cut from a twist of paste with a knife and stuck inside the lower teeth and then sucked and spat at regular intervals. Men, women and children all 'ate *chimó*' as they said. I had come across it with Coromoto and Goyo, mistaking my first sight of it for advanced TB. It stained teeth dark brown, and sepia'd lips. It staved off hunger and produced, so Coromoto insisted, a sense of comfort. It was addictive. It divided people into the slovens and the smart. Slovens spat all over the floor, smart people spat into the ubiquitously used powered milk tin.

It was during the first *molienda* that an old man called Natividad came and sought me out on the bridge. He not only greeted me, he thanked me for returning Jaime to the *hacienda* and blessed me for the *molienda* without which all the *gente* suffered want. He told me that he had once been the goat-herd to the Teráns. He told me where he lived. He said that he knew I had been three times to visit Zara, and next time he would like me to drink coffee with him and his wife. When he had finished speaking, the effort of having said so much brought on a spasm which left him gasping as he leant on the bridge. He had wheezed as he spoke, but afterwards he wheezed himself into a fit. When it was over, he smiled a *chimó*-stained smile.

'I have been ready to be called for a long time, Doña, but God doesn't want it.' He shrugged, puzzled, and then went on his way, clinging on to the barred sides of La Povva as it rattled back over the stones to gather more cane.

I gathered up all such kindnesses and found more sustenance in them than in the black beans that took four hours to soften as they boiled and did not lend themselves to my inexperienced hand. The ground around the house became littered with my attempts to cook the staple food and make it palatable. Inside, I sat at the big desk that had been my father-in-law's and which Antonio Moreno had dug out of the mud and had brought to me. It had been half-buried in the dynamo house beyond the factory. He had also brought me a 1919 Underwood typewriter. He said, 'I always see you writing, Doña, it writes: Don Rodolfo used to make it write.'

It too was covered in mud, its long curling keys were caked together and the reel, which was about two feet long was encrusted in its carriage. I spent hours trying to clean it and make it work to no avail, but it looked good on my desk as I wrote my letters home.

Abrán, who drove La Povva brought me a letter from London at the end of my first month. It was from my mother. Two weeks later, he brought me another from her, she was depressed. She had received none of my cards or letters posted from the ship or from Caracas. I wrote to her, often, giving the letters to Abrán to post. It was a further two months before any letters of mine reached London. So, at first, I wrote them and handed them over to Abrán, who told me he took them to Mendoza Fría where there wasn't a post office but there was a lady who knew about such things and at whose house my letters, although addressed to the *hacienda* and to me, would always arrive. It felt a little bit better than writing and putting the letters in a bottle and throwing them into the River Momboy, but each time I handed over a missive I wondered if it would ever arrive. It was only through writing to my mother that I made any kind of sense of my life. We shared an affinity for flora and fauna, a love of literature and also, she was the one person, other than myself, who believed that one day I would be a writer.

Gradually, by the receipt of her letters, I regained a sense of time. It was the only almanac apart from one guideline on the plantation as to when the week ended after regular work recommenced. Even after Jaime's interest in the running of it became sporadic, Antonio Moreno maintained the pattern. The men were paid on Saturdays, and whether or not I was present at that handing over of funds, I knew when it was Sunday as surely as though church bells had rung. On Sundays the tracks of the *hacienda* were littered with bodies. The men drank some of their wages. They drank rot-gut rum made from our own sugar and distilled elsewhere on the *hacienda* in copper stills. The alcohol ripped the copper from the pipes and added a kick to the drink that rendered the men semi-comatose for anything up to twelve hours. Saturday nights were for drinking. Sunday mornings found all the ones who hadn't managed to stagger home unconscious on the paths or under bushes turning the hillside into a temporary no man's land.

9

MANY YEARS LATER, after my mother died, I found she had kept
all the letters I wrote to her from the *hacienda*. I have read
them again and am struck most by three things: the lies of
omission, the evidence that fewer than one in ten of my letters
ever did arrive, and lastly the lines I slipped in, often jokingly,
which were a confession of my real state of mind. My first
letter, dated 'June/July 1972' begins,

Dear Joanna,
  Where to begin and where to end has delayed this
letter since my arrival here last week; that and the work
and the wars here which keep us on our feet . . .
  Our house is beautiful and spacious with an enormous
overgrown garden and a river, and a stream and a fresh
water spring, bamboo, fruit trees, pillars and crumbling
beams . . . I find I can hardly write for tiredness, so having
said nothing, I shall say no more. When the pace slackens
a little I have a store of things to write about – Ross and
Megan (both well and gnashing their teeth thoughtfully,
no doubt, wondering what to destroy next) . . .

Good night, sleep well, and if you find it in your heart to do so, then think well of me, even if I don't deserve it; for if you don't, who else will?

Love to everyone . . .

Lisaveta

Then, on 12 July,

Dear Joanna,

I have just received two letters, one from the hosp. one from you . . .

There is no public transport roundabout these parts, no telephone, nor telephone wires even, no postboxes, and ten minutes drive in one direction and 15/20 mins in the other to a town and people. I am writing to you once a week, so, on receiving the first letter you will know that another will follow in seven days if not before.

Although we are isolated, there are lots of people here, workers who live on the estate and their families and elderly relations. The estate has a main road running through it, most of the land is high, wooded hills and waterfalls. Looking from our porch, across the road, to the south all the wild hills and land in sight are Santa Rita . . .

The *trapiche* where the cane is converted into sugar is an enormous building about 50 yards × 70, most of it being filled with dry empty canes (used for fuel for heating the liquid sugar). Then there is a series of huge copper tubs, immense rectangular basins, connected to each other and forming a channel through which the boiling syrup runs. The actual *trapiche* (crushing-machine) is a beautiful, solid iron black beast, put there by Don Rodolfo Terán at the beginning of the century . . .

I do what I can with the garden which has a will of its own and is wild, stony and overgrown, and tackle the house, the crabs, rats, toads, lice, ants that sting, cockroaches, spiders that bite and the dust, shit and damp of years of neglect. The house is already quite different from when we moved in about ten days ago (or more).

Ross and Megan are as lovely and as awful as ever.

It is hard to imagine how feudal life is here . . .

I have met hundreds of Jaime's family . . . most interesting of whom have been Luis Daniel Terán, Jaime's father's cousin . . . Then Doña Rosa Madrid, an old lady, fat and probably once beautiful who sits splayed in an enormous, saggy whicker chair . . . talking of times past, and her cool still stone house is like a haven of quietness and musty calm in the midst of a madhouse with no keepers (the world in general but especially Caracas) . . .

Everyone here is kind to me (so far) and his family seem to accept me (though as something of a monstrous rarity) . . .

Little dogs are hungry, and so am I, and my fist is all screwed up with cramp . . .

When we have a little money (at present we live almost entirely on tributes and presents of food which generally stock our stomachs liberally) I shall send you some *panela*, i.e. the sugar which is made here and comes in rectangular lumps about 6″ × 4″ × 3″ and very hard indeed it is to break up . . .

As to presents, I don't rightly know. I know a dressing gown is not needed for a bit, nor any clothes really.

A book on herbs and their medicinal uses would be nice if there is one.

Apart from that, little somethings for the house, it is such a rambly half-empty house . . .

Lots of love to everyone and lots of love to you and I miss you a lot,
        Lisaveta

The next and almost all subsequent letters are written on the headed paper of the Aeroclub de Valera, founded, as the heading states, in 1945 and reorganised in 1960. Antonio Moreno brought me a stock of it which he found in a cupboard in the dynamo. The paper was as thin as an onion leaf, and slightly discoloured by time. The letters are all headed by me, 'Hacienda Santa Rita, Mendoza Fría'. Santa Rita was the name of one of the estates that made up the *hacienda* as a whole; it was the core.

4th? August

Dearest Joanna,

. . . Time slips by here and people and things too.

This afternoon a girl is coming, Nieves, to help in the house, live in and do errands. I was not going to have any servants here, but this girl came to Jaime asking for work – her father works here – she is only thirteen, poor thing, and ran away from her last job because she was being beaten so much. Her pay, 60 *bolivárs* monthly (£6) no holiday, no days off, no fixed hours of work. At least now she won't have to work much and I can pay her more (not much more or all the other women will jump down my throat) and she is nearer her home – she has 13 brothers and sisters.

The agricultural workers here earn about £4 a week, on other estates, less, 5½ day week, 8–11 hour day. The cost

of living is as in England and fast rising. There are
rumours that meat will go up from 10 shillings per pound
to nearly £2 per pound. Imagine the poverty here.
Families of 10 to 20 persons living off a few meagre
pounds a week. Clothes are terribly expensive, the rest as
in England, except that all illnesses, medicines, births,
deaths, marriages and first communions cost a fortune.

Witchcraft and superstition grow with the ground and
the grass here. I have discovered some elderberries here
and am madly planting them around the house – a touch
of home. Also they keep the flies away. Notice how I keep
saying 'here' . . .

Jaime and his mama can't stay half an hour in the same
room without flying at each other and Jaime trembles
with rage and Antonieta (his ma) digs away . . . she was
exactly the same with his father and had *him* trembling
with rage and frustration from dawn to dusk even after his
heart attack, even when he was dying. Most people here
blame her for that – his papa died very young . . . *nyak,
nyak*; nag, nag, no. It does not work with me though
because I don't rise to her. I just let her juggle with everything, move everything, poke and advise endlessly. Really,
I feel sorry for her . . . she is very kind to me and to a
chosen few.

Nieves, the maid, went to Gabriela's house (my sister-
in-law's) yesterday to work there until Christmas, but one
day of being treated not only like dirt, but dirt with an
automatic motor and ten pairs of hands, had her desperate
to leave and begging us, who had taken her there, to take
her back to her home. Why? Antonieta is staying with
Gabriela . . .

Last week I went on an expedition with some children.

The foreman here is Antonio Moreno, he is in charge
of all the other workers and is Jaime's right-hand man as
he was Don Cesar's before him.

So, I went with three of his children who are all under
12. We walked for about ¾ of an hour with Ross and
Megan through woods, up hills, down dales with streams
and brooks, beautiful flowers and birds. Came back with
our pockets full of rose hips and lots of oranges in a
basket (because oranges don't fit in *normal* pockets I
believe). I had not realised until this week just how big
Santa Rita is. I walk for hours on end and I still have not
reached the other side . . . I picked my first avocado pear,
the size of a medium melon, and it is ripening now.

Dear Joanna,

I have no idea what day it is, but I have a sneaking suspicion that more than a week has passed since last I wrote.

We now have water right up to the house . . . The
actual lavatory will be fitted tomorrow . . .

The water we drank at first was from a natural spring
in the back garden, but the pool that it collected in before
falling into the stream was full of crabs and toads and
many another beast – which fact we had not realised. So,
we have both been rather sick this week (ever since we
arrived) . . .

While his mother was here, about ten days ago, she
invited us to visit one of the many millions of aunts . . .

Went to eat, couldn't eat, then felt it come again . . .
Someone dragged me to a bathroom, passed out again
then they gave me sugar and water, camomile and I
don't know what, it got better and has not come
again . . .

The water?

I can't think what else it could be, it felt like a being inside me, it was one of the most unpleasant experiences I have had. All that morning my thoughts turned to Cornwall, the bus, Mabel's, my appendicitis there. And *To the Lighthouse* which I was reading then, and ever since, severe pain gives me the sensation of waves crashing inside and around me . . .

Speaking of trembling, there was a big tremor here some weeks ago, and the house and hills shook in the middle of the night, a tremendous tremor . . .

VERY IMPORTANT

INSIDE NEXT LETTER

JAM-JAR TOPS . . .

If you see or hear from Casanova send lots of love and remind him that he was going to find lovely books and send them here. I (you may prod him) would like books on biology, SHEEP REARING, HERBS, their uses, care of, all those old-fashioned witch books, also, anyone who sees it, please buy *The Golden Bough*, it comes in about twelve volumes, please send any you find, I know of Adonis, Attis, Osiris, it is all about anthropology . . .

There will now be a short intermission.

An hour or so later

Our first hand of bananas is ready and they are exquisite.

Already I have lots of time quietly sitting at home writing or studying. I am quite surprised at my lazy slobby old self, for I study several hours a day, English, French, Spanish, Eyetie, and a bit of Latin, also translating. I have begun to translate some of G. Manley Hopkins, beginning with

The Hacienda

'My own heart let me more have pity on'

Just an exercise really, I suppose, since his particular poetry is hardly translatable, loses most of its beauty and power – still, more the challenge.

I am writing some nonsense myself, pages and pages of things I had been pondering since Bologna. Then in the night time I see through the rushes. However it is very rough and changes almost entirely almost every day . . .

I suppose you have heard nothing from Jan? Well, that is as expected and finished in some ways and open in others, at least, the wound remains open, just a little and dust gets in. Please send lots of news and chatter, anything interesting, even usually boring things interest me right now.

Christmas is coming on. I can hardly imagine Christmas without cake and mince pies and all such things which do not happen here, and no oven to invent them . . .

I am getting rather drivelly by now and hot. Until approximately next week, or, let us say, until the moon has half-waned.

Love to you and to you all (jam tops) lots of news,
Lisaveta

Stranger than anything I ever did or said was my absence of family. No one had ever met them or heard of them. It was as though I were a homunculus, a life-form which had sprouted spontaneously from the mounds of *vagasse*. I had, or seemed to have, no family behind me and I brought none into the future. My father, Jan, had disinherited me when I went off with the Venezuelan trio instead of going to university, and I had not heard from him again. In Venezuela it was unforgivable to have

83

no family, no father, no grandparents. Even if, as I claimed, I did have a family, what kind of family would send their daughter unaccompanied to a foreign land? These matters hung in the air and translated rarely into words. The more immediate question of why I had not produced a son and heir was repeated at every available opportunity. I had been married for two and a half years, long enough to be carrying my second child. It was my duty to give birth. I should never have married the last of the true Teráns if I was not going to bear a son immediately and continue the line of Don Jaime and Don Cesar, Don Rodolfo and all the dons who led back to the *conquistadores*.

I didn't dare admit that I was sterile; I lived with the lie, knowing that *la gente* would only accept and respect me if I gave birth.

I discovered that I was living in a place where women outnumbered men by five to one. It was standard practice for all men to sleep with more than one woman on a regular basis. A man had a wife, a mistress or two and any number of casual friends. With the shortage of men, this was not only tolerated by women, it was considered public spirited. Men, in society and at home, were pampered; women were ignored. Daughters were what you had while waiting for a son. The families were large – a small family would have five children, a large one twenty. This applied to rich and poor alike. Girls were trained from infancy to give precedence to the boys, to wait on them, to serve and please them. By the time a girl was seventeen, if she wasn't married she was on the shelf. Nobody's husband was faithful and it was common practice for the men to wander off for a few days at a time. It didn't seem to surprise anyone that my husband was so rarely at home, but it shocked and worried them that I was such a bad wife that I didn't give him a son.

I had, as I wrote to my mother, much time to read and write. I had all the time in the world. My social life still revolved largely around the eight-year-old Coromoto. When she and her siblings came, I dressed and disinfected their cuts and running sores. I had my first-aid badge from the Girl Guides; it hadn't specialised in tropical skin infections, but it helped, and gradually the three children's many blemishes began to show a marked improvement.

The *hacienda* seemed to be running reasonably smoothly between the able hands of Antonio Moreno and the sporadic overseeing of Jaime, *el padrón*. I knew nothing about farming or sugar-cane or avocado pears. I saw what went on around me, gathering images like magic lantern slides of the bits of plantation life that paraded past me.

I noticed, with regret, that Los Pollos de Eladio returned to the Casa Grande and beat out real Mariachi music and served innumerable grilled chickens, whose scent filled the air at night.

If Los Pollos de Eladio was in the big house, then I could not be. I'd been told that my sojourn in the cottage would be for eight weeks. I had fallen in love with the simple elegance of La Casa Grande and its pantiled roofs – crouched like a hare under the mountain. I thought, if I was to live in solitude, I would have rather been there. I asked Antonio about it, he shrugged and made a face as though to imply that he thought the continuance of Eladio in the family house a madness. I asked my husband, but I might as well have asked the bamboo. The bamboo, at least, whispered back to me when I spoke.

I heard nothing from Otto and nothing from Elias, not a word. Being cut off from newspapers, or any media news, I didn't know of the troubles in Chile, I only knew that Otto had promised to write and send me books. When I wrote to my mother I asked after him. We called Otto Casanova in our code. I hoped that he had been to Chile and returned. I hoped that he would turn up one day, park his truck by the *trapiche* and come and find me and take me away.

Meanwhile, piecemeal, through Coromoto, I began to compile lists of herbal cures. They didn't use patent medicine on the *hacienda*, except very occasionally. They couldn't afford it. They used herbs and grasses, bark and seeds. They divided all foods into the categories hot and cold and applied them like internal poultices to all their needs.

The maid, Nieves, who had come to the *trapiche* to ask for work and then been taken to one of my sisters-in-law (Gabriela) was returned to her home. She had been sent out to work because her family needed the money. Thirteen was old for a girl to be at home. Work started at eight. An eight-year-old could stand on a box by the sink and wash dishes or she could stand on a box by a stone sink and thump linen clean, then wring it through an old-fashioned wringer. An eight-year-old could pound out *arepas*: the corn meal that was eaten instead of bread and had to be made, like a Mexican tortilla, twice a day. The small balls of dough had to be pounded with the heel of the hand into perfect circles, and piles of dozens of these little discs had to be prepared. And an eight-year-old could run around after a toddler and keep it out of harm's way. Nieves, at thirteen, had to find work as a servant and give her wages to her family. The day after she had been accompanied high up the hill to a mud shack with a dusty yard full of children, she came back to the *trapiche* and asked if she could work for me.

This had been her original plan, thwarted by the Venezuelan habit of *sonsacando*. This was a crucial element in the life of the idle classes, who were not, as I learnt, idle at all. Everyone had servants, anything between two and ten of them. Each household bribed and stole the servants away from its neighbours and friends. This act is called *sonsacando*. It is an intricate and often dangerous game. To be caught in the act could lead to feuds and feuds make for vendettas. Plans as intricately laid as military strategies were devised and executed to lure away the working girls from one house to the next. It was done as much for the challenge (and sometimes spite) as through necessity. As soon as Nieves arrived at the *trapiche* with her bundle of possessions wrapped up in a shirt and tied on to a stick like one of the three little pigs off to seek her fortune, my sister-in-law descended and whisked her away. It was an easy victory since I was so unskilled in the rules of play.

The swapping of cooks and maids, laundresses and nannies was like a great game of musical chairs. Once a girl was out, she was out and couldn't go back to the place she had been lured away from, even if she had been summarily dismissed from the victorious *sonscadora*. The bribes proffered were rarely honoured – it would have disrupted the entire wage scale of domestic service – but this was not something that the girls themselves tended to grasp until it was too late.

However, Nieves came back to me and I took her on. I had swept out one of the dark storerooms for her, clearing out the small bones and droppings of innumerable rats. I proved to be a mistress of great ineptitude. Nieves didn't know how to do anything without being told, and I didn't know how to tell her.

Spanish is a language of direct command. In English, orders are given indirectly. 'Do you think it would be a good idea to make some coffee?' actually means 'Make some coffee.' In

Spanish, it means what it says; so to someone who wasn't thinking about coffee and doesn't think of it as a particularly good idea, no command has been given. 'Perhaps you could make some coffee,' is also a statement rather than a command. In Nieves's case, yes, perhaps she could, in fact she'd learnt to make coffee as a child, but since I still had not asked her to do anything, she continued to hover around me, sulking. 'Make some coffee,' is the only way to get it made and 'Bring me coffee' is the only way to get it out of the pot and into your cup. Everything I said to Nieves was tangled in a web of translated misunderstandings. It seemed rude to me to command; it seemed rude to her that I didn't.

Coromoto hated Nieves. She came to the corner of the workshop and refused to come in. She just stood and glowered. Nieves occasionally went out to speak to her and I overheard them having vicious arguments which stopped as soon as I got near enough to break them up. After five uneasy days, a woman from Mendoza Fría who came to the *trapiche* to see if there was any sugar to buy and wandered down to the house to say hello, set a trap to steal Nieves away. I watched and listened carefully, allowing them enough time on their own for the *sonsacando* to take place, but not so long that either of them could learn that I would be happier than the *sonscadora* if she took the resentful Nieves off my hands.

At seven o'clock the next morning, the same car cruised on to the bridge. Nieves, bundle in hand, announced that she was quitting. I made a show of regret and let her go gratefully. By mid-morning, Coromoto came down to celebrate. She brought me a bunch of wild busy lizzie flowers, pink and red and white *impatiens*. She held my hand and kissed it. She helped me prepare a picnic of sorts and we set off into the hills with the dogs and Napoleon. Coromoto confided to me that if any other girl tried to come into my house to touch my things, she would scratch their eyes out. 'I'll be your maid,' she said. 'You don't know how to shout, you don't know how to talk, you don't know how to do anything, anyone else but me will just steal your things and laugh at you.'

10

THERE HAD BEEN moments of sunshine, and hours of sunshine, then by August there were entire days of sunshine. It still rained in between, and the rain was torrential, but gradually the balance of dry and wet tipped over to the dry side. By September the tin roof of my house, which had momentarily become hot enough to cook on on arrival, stayed that way for most of the day. To be under it, was like sitting in an incubator. The mud caked and cracked and released inexhaustible swirls of dust. At night, though, it continued to be cold. It was cold enough to feel chilly, to need a jacket, shawls, jumpers: all things I had omitted to bring.

Because day by day the temperature dropped and soared, everyone caught colds in the contrast. Colds, coughs and sore throats were endemic and any given family on the *hacienda* would tend to be struggling with at least one bronchitic child at any given moment. Without antibiotics, the bronchitis turned quickly to pneumonia and was a common cause of death, particularly in babies.

The builder who continued to make leisurely improvements to the house and, more often, on the *trapiche* buildings, began to talk to me when nobody else was around. He told me about the hospitals in Valera. There was no doctor on the *hacienda* and no doctor in Mendoza Fría. There was a witch-doctor in the hills far beyond where Antonio Moreno lived. There was a man called *el bachiller* Simanca, who lived half-way to Valera in a place called Carmania. He could diagnose any illness from holding a sample of the patient's urine up to the light. He was famous for it. He charged, so *la gente* could-n't go to him often, but *el maestro* Ramón Rivas assured me, when you did you got results. If people fell ill on the *hacienda*, they were treated with herbal cures. When they got fevers, they were given a broth made out of guinea pig. This too, he assured me, was very efficacious. Sometimes though, certain fevers were more powerful than any home cures and defied even the witchdoctor's spells. Then there was nothing to do but watch the person die and bury them.

'Sometimes though,' Ramón Rivas explained, 'you can't stand by like that.' As he spoke, he pulled his little son towards him. He was a small boy of about four years old. He came to work with his father most days, sitting quietly beside him, happy just to be near. When the day ended, the two would walk away, hand in hand. The boy never spoke to me, he was too shy despite seeing me so often, but I liked him, more perhaps than some of the other estate children at first sight because he had no sores or scabs on him. His hair, which was short and blond, was free of lice and his clear grey eyes were wide and trusting as they looked at his father. The habitual expression of suspicion and resignation of most of the estate children was not there. Ramón Rivas pulled his son to him and squeezed him affectionately.

'He's a twin. There were two of them, identical, but the other one died. They killed him in the hospital. He was six months old and the fever was racking him. I couldn't stand by, so I took him to Valera, to the hospital, to the children's ward. They took him away, they said, "Go away. What good can you do by staying? We don't want you here, you'll bring germs into the ward." I wanted to stay and help, to nurse him. They told me I couldn't come back till the next day. So next day I returned. They said, "He's in there, he died." Just like that, like nothing. When I went in, my baby was on a big high bed, a metal bed, a metre and a half high off the ground. He was lying on it in a funny way. His face was all smashed in, and his shoulder was broken. He had a fever when he went in, he was thrashing about. I could see they put him on that bed and left him there. And you know, Doña, they didn't even wipe the blood off his face for me to take him home. They didn't care. Well, we all know they don't care, but they didn't even pretend . . . We are unprotected here.'

I felt helpless and inadequate. What was I supposed to do? Several times, as the months went by, Antonio Moreno would come to me and ask if I could remind Jaime of something, mention something else, get him to do things that needed doing. I told him the truth: my husband wouldn't listen to me, he wouldn't do anything I asked or wanted. It was better if Antonio asked directly; my intervention would hinder, not help. Antonio shrugged and hurried off shaking his head.

When a new red International tractor arrived, he seemed much placated, but after the first month, when it sat idle by the *trapiche*, he again asked me to intervene, to allow someone else other than *el padrón* to drive it. There was nothing I could do. In fact it was Napoleon, my pet turkey vulture who eventually solved the problem of the redundant tractor. Napoleon had a Valerano heart, he nursed grudges and enacted innumerable vendettas, scoring points against his enemies in carefully planned revenge. He was wont to attack people he didn't like. He was jealous of my attention and company and jealous of his own privacy. When crossed in any way, such as being reprimanded for trying to take bites out of visitors' shins, he would flap about in a great rage and beat his long beak against the floor, eyeing any spectators with an evil expression. He conducted a running battle with *el padrón*. Napoleon was unimpressed by ancestry and the much-vaunted Terán pride. When it came to pride, no man or beast had more than Napoleon himself. When he wanted to upset me, he went into my extremely primitive kitchen and wrecked it, throwing down everything from the two mean shelves I had in lieu of furniture, opening tins and tipping out beans and salt, rice and coffee and then mixing it all upon the floor. When he wanted to hurt *el padrón*, he took his favourite clothes, shoes or hat and tore them apart, flinging the pieces disdainfully across the garden. When Jaime got close enough, Napoleon would also take pecks at his hands and legs. He would wait beside him sometimes, offering a false truce and then go for him, usually drawing blood. One day, after a particularly heated altercation, in which each chased the other for a while up and down the *camino real* in front of the *trapiche*, Napoleon was finally overcome by a stone aimed skilfully at his head.

El padrón, as was his custom, took his pick-up truck and drove off towards the city lights. He no longer bothered to say he'd be right back, and I no longer expected him. We lived our separate lives and he continued to keep some of his clothes in the little house of the *trapiche*. During the night, Napoleon rallied and set to work on the standing tractor. He ripped out every wire exposed on its side and he tore the stuffing out of the seat and scratched as much paint as he could reach.

Two days later, when the *padrón* returned, he was so angry that after thrashing Napoleon with his belt, he declared, to the Momboy valley in general, that he didn't want to drive the tractor again. I had to enlist a disgusted Antonio Moreno to help hold the wounded Napoleon down in order to mend his broken leg and wing. As I worked the plaster of Paris on to the splints, Antonio kept offering to kill the bird.

'I was watching, Doña,' he told me, 'as soon as I saw the tractor, I knew there'd be trouble when *el padrón* returned. You did well not to try and intervene.'

I shook my head, I wasn't proud of my cowardice.

'No one can intervene when the Teráns fly into a rage. It's like a fit they have, they go wild. If you can knock them out for long enough, they get over it, but if you try and interfere, they'll kill you. Remember that, when he has a rage just hide; we do.'

Napoleon's leg took a long time to mend. Meanwhile, I chained him by his good leg to the bamboo tree. He refused to have anything to do with me. For the first two days he also refused to eat, after that, he ate when I was out of sight. Everyone who came by during the time of his sickness said, 'Kill him.' I hated to see him suffer, but I couldn't kill him, not least because he had been my friend and I had so few friends.

11

Time stood still on the *hacienda*. It seemed that it had stood still for at least a hundred years. Only the occasional cars and the tractor, the rattling Povva wagon and the tiny transistor radios crackling music, gave evidence that the twentieth century had impinged on the hills. The road ran through like a taunt. Only twenty minutes away were the sprawling suburbs of Valera: a concrete maze leading into the wide Avenida Las Acacias, where the rich had their own individually designed dream houses like ships moored on a tropical green sea of plankton. In lieu of grass, which died in the heat, the lawns were planted with a round-leafed plant.

In Valera, there were slums in the *barrio*, there was the red-light zone and then there were the big houses. These last had bathrooms, in fact they had one for each member of the family – to have fewer would have been inconceivable. The dream houses had pools and fountains, marble floors and gold taps, chandeliers, polished wood and acres of plastic. These houses were full of gadgets and televisions. The televisions were constantly tuned to soap operas interrupted every few minutes by a barrage of advertisements. Every three hours there was the news, one minute of news sponsored by a product. If it was Colgate toothpaste, then, out of the minute, two mentions of the toothpaste and its powers were carved. In the intervening seconds, a flash of information about the rest of Venezuela would squeeze on to the screen.

Several of the houses had radio transmitters, by means of which it was possible to link up to telephone numbers abroad. By radio, I called home to Joanna. The line crackled and wheezed so loudly that it was virtually impossible to hear or speak. It was also overcut by other voices. I had not been able to warn Joanna either that I would call her, or that when I did, out of the blue after three months, it would be by radio. We didn't manage to establish that only one person can speak at a time and all the 'overs' and 'rogers' had to be observed and the radio switched to the other person. Joanna was slightly deaf which, added to the other problems inherent in the line, distressed her so much that the call ended with her crying and hanging up. It had taken hours to establish the connection. I didn't try again. Even if the line had been good, I don't know what I would have said to her. In a way, it was a help not to have to either lie or confess.

I was living in a cocoon. None of my plans, so fondly devised in London, for improving the *hacienda* had even begun. My partnership was over and the only sex that took place in my house was between the dogs. My acceptance at almost any level was suspended until I became pregnant. What I had once imagined as my brilliant career as a writer had also turned to dust.

Meanwhile Megan, my beagle bitch, was pregnant and dozens of other mongrels were being brought to my house to mate with Ross. This custom had developed before I had given it any thought. However, as the months dragged on and my own state of isolation and ostracisation entrenched, I grew to resent it. If I, the Doña, didn't have sex and couldn't get pregnant, then the last thing I wanted in my life was to be constantly reminded of it by the presence of dogs fornicating on my veranda from dawn till dusk. I banished the mating sessions up behind the *trapiche*, out of sight and earshot of myself and I sank even lower in my own esteem for envying the poor dogs their pleasure. On the few times when I refused to lend Ross out, I had my foreign crimes thrown in my face.

It appeared that many years before, in the 1930s, a Chinaman from Trinidad called Mr Lee had lived in Valera. Because he was a Chinaman from Trinidad, I was told, he was English. And since I was English, it was obvious that all English people were mean. For Mr Lee had bred prize canaries, and he too had refused to lend out his males. No good had come to Mr Lee.

There are no letters extant between August and October although I know I wrote them. They start again on:

October 2nd

Dear Joanna,

Please give your honest opinion of these two poems. The shorter one I am pleased with (I have had a year to pick it over) . . . The longer one I am very unsure of. Please tell me what you think, alterations, eliminations, scrap it etc.

It is my birthday today and it isn't – no letters arrived; Jaime forgot, no one else knew . . .

I think I shall publish something (with your help) soon. My morale is at nil . . .

Nothing like a birthday moan.

How is your new job? I expect a letter will arrive tomorrow with news etc.

Every day we live better, more friends, kinder people, everything beautiful and every day I sit and stare at the timbered roof going quietly insane (this morning rather more noisily insane) which shows what a contrary nature I have.

Whatever happens come next summer, please. Write to me, please. – Sometimes it is lonely here – often. I know this depression is useless. I just feel completely useless here (and lonely).

Two dogs, 3 cats, 2 hens, a cockerel and a tortoise and Jaime and I.

P.S. Don't tell Jaime's friends this.

Hda Santa Rita, Mendoza Fría, Estado Trujillo
mid-October

Dear Joanna,

How are things? . . .

Jaime is going to Barquisimeto today and coming home with our brand-new (red) tractor (cousin president of Farmers' Bank – very handy). Then we shall prepare all the level land for replanting: sugar-cane, tomatoes, lettuce and cabbage, etc., coffee, various fruits. Later we shall have flocks of sheep on the hills – there are more than a thousand acres of wooded lovely hills put to no use here . . .

I had my hair cut short this week.

Sorry about the fiasco phone call . . .

I feel well already.

Please keep writing,

Love,

Lisaveta

Then there is a gap in the letters of a month. It was a month when Antonio Moreno and the workers made headway on the *hacienda*. They mended ditches and cleared away years of silting in the irrigation channels that ran through the fields. They planted sugar-cane, sticking segments of the cane cut for the *molienda* and saved from the sugar-crusher, in the ground. Antonio Moreno told me that sugar was a noble crop. It grew despite what anyone did to it. He said you could plant the sticks upside down and they'd still grow, you could forget it, neglect it, starve it and it would still grow, like a weed with a strength of its own.

Since this was the case, I asked why they bothered to weed, irrigate and tend the crop at all. Everything came down to the colour of the sugar. Left alone, the canes grew wild and the sugar content was low: when it came to a *molienda*, the sugar would be dark and cheap. Tended, the sugar content would be high and the sugar made, the *panela*, would be the desired beige sporting that nap of white crystals.

Venezuela is a country, like so many ex-European colonies, that is colour-conscious. In life, as in sugar, light is best. On a scale of beauty, fair hair is considered better than dark, light eyes more attractive than dark. A fair skin is a sign of breeding, a mark of beauty in itself. A dark skin is the Indian strain coming out. At the bottom of the social scale is any trace of African blood, because the Africans were slaves until Simon Bolívar enlisted their help in his War of Independence and liberated them in 1810. Since the slaves fought side by side with the other patriots, including many women, and passed through great swathes of Venezuela, there are many traces of their genes which throw back genetically, to the consternation of the families involved. New-born babies, even before their fingers and toes are counted to see if the tell-tale signs of inbreeding show, are turned over and examined for signs of the Samba: a dark shadow at the coccyx and purplish half-moons on the finger-nails.

My forays into town or to the village were a constant revelation of the innate racism in that place of such palpably mixed race. I had assumed, fondly, that I, who was of mixed blood, would feel at home among a nation of similarly stirred genes. Yet every family was crossed somewhere with Indian blood and most of them were obsessed by the notion that they were not. There was ethnic snobbery. Many of the families, like the Teráns, were descended from Catalans, but all were mixed. I heard the proud boast of the Teráns who had inter-married cousin to cousin for 400 years repeated over and again. I heard how the first Labastida (the family which pre-ceded the Teráns, eventually marrying its last two daughters to two Terán brothers and thus incorporating what was left of the Labastida family into another clan) refused to marry any of the Spanish women on hand and grew to old age, celibate, until, in his senility, a young cousin was sent from Spain to bear him a son.

It seemed ironic that the cultivation of sugar-cane should bear, inherent in its growth, the seeds of this colour coding. I had tasted the dark *panela* sugar, and liked its thick moscovado taste. I asked Antonio Moreno why the *hacienda* could not produce pure dark sugar. He laughed.

'No one would eat it.'

'Why, though?'

'The fairer the better. That's the way it is. Look at me, black as molasses, and Zara as fair as elderflowers; who is the prettier?' He shrugged and smiled, twisting his thin lips crookedly. Then he paused to spit *chimó*, turning away to do so. 'Life isn't fair, Doña, it's just the way it is. Here's an example. Take Coromoto, she's a fine strong girl, too head-strong, I know, but she gets that from me and I love her. Now Coromoto isn't pretty. She looks like me. I was handsome once, but what a man can carry, a girl can't, and then her face is a bit squashed. Then take El Capino, Doña, my little one. He's white with golden hair. Tell me Coromoto wouldn't have a better and an easier life if she too were white instead of molasses. You can look like a toad squashed by a stone if you're fair. That's the way it is. I love Capino and I'm proud of him, people touch him for luck. Then, you see, we work here for the family. We've all worked for them, our fathers and grandfathers and greatgrandfathers worked for them. The family is fair-skinned, fair-haired, and they have mixed blood with ours and we like to see it surfacing.'

Some days I could talk to Antonio Moreno for hours, or rather I could get him to talk to me. Sometimes, he was locked in silence and it wasn't possible to say more than 'Good morning' to him. On other days, I felt he sought me out a little and tried to explain the ways of his world to me.

I asked him if he ever tired of working so hard and wanted to give up, to retire. He had been working on the same piece of land for eighty-one years.

'I'm an old man, but I have a young family.'

'Couldn't you have some kind of pension, though?'

Try as I might to explain what a pension was, Antonio Moreno just did not believe it existed. I went on to elucidate such matters as unemployment benefit and sick pay. Mid-stream, Antonio interrupted me.

'Do you really come from a world like that, Doña? No wonder you are lost here. Such a system would crumble within a few years and there would be nothing but chaos . . . There are things that need doing here, Doña, things that need seeing to; someone has to be in control. While *el padrón* was away, I was in charge, now he has returned; it has to be him. I cannot do things without orders any more, it is not our way. There are things that just have to be kept going. If you could help, you know, speak to him, get them done, it would make a big difference.'

I told him again that I had about as much influence as a fly.

'There's little more powerful than a fly that plays dead. You hear, you see, and you've still got your sting. Never underestimate *la mosca muerta*.'

Improvements inside consisted of a bed and a refrigerator. On the veranda, taking up almost its entire length, was a big carved settle which came, I shall never know how or why, from the cathedral at Trujillo. By sprinkling powdered lime on the floors and raising it up in the daily dust cloud, the invading cockroaches were kept at bay. My books, which had been much chewed over by both the dogs and the cockroaches, were now prey to bookworms which guzzled with bulimic haste through the pages. A cousin from Barquisimeto who treasured books told me to soak them all in a vat of kerosene and then stand them to dry, turning the pages to stop them from sticking. This process took a very long time. Seven years later the books still stank. Had a smoker ever tried to read one, he would have gone up in flames, but books were the one part of my luggage that aroused no curiosity. Nobody wanted to take them or read them or even touch them. They were mine, smelly and safe even from the insects, which spurned the petroleum pages.

Natividad, the old goat-herd, invited me again to his house. He lived on the hill immediately above La Casa Grande, five minutes' walk up the slope from the edge of the big house's orchard. To reach his house, I had to pass Los Pollos de Eladio, now back in residence and in full swing. There was an irrigation ditch running round the outside of the Casa Grande, like a small moat. Its courtyard, enclosed by high wrought-iron railings at one end was shaded by a magnificent ancient avocado tree that rained down small nobbly avocados by the hundred. Antonio Moreno insisted that this tree had been planted by Don Cesar Terán and himself at a time, which by sifting through both earthquakes and politics, floods and neighbouring births, I pinned down to being about 1935. This meant that the tree, which looked as though it were at least 200 years old in its massive, gnarled state, was exactly thirty-seven years old. A person could plant an arboretum here and live to see it mature. I personally could plant out great avenues of trees, of jacaranda and *puma rosa,* rubber and *ficus* and a hundred other varieties; and before my old age I could see them pass the point where my arms could wrap round their trunks, I could see them pass the point where I and another person could girdle them between us. I loved the idea of making a mark as solid and as visible as a forest, as avenues of trees, on this land which had so far refused to let me so much as scratch its surface.

Natividad and his wife, Josefa, were old and gentle. Their two-room cottage had some of the charm of an English country cottage. I imagined myself somewhere in Devon or Cornwall, surrounded by the flowers of a cottage garden, which here were the blooms of a tropical pot garden, with each plant in its bucket or tin. Within the confines of their poverty, they had accumulated a certain wealth. The oleanders in their pots were big bushes, their rosemary plants had grown into a hedge, their frangipani sticks were two exquisitely beautiful trees, bare of branch until the offerings of the waxen flowers on their crowns of thick green leaves. Beyond the cottage a stream had been diverted to run a trickle near their house. The arrangement had been made so long ago that all along the stream mature orange trees grew and shaded it. Their tiny plot of coffee bushes was as orderly as the corner of a plantation. Their circles of banana palms had edged away from the house of their own accord, leaving the blue plumeria and the brilliant orange trumpet vine which everyone called tango, to cover the wasp-drilled mud, which was the sun-baked clay of the walls. Natividad's house had proper doors in frames and his window had shutters. He had wooden three-legged stools to sit on, a table, a big roughly carved chair and in the kitchen there were shelves for Josefa to keep her pots on. Her cooking pots were of copper, lemon-polished to a shine. There was a picture of St Anthony in a 1920s frame hanging over a shrine of the Madonna complete with candles, tinsel and a number of small test-tubes.

Josefa, who was also in her eighties, had worked for Don Rodolfo as a girl. She had been at the Casa Grande for years, she had been the recipient of many unwanted and used-up utensils. They lent her kitchen an air of comfort. Natividad had filled his hours out watching the goats with whittling. He carved the furniture and ornaments. Over the years the bits and pieces had accumulated. Where other huts were empty, theirs was full. This sense of well-being was contradicted only by the presence of four small children all under six, who were sitting out among the pots of flowers like garden gnomes. Josefa had stitched them frocks, brushed their hair and kept them clean. She fed them, but she didn't know what to do with them. She was old and arthritic. She mentioned her daughter, Maria, and tears came to her eyes. She turned away and limped into her kitchen where she sat at the table, head in wizened brown hands.

Later, on other visits, I learnt that for forty years, Josefa and
Natividad had scrimped and saved. He had made extra money
by carving, she by sewing frocks for *la gente*. Of their four children, only one had survived infancy: Maria. Without the
burden of mouths to feed, they had saved enough for
Natividad to stop cutting cane. He was old and frail and his
eyesight was failing. He was a menace in a line of cane-cutters
both to himself and to the other workers, wielding a razor-
sharp machete across his own and other people's arms. They
had planted out their plot of land in such a way as to glean
enough beans, coffee, corn, tomatoes, onions, yucca and other
things to be self-sufficient. They had hens and ducks and a pig.
They had goats left over from Natividad's goat-herding days.
They sold milk and little flat cream cheeses. They sold eggs
and the occasional hen. They had dreamt up their own retire-
ment. As soon as Maria left and married, they would enjoy
their last years in the comfort they had always denied themselves before.

Maria didn't marry then and, later disgraced, she never
could. She eloped with El Bobo, a slow-witted man who had
seduced her. When I got to know Josefa better, she would
brew up lemon balm which she drank for her nerves and the
despair that gnawed her, 'Maria was always slow, but she used
not to be so bad. She helped me. She was a good girl. She
helped me, and then, one day, she was moonstruck and she
took to the path, just sitting there all day, so people had to
step over her to get up or down. We used to pull her away,
but she was spellbound. We tried everything. We even took
her to the witchdoctor.' Josefa shook her small bird-like head
with its mane of long grey hair as thick as horsehair tied back
tightly into a bun.

'She just sat there until El Bobo came and took her away,

without so much as a by your leave. Our only daughter. Our only hope. Took her, if you please, to live under the bridge at Carmania, like a vagrant. He took her on his donkey, but he sent her back alone . . . Four children in that yard, and three stillborn and one gone with the gripe. Tell me, Doña, is it right? What kind of a man is that? They say he loves his donkey. They say he loves her more than my daughter. They say all sorts of things. I don't care what they say. It's the disrespect. She's gone again. The first time, Natividad went after her, to bring her back or to make El Bobo marry her. They laughed him away. Our Maria is in a trance here, but she laughs and talks under that bridge . . . and more, Doña, always more, because she always comes back with a belly.

'When my son died, I thought I had felt the greatest suffering a woman can feel. I must have been so bad, Doña, so bad in ways I don't understand, because God has punished me, he is punishing me still. Nothing hurts more than this shame, more than this looking ahead and seeing nothing.

'Now she's gone again. I've used up all our savings. What will we do when she comes back with another belly? Those bellies grow and eat. She's our flesh and blood, the children are too, for all the shame, we have to keep going. She is our ruin, one of these days, she'll get us turned off.'

Antonio Moreno ruled the *hacienda* with this ultimate threat. If the man was thrown off, then his family had to follow him. This meant not only the loss of work but also of house, land to grow food for his family and, almost as bad as all three, the loss of face. Few *haciendas* took on new people, they had their own. To be thrown off was virtually to be condemned to dire poverty and danger, the danger of going it alone in the slums of the *barrio* that surrounded the town. It left little choice to peasant families other than prostitution and petty crime.

Antonio used the threat often, reminding every man and boy that they had to toe the line. It seemed to me that he humiliated the men gratuitously with this frequent menace. I tackled him on the subject only after I was sure of both his affection for and loyalty to me (so only after some years). Antonio was the key to the running of the *hacienda* and I could not risk offending him.

He said, 'Almost every man and boy whom I command is younger and stronger than me. They are all armed. As you see, Doña, we carry our machetes at all times. Half the time, as you've probably noticed, they're also drunk. If I were lax, they would not respect me. If I were lax, Doña, I would be dead. There are many among them who would gladly take my job, my house, my cows, my salary. If I don't make them respect me, I'm finished. I'm an old man, a bit too old for this job, I don't see as well as I used to, and I don't hear so well. I miss the mutterings, the goings on that were always the signs of trouble brewing. I have to be hard with them; and even so, every night when I walk up to my house and Zara, I wonder if, when I go out to see to the cows, one of the men will be waiting for me. I wonder if I've been hard enough . . . These are good people, Doña, but they don't think, they react. We all do. I have to think for them, but it isn't easy.'

12

EL MAESTRO RAMÓN Rivas and Antonio Moreno's oldest son, Antonio José, made an enclosure for the dogs. By mid-November Megan, the bitch, was heavily pregnant and I had decided to keep the litter and breed beagles myself. Every cousin seemed to want one, and there were hundreds of cousins. The enclosure had, as I told Joanna:

> 6ft high fences and a kennel with a cement floor; door with a padlock (and a drain in the floor). Both dogs are much happier there and safer. They have a little house to sleep in, two trees inside their enclosure shading them from the sun.
>
> Every morning I take them walking up into the hills and then let them loose for an hour or more. After break-fast, I put on my gloves and sunhat, lock up the house and open the kennel. Then the two of them, with collar and lead, drag me up the garden path, over the bridge, down the avenue to the main road, great effort to hold them till all is clear, then rush to the other side, up a crumbly slope, past the big house . . . across the garden,

up a narrow path between the magnificent sugar-canes, over a stream, uphill, over another stream – and I let them loose . . .

I take them to a beautiful dell filled with wild plants, banana palms, orange trees and birds chanting overhead . . .

All this writing and I still have not said that I am very well and four months pregnant. I was wondering if you could send a trunk. I shall send money for things that need buying. I do not really know what I shall need in the way of clothes, perhaps you could help me. I have the lovely shawl you made, but it is so cold here at nights and in the morning that I shall need at least another one, and woolly things too. I am rather ignorant in these matters, would you please send me a book or two about babycare and the things one should know – nothing too drastic, eh? A couple of weeks ago we went to the *páramo* and stood at the highest point of the Venezuelan Andes, a moment, no more, because it was so freezing that we had to leap back into the car and knock off half a bottle of rum to recover our senses. The flowers (in the postcard) are called *frailegónes*, and are almost the only plants to grow on the cold stone at that altitude (5,000 metres) more than 15,000 feet – much more, but maths rather poor.

Did you know that we live higher than Mt Snowdon here in Santa Rita – well, we do!

As I was saying, when the *frailegónes* are not in flower, one sees only the white sheen of the leaves which from a distance look like so many sheep crouched on the mountain side . . .

I forgot: went to the beach (the edge of Lake Maracaibo) a little while ago. Swam in tepid beautiful water, sandy beaches, coconut palms etc. . . .

Our highly despised tenants leave in March . . .

If I have any old white school shirts, send them in the trunk for the children here.

Write soon, with much love

Ever since my arrival, despite all the material improvements, I had been in a social deadlock. In order to be accepted, I had to bear a child, to bond physically with the clan I had married into. In moments of panic, I had toyed with the idea of adopting a baby and passing it off as my own. To do so, I would have needed my husband's full co-operation. I had reached a point where, by keeping myself to myself, keeping out of his way, and asking no questions at all, I lived a reasonably peaceful life; no more or less. I had resigned myself to expecting neither more nor less. I grieved for the lack of a child, not just as a passport into the *hacienda* and the hearts of *la gente*, but for myself as well, to ease the loneliness. I grieved, but I didn't hope for or expect a miracle.

It seemed like a miracle when I found I was pregnant. I was supposed to be sterile; and, also of some relevance, I was celibate. For some months before I went to see a doctor, I had suffered from intestinal worms. Coromoto filled me with horror stories about what happened when worms got out of hand. First, they hurt, every morning when you awoke they ached and made you feel sick. Then they began to grow and multiply and you swelled accordingly. All the children on the estate had worm-bellies, hard and distended, Goyo and Capino came regularly to see me, disfigured by their own implanted drums. Then the worms began to churn.

'You can feel them writhing inside you,' Coromoto told me. 'When there's no more room for them, they start to climb out. If you cough, they come out of your mouth. They crawl through your nose and you have to pull them out, but you mustn't break them, because if bits get left inside you, they go off and you die.'

Coromoto was fond of graphic descriptions of the many ailments that afflicted *la gente* and herself.

I had, for at least a month, felt the worms churning inside me, when I developed a cough. The appearance of the creatures through my nostrils seemed imminent. Two cousins, who were identical twins, known collectively as Las Morochas, had befriended me. They took me out and about: to the *páramo*, to the beach, to town, to a bar to drink banana wine and listen to Elvis Presley on the juke box, and into town. I had tried a number of Coromoto and Zara-recommended purges to no avail, and decided to see a doctor and rid myself of my portable zoo. I asked Las Morochas to take me. They chose a doctor called Dr Briceño, who was 'almost a Terán' having been brought up by one. He had studied gynaecology at the Royal Free Hospital in London and was to be a man of great importance in the rest of my time in Venezuela. However, on the first day I met him in his surgery, he was a stranger to me and I to him. He asked me what the problem was; I told him about the *hacienda* and the worms. He told me I was pregnant, four and a half months at least.

From the moment he told me, I felt infinitely grateful to the child inside me. I had never told my mother about the pressure on me to procreate. I believed it to be an impossibility, so help and advice would have been pointless.

There is always something miraculous about conceiving a child, and about the moment at which the mother knows it, and the moment at which the secret is told. I asked the doctor not to tell anyone yet. He was reluctant and wanted to know why. He spoke English, the first person to do so since May.

He surprised me, making words in the language of home in that alien place. The combination of the news he had given me and the language he spoke, threw me off my guard, and I confided to him that I had been having a hard time. I had, in particular, been spurned for not getting pregnant. I had been forced to live alone.

'But you're married.'

'On paper.'

He looked at me for so long, I felt afraid he would tell on me, he was, after all, 'almost one of them'.

'I want something for myself doctor, to get used to this first, before I have to share it. I want to have a secret for a week before it's picked over by everyone else.'

He agreed, and I left. The Morochas were waiting for me outside. They took me to buy paw-paw milk-shakes and chilli fritters, then they took me home. As we drove past the ragged clump of banana palms that I knew to be the frontier post of the *hacienda*, I noticed that for the first time since I had arrived, I didn't get the sensation of being taken back to prison after a turn round the yard. I was carrying inside me a way out of the silence. I imagined all the huts in the hills beyond Antonio's and Natividad's being open to me, and all the people saying 'Good day' to me when I said 'Good day' to them instead of scowling and turning away. I wanted to stay.

I had one week to gather my thoughts and to rid myself of the bitterness that had been growing in me over not having been accepted. I had one week to live as I had done for the last half year before everything changed. I knew that virtually nothing would be the same again afterwards. My key to initiation into the clan was there; as soon as people knew, I would become a blood relation and the world revolved around blood ties. In Valera, over my milk-shake, I worked out that the date coincided with the three-week amnesty of the August before. This was not, as I had momentarily supposed, a case of immaculate conception. Nor was it the consequence of my sleepwalking.

In my first few days on the *hacienda*, I had begun to sleepwalk. It was not something I had ever done before. Yet, night after night, I found myself wandering out of doors. The cold woke me. It was extremely cold to be standing barefoot in a nightdress by the edge of the river at three o'clock in the morning, particularly if it was pouring with rain. Given the abundance of snakes, scorpions, poisonous spiders and other hazards, I tried to lock myself in. I was more worried about insects or drowning than rapists, because the mythical Coco seemed to keep the entire place deserted at night. Before retiring to my hammock, I locked and padlocked the door to the room, barricaded the window, moved the old desk to block the door, locked the gate to the palisade with another padlock and hid the key. Sometimes, I woke up in the process of escaping, yet still, often, I found myself wandering around the *trapiche*, or anything up to a mile away along the stony *camino real*.

When the dates fitted what Dr Briceño had told me, I felt a lot calmer and better. When you live with someone but you haven't slept with them for over four months, it isn't the easiest thing to say, 'Oh, by the way, I'm pregnant.' When the person in question has trouble remembering who you are, it is more difficult. I had learnt that to gain *el padrón*'s attention, I had to say what I wanted swiftly. During my week of grace, I mused over how to break the news. If I just told Coromoto, he and the entire *hacienda* would have known within minutes by whatever telepathic tom-tom gossip was relayed around the hills, but I felt I had to say it to him in person.

He ate breakfast with Antonio Moreno out of billycans in the *trapiche* when he was at home. I had overheard him making an arrangement for the following morning. I woke early, helped by the inane screeching of the Cuban cockerels who strutted their miniature crests around my yard. It was day five. I would get up, get dressed, wait for him on the veranda and then tell him. If he didn't listen, I'd shout it after him. And, if need be, in the evening, I would leave a note on his hat. He never went anywhere without his hat. It was half-past five and barely light. Antonio Moreno would be down at seven.

When things happened on the *hacienda, la gente* just seemed to know about them. That morning a man had died on the road at the entrance to the path to the *trapiche*. Coromoto and her friends knew to go down early. I cross-examined her as to how she knew, when she never came down before ten, and she said, 'It's just a feeling, a fizzy feeling like Paysi-Cola in the back of my neck, inside, and then you feel itchy, you know, like lice crawling over you and you just head to wherever it is.'

Coromoto and several other children from different parts of the estate had simultaneously experienced this Pepsi-feeling and converged on the corpse of an old man lying across the dirt road that led both to the *trapiche* and my house. One of the man's cloth slippers was lying away from his body. Nobody wanted to touch his body, he was a stranger and therefore brought bad luck, but the *cotiza* slipper was fair game, and Coromoto and her friends all claimed it as a personal trophy. Their heated bickering slung across the river to me. It was six o'clock. I went to investigate and was met by Coromoto and the other girls marching across the bridge. They were all excited. 'There's a cadaver, there's a *cotiza*, there's a cadaver!'

They all talked and shouted together, five of them, including two I had never seen before. My presence finally subdued them, leaving Coromoto, uncowed, to speak. She insisted it was her right to have the *cotiza*. She reminded me that she came here every day and so would naturally have found it. It was hers and she wanted it. The other girls looked at me shyly, comparing me, I felt, to the stories they had been told. When they had decided that I didn't look half as menacing as I was said to be, they joined in, squabbling. Meanwhile, the dead man lay at our feet, arousing no interest at all.

Much to Coromoto's annoyance, I made her put the *cotiza* back beside the corpse. I'd never really seen a dead person before. I'd been to a funeral for a still-born child and seen his dead, staring face wreathed in white satin in his white casket. That had seemed bad enough, but it had been quick and was followed by a mug of hot chocolate and a pile of ginger biscuits and had all taken place inside someone's sitting room at a formal wake. The corpse at my feet was much more distressing.

'Don't touch anything,' I said over my shoulder to the children, remembering innumerable films where the police always said that. I hurried home.

'Where are you going?' Coromoto asked me.

'To call the police and ambulance.'

She looked at me as though I were in the throes of a convulsion. I kept hurrying to maintain my dignity, but it was true, who could I call, and how? I had no phone, as far as I knew there were no ordinary policemen and I hadn't seen an ambulance since we left Caracas.

It wasn't long before Antonio Moreno came down for his breakfast rendezvous. He didn't come to the house, so I went to the *trapiche*. I told him there was a cadaver on the road.

'I know, and right across the path, I had to step over him to get here.'

'Who is he?'

Antonio shrugged elaborately. He was a stranger, a tramp. The National Guard would come by and collect him at some time during the day.

'Do you mean you're just going to leave him there?'

'Of course not, he's blocking the road. I've already moved him to one side . . . and you'd better hold on to Napoleon, that's just his sort of thing out there, he'll be thinking it's a picnic.'

Napoleon was safely locked up in the bathroom, which was where I chased him when he got too out of hand. His fits of jealousy were a recurring problem and he often needed time to calm down. As Antonio had already pointed out, Napoleon, with his sudden rages, was almost a Terán.

I crossed Jaime on the track back home. I had missed my chance to tell my news. At some point during the morning, the body was taken away. I didn't see who came for it, people said it was the National Guard.

That night, I was alone. I brought the dogs in for company, and let them sleep in the room. I seemed to have forgotten how destructive they could be. While I was sleeping, they chewed their way through several books and records and a pair of Oxford brogues. I overslept. The sun was over the hill when I woke. There had already been several scenes including the dogs and I knew that if anything else was spoilt they'd be in for more than a thrashing. Jaime actually loved the dogs, he played with them, cuddled them and lavished presents and affection on them. But when he got angry he didn't think, he reacted, as Antonio would say. It wasn't wise to stand in the way of his reaction. I decided to hide the dogs in a brick room in the *trapiche* where the sugar was packed. It was high up and out of sight, and, I hoped (over the rush of the millrace), out of earshot.

I took Megan up first and locked her in. It was several minutes' walk away and as I ran back, Jaime returned. Since he was driving and I was walking, he got back before me. I went in to find him surveying the mess. He picked up a leather shred from the edge of his shoe, then he leant down and picked up Ross. He held him up and hurled him across the room. The dog hit the far wall with a thud. The tin roof rattled. Jaime's face had set half-way down in the rigid grimace I dreaded. He bent down to pick up the dog again. Then, I didn't think; I reacted. I clasped my hands together and brought them down as hard as I could on the back of his neck. The dog was whining. Jaime keeled over. I stepped back and back again. He turned over and got up. He too had clasped his hands, he held them high up over his head, poised to come down on mine.

I continued to back away from him. I shouted, 'I'm pregnant, don't hit me, I'm pregnant.'

He didn't seem to hear me, he kept following slowly round the room. I held my stomach to accentuate the bulge, 'Look, I'm pregnant; You'll hurt your baby if you hurt me.'

Ross was still whining. He too had picked himself up and was staggering across the floor to the door. I was so sure Jaime would get me, I started to laugh, a nervous laugh that has been the bane of my life and tends to crop up at the most tactless moments. As I laughed, he paused, puzzled.

'What did you say?' he asked me.

'I said I was pregnant, four and a half months' pregnant.'

'But that's wonderful, Lisaveta. Why didn't you tell me before? How do you know, how can you be sure?'

He turned to where Ross was struggling to get out of the door.

'What's the matter with Ross? Why is he whimpering? What's happened? You should tell me, he might have been stung by something, he's limping.'

He knelt on the dusty floor and fussed over the dog.

Like a tap that turned from hot to cold, or a railway signal that could make an engine change course, the next three months fanned me from friend to foe with a regularity that began to make such behaviour predictable. In the good times, there was no recollection of the bad ones, and in the bad times there was no recollection of the good, at least for Jaime. It made for a surreal emotional pendulum. I rocked backwards and forwards, paying lip service to whatever phase we were in.

Meanwhile, I was writing, I wrote long dreary poems about dead newts and dead bats. I wrote fragments on loneliness, rejection and fear. I tried to find the perfect adjectives to describe the gnawing of rats and all the other sounds that invaded the human silence of life in the little house. I continued to write out the colours green, the different shades. I also wrote all the things I didn't dare to say, then I burnt them, reassured by the pretence that anyone would be interested in anything I thought or said.

For much of each day I read. When the surviving books in my trunks seemed too recently recycled through my brain to tempt me, I read the *Concise Oxford Dictionary* and the *Cordon Bleu Cookbook*. Joanna had sent me *Gray's Anatomy* and several other medical books, which I grappled with. I was chastened by my attempt to mend Napoleon's leg. He limped. I had a grey, cloth-covered vade-mecum of all the antibiotics, their uses and interreactions. I tried to memorise it. No matter how many herbal cures I learnt, I was sure I would always need antibiotics.

I dreamt of one day running a proper dispensary. I wanted to be the healer of the running sores. Without encroaching on anyone else's territory, I saw a niche for myself as the curer of the terrible outbreak of cradle cap that scabbed and festered on almost every estate baby's head. Later, I mused, I would tackle internal parasites and more complicated things. I spent hours testing myself on the theory of how to amputate a leg above the knee with a special flap that was sewn at the back of the stump and therefore didn't rub its scar on an artificial limb.

While I perfected this technique, I was concentrating on festering sores. My patients were limited to those who came within range of the *trapiche*. Even so, the sores I treated improved. I had amassed a stock of patent medicine, but I hadn't the courage to prescribe it yet, with the exception of a few topical antibiotic creams. I concentrated on herbal remedies, learning what I could from Zara and old Josefa, adding cures I found in the book Joanna sent me.

I had always enjoyed gathering flowers and herbs. Where once I just drew and pressed them, I now made pastes, potions and powders. The success I had with tincture of arnica on Antonio's badly sprained wrist won me his admiration. I had learnt to bandage in the Girl Guides. By tearing up a sheet, I replaced the local bandages of a wrapping of banana fibre for my own more clinical version. Coromoto showed me how to bind finger-cuts with cobwebs, and I showed her how to disinfect her and her brothers' wounds with salt and water.

When I became pregnant, I dreamt of a life of being Lady Bountiful; of living in the Casa Grande and dispensing nourishing meat jellies to the sick. I planned to keep the endemic conjunctivitis under control. I would treat worms, lice and sores, skin infections, the endless diarrhoeas, and some day, when I felt qualified, I would tackle all the bronchitis on the *hacienda*. I had a big supply of aspirin which Joanna replenished for me. She sent me parcels via Venezuelan friends of friends travelling from London back to Caracas.

Most of the well-to-do people I met had *haciendas*, but they didn't live on theirs. They were run by foremen. The men visited the estates once or twice a week, on the principle that the eye of the owner fattens the horse. Under the veneer of frivolity, some of the wives did a lot for their workers and their families. I noticed the ways in which these other women helped and tried to copy them. If I asked too many questions, though, they warned me not to get too involved. It would look bad. *Qué dirán?* Word reached my mother-in-law in Caracas that I was getting philanthropic. She wrote me an affectionate letter warning me not to. She said, 'The ruin of a house enters through the back door, through the kitchen.' She hoped I wasn't giving away any food. To do so would be fatal.

The days slipped by and I lay in my hammock and embroidered beautiful gowns for the baby, which was to be born by the first week of April. The sun beat down on the tin roof. People drifted in and out, and I drifted in and out of the game I was playing. I kept my dusty house swept, and the box of bandages clean. The lazy days could easily have become years, and perhaps would have done, were it not for a jolt into reality.

13

ONE MORNING, COROMOTO came early to the house. Instead of coming in, she hid by the corner of the workshop like she used to. Her face was puffy and her usually shrill voice subdued.

'Doña, come here,' she said. 'Come here, I've got something to show you.'

I wondered what she'd brought this time. She always tried to find things to surprise me: a blind snake's discarded skin, a gecko's tail, a wild orchid, birds' eggs, stick insects mating, a tree-frog in a jar.

'Come here,' she insisted, flapping her arm down in a semaphore signal which stood for the same request.

I waited for her to come to me. She didn't move. I went to her. As I approached, she pulled El Capino, her youngest brother forward and pushed him in front of me. He was green. As green as a sick lizard. The varying shades of green of his hands, his face and his spiky hair were reptilian. He was three years old. The whites of his eyes were marbled green. Coromoto re-arranged a grey towel on his head to keep the sun from his forlorn face.

'Mama says do something.'

I'd never seen a green boy before, I didn't know what to do or what to think.

'Mama says to do something,' Coromoto repeated. Her voice cracked.

I thought Capino had been dipped in dye. I thought perhaps he had gangrene. I didn't know what to think.

Coromoto was asking, 'Will he die?'

'What is it?'

'El Capino, he's taken a paper.'

Medicines came in papers. People took fruit salts and Epsom salts and bicarbonate of soda. None of them were green.

'Loosen the wheel. Call Antonio.'

Coromoto ran off, relieved to be doing something. El Capino was poisoned. I had a book on poisons. I rummaged through it; there was nothing as extreme as the child's green-ness. It offered egg white beaten with water as a general emetic. 'Seek medical help immediately.'

'Drink this, Capino, it will help you,' I said, touching the towel on the child's head.

'Will I die?' he asked.

I tried to spoon-feed him some of the mixture. He resisted, shying his head.

'Will I die? Will I die?' he kept asking.

The loosened wheel clanged and crashed, rumbling across the valley. Antonio Moreno arrived quickly, followed by a number of other workers. Antonio came up, but he wouldn't look at me, 'Can you do something, Doña?'

I shook my head, 'I'm sorry, he'll have to go to the hospital.'

Antonio's face tightened and a muscle in his hollow cheek twitched. He turned to fetch La Povva. He backed the lorry down the broken track to the little house and lifted his son into his arms. The green boy sicked up a trickle of the egg white

122

Coromoto had succeeded in feeding him, it too was green.

The wheel clanged on, rumbling round. More people gathered, the more the wheel summoned, the more workers came. They were whispering 'hospital'. The word was like death itself to them.

Jaime arrived, saw what was happening and climbed into the driver's seat.

'Get in, *compadre*,' he said to Antonio.

Antonio walked round to the other side of the lorry, and climbed in. Capino's voice cheeped from his father's arms, 'Will I die, will I die, will I die?'

His eyes were glazed now, as though he saw and heard nothing. Only the question seemed to link him to his former life. I watched them drive away. Months later, remembering what he had looked like then, I wrote, 'All the different greens seemed to glare forward that day, comparing themselves to El Capino's vivid skin. He was the colour of lettuce leaves and young banana palms, of marsh grass and ripe passion fruits. His cheekbones and knuckles seemed almost as dark as the cane itself and the convolvulus that grew around it. And his thin eyebrows were like dull lichen.'

After La Povva left, a puddle of albuminous water transformed to pond weed remained on a worn cobblestone. We who were left stood awkwardly around the pool and the space where the lorry had been. More and more workers gathered. I felt oppressed by their crowd, by our mutual uselessness. They kept arriving. I heard them asking each other in loud whispers, 'Did she do something?' Coromoto was leaning against the wall of the workshop, almost buried in the jasmine bush. She looked as though the wheel were turning through her head. Eventually she sidled up to me, 'They'll keep coming and they won't go away until you tell someone to tie up the wheel.'

The wheel was tied and the crowd dispersed. Everything in the valley seemed to be asking, 'Will I die?' The *hacienda* begged the question all afternoon. Jaime and Antonio returned at about four o'clock. El Capino was in the hospital; a doctor friend was looking out for him. Capino would be all right. He would get well. It would take time and the green would fade. They had returned in the juddering Povva together with a convoy of trucks. Antonio sat heavily down on the old cathedral bench on my veranda. '*El padrón*'s going to stay in town, he'll be on call. I'm going up to get Zara. Coromoto can look after the baby. I need Zara to go to town.' He spoke dully. His voice was completely flat. His sunken face had aged and caught up with him suddenly. He stood up to go and then slumped down again.

'I gave it to him, Doña. I poisoned my son.'

I tried to say something to soothe him, but he had made up his mind to speak.

'Capino had worms, bad worms. He was pining and I hated to see him lose all his strength. We tried everything, but he kept on being sick. So I took him to the *brujo*, the witchdoctor. The *brujo* is my friend, I've known him for years and he's famous for some of his cures. He has been a help to us many times. The *brujo* used to be a simple man like me. I had faith in him. There is little left to have faith in.'

Antonio was jabbing at the floor with his talon-like toe, marking time as he spoke.

'Everything is changing here. Even the *brujo* has changed. He's grown too proud to speak his cures any more. He has to put on the airs of a hospital doctor. When he sent the medicine for Capino's stomach pains, he wrote it down on a scrap of paper.'

Antonio waited.

124

'I can't read, Doña. I didn't know it said copper sulphate.'

'Didn't they ask what it was for at the chemist's?'

They had, and Antonio had told them it was for the *hacienda*. On the *hacienda* it was used for baiting rats in the *trapiche*.

'You see,' he said, stabbing at the floor, 'you don't expect medicine to taste nice. When Capino wouldn't take it, we held him down and I made him drink it. I purged him with death, Doña.'

'But they've said he'll be all right.'

'Will he, though? I want Zara to see. She'll know if he's improving. He's on a drip, they're doing things. Who knows what things they do there? It's another world. It's not our world.'

Coromoto came running along the track, she had seen La Povva returning and the cloud of dust from the accompanying cars. Antonio told her what he knew and sent her straight back for Zara. When she had gone, he continued, 'We thought he'd stop crying after a while, but he didn't; he cried all night. The neighbours came. The women said it was the evil eye, but I knew it was the paper.'

Antonio sighed, and his rheumy eyes scanned the cobbles, the bamboo, the ochre escoba bushes with their untidy leaves.

'I have known shame, Doña. I have lived with it and chewed it in my food, and I've known loss, but I never thought I'd live to see the day when I'd kill my own boy.'

The *brujo*, scarcely more literate than Antonio, had learnt the fancy names of certain drugs. These he copied out. He wanted to prescribe Epsom salts to Capino: in the old days, he would have said 'Sal daysom', sal de Epsom, and everything would have been clear. But from a book he could scarcely decipher, he had discovered that 'sal daysom' had a longer name, *sulfato de magnesia*. From *sulfato de magnesia* to *sulfato de cobre* his memory must have slipped. Magnesium was not the stuff of every day, copper (*cobre*) was: the vats in the *trapiche* were made of copper, lots of things were, and copper must have slipped into his mind, been written down to be passed from hand to hand by people who couldn't read. Only the chemist would have known he was selling a paper of poison, chemists weren't allowed to sell poison to just anyone, but Antonio Moreno wasn't just anyone, he was the foreman of the Hacienda Santa Rita, the Terán plantation, so no one asked him what the poison was for.

Zara came down to the road for the first time in nearly a decade. Antonio sluiced Capino's green sick out of the floor of La Povva and drove her into Valera, to the hospital.

Early next morning, he returned. I heard the lorry battling up to the *trapiche*. I went to find him. He was alone.

'They're letting him die, Doña. I beg you to do something.'

'What can I do?'

'Go to the hospital. Make them notice him. Make them help. You can, you're a Terán.'

I climbed into La Povva. I had never been in it before. It was high and hard to get into with the weight of my seven months' pregnancy. *En route*, Antonio didn't speak until we reached the slums on the outskirts of Valera.

'Do you believe in God, Doña?'

'Not really.'

'Nor me. I've seen too much. But . . . if Capino lives, I will believe in him.'

He was close to tears.

Outside the hospital, rows and rows of women and children sat in folding chairs or on the ground, surrounded by bundles of provisions. All looked towards the door, as though towards a stage. The hospital was a last resort, it was where a peasant came when all else failed. It was customary to see each patient by turn for a few seconds, issue two, four, or six, identical little pills and tell the sufferer to return in three months. In three months, almost all would either be dead or spontaneously cured. Every Venezuelan was entitled to free medical care at the hospitals. It was the law. With fortunes to be made by doctors in private practice, few cared to carry out the statutes of the welfare state. The peasants were not only neglected, they were treated with overt disrespect. Only the intervention of the landed classes could get them any service. Most of the public hospitals were purloined for private practice. A few good doctors battled against the system. Dr Briceño was one of these, and I was to meet several others. Their work was a drop in the ocean. Numerically, there was not much they could do, spiritually their honesty and dedication gave hope and kept faith for better times to come.

Antonio guided me to the doctor who was in charge of Capino. We found him among an obstacle race of trolleys, each filled by the victims of gunfights, knife fights and terrible burns. Dozens of people were shouting, groaning and crying at once. Further along the corridor, men and women were heaped two per single trolley, some with bandages, some with drips. There was no room for all the sick, not enough doctors or nurses, not enough beds. The doctor, in a stained white coat came straight across to me. I asked after Capino. He told me the green boy was as well as could be expected, he was doing well. He told me where to find him. He told me what was in his drip, what drugs he had been given. He told me my husband had been in to remind him to take care of the child. He shook my hand and turned back to his sea of weeping patients.

Antonio and I went up to Zara. She told Antonio to go and rest, to come back later. I sat with Zara beside the green child in a corner of the children's ward. His drip was dripping. His catheter bag was filling with drips of black blood. Capino was barely conscious. Zara dabbed wet cottonwool on his lips. He was whispering something. When I leant closer, he was still repeating, 'Will I die?'

In the afternoon, Jaime came up to the ward with the *compadre* who had given me Napoleon. They summoned me outside. I explained what the doctor had said.

'The bastards!' the *compadre* said, 'if that's all they've done, the bastards! Did you ask about a stomach pump?'

I shook my head.

'You can't just sit there and assume things are happening. This is Venezuela . . . Come on!' We went back down to the casualty hall. The *compadre* pushed and shoved and shouted until he had located the young doctor I had spoken to.

'Did you give the green boy a stomach pump?'

'Yes.'

'When?'

'I don't know, I was off duty.'

'Show me his chart.'

'It's upstairs. I'm busy. Can't you see what hell it is in here?'

Upstairs, the chart showed no stomach pump had actually been given. It had been recommended and forgotten. Treatment was ensuing as though the intestinal wash had occurred. The *compadre* turned to me, 'Why didn't you check? Can't you see what it's like here? Nobody gives a damn, nobody cares. That child is dying, can't you see, *musiua*, that-child-is-dying. He's poisoned. He needs washing out and a change of blood. Have you got a stock of blood in for him?'

I shook my head.

'The doctor downstairs has just said he told you they might have to do a transfusion.'

I nodded.

'Well?'

I thought, 'Well, what?' What could I do? Transfusions came from blood banks not from me. The *compadre* stormed out of the hospital, he was furious with everyone, me, Jaime, the hospital and himself. That afternoon he took Jaime to the local radio station to send out an appeal for the rhesus negative blood. There was no blood bank in Valera. If a transfusion was needed, the blood had to be supplied. The message requested the blood for a member of the Terán family and the donors rallied, some of them coming up to peer at the green boy their blood was actually for. The *compadre* brought in a team of crack doctors and Capino was moved into intensive care.

Antonio, Zara and I were banished from the bedside and waited in a corridor. We were joined by several men who assured Antonio that everything was now being done to save his son. Plasma was flown in in frozen containers. In the morning his kidneys would be linked to a kidney machine if need be. During the night, it was just Zara and me. Capino sank into a coma.

Next day the kidney machine was used. By the afternoon his heart and lungs were on life support. At the last minute, someone organised a military plane to fly Capino to the military hospital where a transplant surgeon was being found to replace his kidneys.

I sat alternately with Zara and with Antonio. Mostly, we said nothing. There seemed nothing to say. The waiting up and the tension induced a curious, feverish state in the watchers. The general standard of care in the hospital was depressingly low. From the care and attention that was now swamping Capino, it was clear that the actual resources of the hospital were phenomenal. Machines I had never even dreamed of were wheeled out and linked up to his frail green body. Several times during the next two days people came and took me away to drink fruit-shakes and snacks in Valera. The contrast between the hospital and the outside was surreal. The only thing the two places had in common was the heat.

Twice, during our vigil in the corridor, the National Guard came up to interrogate Antonio about the purchase and giving of the poison. The first time I corroborated his story that the copper sulphate had been bought on estate instructions as a rat poison and then taken by the child by mistake. When all the attention began to focus on El Capino, and the whole hospital was talking about the green boy on the children's ward, the National Guard came back. They questioned Antonio again, this time more roughly. They had heard a rumour of how the accident had actually happened. The arrival of some of the Teráns ended Antonio's ordeal, and the soldiers were sent away with short shrift. Antonio seemed resigned to anything. When the soldiers had come back the second time, he seemed content to let them take him away, contradicting nothing, offering no defence and no resistance.

El Capino clung on to his life for five days. Twice he surfaced from his coma sufficiently to murmur something, each time it was, 'Will I die?' No one had the courage to tell him, 'Yes.' It was very early in the morning when a doctor came out and took Antonio gently by the shoulder, he said nothing, only jerking his head slightly towards the intensive care room behind him where Capino had died. The doctor half-closed his eyes and opened his hands in a gesture of both apology and defeat. Zara saw the gesture and rose to her feet. She tried to get past the doctor but he held her firmly back.

'I'm sorry. The body will be ready to be taken up to the *hacienda* this afternoon.'

Antonio raised an eyebrow. Why couldn't they take Capino back now?

'There'll have to be an autopsy. I'm sorry. This is a poison case. We have no choice.'

We drove back to the *hacienda* and Antonio dropped me off at the *trapiche*. Zara had sat beside me all the way back holding her sides and rocking in her grief. Antonio climbed down to help me out. He opened the door and half-swung me to the ground. I was searching for something to say.

Antonio touched my elbow and said, 'I killed him.'

Then he staggered back to his side of the lorry and drove away. As I picked my way along the track back to my house, I thought that Antonio had indeed administered the poison, but he had tried everything he could to help his son. Antonio's only fault was his ignorance and his poverty. I wasn't poor and I wasn't ignorant. I had the means to hold power. So if Antonio had killed his son, then just as surely I had let him die. If one-tenth of what had been done at the end had been done at the beginning of his treatment, Capino might have lived.

The story of the green boy passed quickly into the popular myth. For me the death of Capino was the spur that pushed me out of my dream world into reality. From that day I made myself responsible for the welfare of *la gente*.

14

WHEN ANYONE DIED within the community, everyone shared in their death. There was a pre-established ritual that provided a framework for the mourning and the loss. Death was one of *la gente*. It lived on the *hacienda*. It was familiar to everyone. It culled the children and decimated the adults. The *hacienda* was a place of fevers and infections, of amoebiasis, diphtheria and diarrhoeas. In the cane-fields there were accidents along the lines of wielded machetes; in the huts there were burns from kerosene stoves and lamps. There were snakes and forest fires and landslides, there were fights and organised vendettas. And running through, taking its annual tithe, as surely as a hungry anaconda, there was the road.

Death and the grief that surrounded it were too regular guests in everybody's houses to be entertained alone. Their presence was shared. The depth of emotion expressed at wakes and funerals and the annual memorials held for each death was not feigned. Every time someone on the *hacienda* died, the loss of someone else was recalled. Those who survived lived a little bit more intensely for those who had died. And every death brought a little bit of life to other people's bereavement.

Since tradition ruled in all things, it did, too, for funerals. When adults died there was much weeping and lamentation; when a child died there was a celebration. Until the age of nine, children were deemed innocent. A dead child was an angel too good to live, whom God had gathered up to heaven to keep him company. There was no question of hell or purgatory; little children went straight to heaven, bypassing the day of judgement by flying there on stitched satin wings. The first thing done to the newly dead was to prop up their chins and close their eyes, but children met their maker with their eyes open. The corner of each eyelid was propped open with a thorn. At most wakes the faults of the deceased were hastily forgotten and a list of their good points was proclaimed by members of the assembled mourners. Each attribute was introduced by 'because'. Because he was a good father and because he was a generous husband, because he was tall and strong, because . . . When the becauses ran out (or when they made too blatant a contrast to the universally known truth: because he was a neglectful father and a mean bastard of a husband, etc.) the night of the wake would be whiled away recalling anecdotes of the more enjoyable or unusual events of the deceased's life. Wakes were never entirely gloomy for very long. Fifteen hours is a long time to sit solemnly round a coffin. It is long enough for life to go on: meals are cooked, snacks served, endless mugs of hot chocolate made from greasy pellets of Criollo cocoa are handed round. These were hot, sludgy gulps of dark porphyry with droplets of oil sliding around on top. Chocolate was traditional only for wakes and after funerals. Local firewater and sometimes rum were also served. Towards dawn, relays of mourners sidled round the coffin of their friend or relative to be sick on his newly vacated porch. It was bad form, as the morning dawned, to mention or even seem to notice the transformation in the corpse. Funerals were never more than twenty-fours hours after the death, usually they were less. Even so it wasn't usually soon enough to stop the corpse from decomposing. Although it was not done to be the first to comment on either the smell or the visible discoloration of the newly departed, it was usually a surreptitious diversion among the mourners to monitor their progress.

Wakes were the most socially unifying events in the year. Everyone gathered for a wake. Only the paraplegic, the desperately ill or newly delivered mothers were excused from attending. Since it was the only time when distant cousins met *en masse*, inevitably wakes had a certain festive quality to them.

El Capino's wake was the first I ever attended. Being still unversed in the *mores* of Andean deaths, I was surprised to find myself at what seemed to be a party. Having seen both Antonio's and Zara's grief earlier in the day, I didn't understand how it could have vanished so suddenly. Their hut was swarming with friends and neighbours. The women were cloistered in the kitchen, spilling out into the back yard, while the porch, the front and the bedroom were full of men and boys.

The wake had started early and was in full swing by the time I arrived, stumbling up the steep track with my torch. Wakes on the *hacienda* would always start early to cheat El Coco, the Bogey Man, of wandering prey. At one end of the porch, a sawn-off kerosene can was filled with local *aguardiente*, the firewater beloved of the country. The kitchen, packed with women and young girls, had become an *arepa* factory. A production line of thin round maize cakes was under way. One woman, with upper arms almost as muscular as Zara's, was kneading a great snowball of ground white Indian corn and water, twisting bits the size of ping-pong balls methodically and piling them beside her. Others were flattening these, swirling them round expertly under the heel of their hands, then piling their discs up on an enamel plate. A cast-iron hot plate was covering the embers of a fire, balanced on the three cooking stones that encircled it. There was smoke everywhere, as there was in every peasant kitchen, since no chimney existed other than the door. The various stages in the making of an *arepa* were deemed to be of manifold importance. It was never enough to make and griddle them, they had to rise, bubble and subside in such a way that the finished article was soft, cooked and also brushed with beige on the outer skin. To this end, they were removed from the griddle very early on in their cooking and finished off over the ubiquitous used milk tin, sawn off to make an empty cylinder and covered with wire mesh at the top. Over a hot stone, the cooking of this staple food continued on this charred drum. A woman who couldn't make a perfect *arepa* was never quite a real woman. (I was instructed in the art of *arepa*-making for so many years before I finally scraped past my *arepa* finals that I was thought to be slow in the head and in need of all the help and guidance I could get.) After the slow grilling was over, the *arepas* were wrapped in a cloth. They were served with dips, the commonest of which was called *mojo de huevos*, and was a variation of soft scrambled eggs cooked with onion, garlic, tomato, fresh coriander and salt. The hot *arepa* was either filled with this or dipped into a bowl of it. Because this was a wake, there were also dips of cream cheese and coriander, sardines and coriander and a preparation of fresh chilli and bird peppers steeped in milk, salt and coriander. This last, known generically as *ají* which covered anything and everything that contained hot peppers, had a kick that made you see stars and weep. *Ají* was served with every meal including breakfast. When times were hard, a meal was simply *arepas* with *ají*. Sometimes the *ajicero* (sauce made with *ají*) was steeped in water.

Only at wakes, and only to concoct the hot chocolate was milk used in any quantity. Milk for human consumption came in blue and white tins with the name 'Reina del Campo' written across them, 'Queen of the countryside'. Despite the fact that hardly any of *la gente* drank milk in any form, the used tins were so prized they were almost collectors' items on the *hacienda* and were, indeed, the queens of the countryside, since everyone used them daily to make their *arepas*, and gardens grew almost exclusively in their tins. The cousin in Valera who was constructing a full-size aeroplane out of these Reina del Campo tins was marvelled at, I am sure, not so much because of the attempted feat of engineering and all the welding and design that, over twenty years, were going into his aircraft, as for his wealth and ingenuity in acquiring so many thousands of tins.

In a place where amoebiasis was endemic, where every man, woman and child carried a chronic strain of that microscopic parasite in their blood, milk was poison to their systems. The intestinal amoeba thrived on it. To drink milk was automatically to bring on a bout of cramps and runs. The acute version of the attack could kill and did so regularly like a first cousin twice over of the Grim Reaper. The hot chocolate, so thick it congealed into dark blancmange, was mixed partly with water, but the powered milk was there, stirred into the recipe: a penance for all who drank it.

In a corner, on a stool, wedged behind the bustling kitchen helpers, Zara sat in a corner smiling wanly. She was not supposed to mourn the loss of her Capino. He was an *angelito*, a little angel saved from the valley of sorrow and drudgery, called in his innocence to a better life. His mother and all who knew him were supposed to rejoice. Capino would not have a life as hard as theirs. He would not know the continual battering of the elements, or have to fight disease and poverty. Antonio had got around his dilemma by getting hopelessly red-eyed drunk, but, like most local women, Zara wasn't a drinker. Convention told her to rejoice. She didn't have it in her. Rather than cry openly (*qué dirán?*) she sat in a huddle like a zombie and stared at a patch of dirt floor by her feet. She was staring at it when I arrived, and as the night wore on, she stared harder and harder, letting her tired head loll forwards towards the studied patch as though it were her own only link left to life.

With Zara semi-cataleptic in the kitchen, Coromoto became the lady of the house. Her eyes were puffy from earlier tears and her face was contorted and swollen, yet by well before midnight Coromoto had risen to the pride of her position and was sidling, straight-backed, and with the slight coquettishness of a natural-born hostess, between the groups of swaying drunken men, carrying hot chocolate and fritters and stacks of steaming *arepas* and wedges of grilled yucca.

In the bedroom, in a small white painted casket, El Capino lay cushioned in satin and smiling with an expression of huge relief on his pinched, tortured face. Despite the undertaker's heavy-handed efforts to conceal the natural hue of Capino's skin, underneath the beige foundation and the liberal dusting of powder, his skin still showed a little green. Like the verdigris that is the base of pigment in Renaissance skin tones, the green glow showed through with age. I had seen innumerable green-faced angels in church frescoes in Italy, with all the colours of life eroded from the pigments of their skin. Now, far away, a child prematurely aged had been corroded and lay in incongruous pomp in the mud hut of his parents. There were tin chalices at either corner of his bed. An enormous crucifix hung from the rafters over his head. The table his coffin was laid on was draped in something which in the half-light looked like cloth of gold embroidered all over with a wealth that seemed Venetian in its sumptuousness. Also at each corner, competing with the chalices, were big church candles.

By daylight, when the undertaker scuttled up to take back his hired finery, neither candle stands or cloth were more than cheap, poorly made imitations of better things. But as they stood in the flickering candlelight, steeped in incense around the dead child, their theatricality worked.

I had decided not to stay long at the wake so as not to embarrass the other mourners. I stayed longer than I had intended because I was thrown by the lack of mourning. The sleepless nights spent at the hospital had made me see the world as through a fever. Antonio Moreno, who had been trembling with sheer exhaustion by night three was smiling drunkenly. While many of his workers, on a regular Saturday night, would get nasty and offer, machete in hand, to slice their way to immortality, or stand out in the scrub and roar like wounded beasts, Antonio seemed to hug the secrets of the universe to himself and smile at the illumination.

I was shattered and would have gladly joined the men and drowned my sorrow, guilt, and grief, but my pregnancy forbade it. I would have gladly sat like Zara and stared, but it wasn't my child who had died and I felt I had no right to show what I felt when they who had suffered the loss had managed to control their feelings. So I stood around, aimlessly, inhibiting the others with my presence. It was a mark of respect for me to have been there. It was a matter of tact for me to leave.

It is always difficult, in English, to know what to say at funerals or when meeting someone who has been bereaved. It is simple in Spanish, the phrase is 'Sentido pesame'. It can be repeated hundreds of times, if need be. It is the same and unvarying to all people and in all cases. I knew that I had to say it, formally, to Antonio Moreno before I left. I had said it upon arrival, but he hadn't heard me, I would have to say it again, much more loudly. He was surrounded by a circle of cronies, locked into the *aguardiente*. I could see no way of getting to him. If I said, 'Antonio, I have to leave,' it would have broken up the group and he would have come to me, thus giving me the chance to say my *pesame*. Form dictated that first I had to say the *pesame* and then tell him I had to leave. The dithering lasted for over an hour. Eventually, I pushed through his encircling friends, grabbed his elbow and gave my *pesame*. It felt as though the tenuous thread that held their grief at bay, snapped as I reminded them of why they were at this party. A long silence followed. Antonio struggled with the muscles in his face. His bloodshot eyes scanned the compound as though searching for some escape. No words came to his assistance.

I told him I had to leave. Leaving or not leaving was safe ground, he trusted himself on it. He insisted I stay, I insisted I leave. His cronies followed the discussion anxiously, obviously hoping that I would not be persuaded to change my mind and spoil their revelry. Antonio José, still in the nebulous phase before he became the master of the world and unsheathed his machete to prove it, was summoned to accompany me to the *trapiche*. Then Antonio said, 'Come with me, Doña.'

He took me back into the bedroom where Capino was lying in state.

'Look what they've done,' he said.

I looked and didn't know what to say.

'Look what a peasant is worth in the Andes, Doña. Look what they've done to my son.'

Antonio guided me into the candlelit bedroom. As we entered, a number of people, mostly women and children looked up and stopped mid-sentence in their chatter. Antonio jerked his head towards the doorway and signalled them towards it with his eyes. Reluctantly, everyone moved on to the chilly, already crowded porch. Once alone, Antonio pulled the hen-pecked door to.

'Look what they've done to my son, Doña.'

We had approached the glossy white casket where Capino lay in a new white shirt with a ribbon around his neck, looking smarter than he ever had in his short lifetime. He wore white satin shorts from which his green, wasted legs protruded. There were white satin roses in the coffin. His naturally green eyes, edged now by their unnaturally green, marbled whites, stared out of the coffin at the ceiling, with his eyes fixed in surprise by the fat thorns that propped open his lids at either side. Antonio pulled the boy's shorts down angrily and he pulled the shirt up.

In the hospital, while waiting in the corridor outside the intensive care ward, I saw, from other visitors, that the most popular newspaper in Valera was called *2001 Dos mil y uno*. In lieu of most of what other papers carried and reported, *2001* specialised almost exclusively in scandal and gore. Close-up colour shots of road accidents, murders, stabbings, fights, burns and other calamities filled its pages. It was constructed to thrill and shock. The newsprint was mostly reduced to captions and short sentences framing the indignities of blood and guts. No one on the *hacienda* had anything to do with newspapers. No one could read, and there were no newsagents nearer than Valera. Coromoto and Zara had somehow found a source of old magazines, whose black and white fashion photographs from 1960 were pasted on to their mud walls. This wallpaper stuck on with flour and water had been much appreciated by the cockroaches, which had chewed a maze of tracks through the pages, leaving only stray hands and faces, feet and an occasional caption.

Antonio Moreno, as foreman and *capataz*, knew about *2001*. He saw it as a disrespecter of death, feeding on the tragedies of the poor for the edification of the rich. As Capino lay dying, a journalist from *2001* had had to be physically ejected from our corridor. He had offered Antonio, two, four and then six pounds for his story and a chance to photograph the green boy. Now, as the *hacienda* paid its last respects to his son, Capino lay in his plywood coffin with a gash across his abdomen that reached from side to side. It was crudely stitched up with a coarse twine and protruding from it, to add insult to injury, was a crumpled headline from *2001*. It stuck out of his flesh, squeezing through the stitches and the wound, flaunting its name and abusing his frail corpse. The sleazy, grotesque and morbid scandal was stitched into him.

The sign of the cross had been carved into his body. Dissecting the lower slash, a long wound stretched from his chest to his groin. Again, through the clumsy stitching, flecks of colour and newsprint showed through where he had been hollowed out and stuffed with *2001*.

On the way down the hill and across the valley to the *trapiche*, Antonio José guided me with the exaggerated steadiness of the drunk. We walked in silence but for his mumbled instructions to watch the stream and mind my step. At the road, as though freed from the restraints of his enforced subordination, he said, to me and to the road, 'Those sons of whores at the

141

hospital shouldn't have done that to my brother. They have treated him like a dog. My mother stitches up chicken necks better. They're supposed to use fine straw if there's an autopsy. If I knew who put that newspaper in Capino, I'd buy another and bury it in their guts. I'd . . .'. He spluttered and wiped the tears angrily from his eyes, waving his oil lantern around his head so that the still night air filled with the smell of singeing hair.

He left me at my wicket gate and staggered home. I crawled into bed feeling sick with rage and guilt and sheer exhaustion.

Next morning, they carried El Capino downhill, singing 'Los Angelitos' in a cracked, half-hearted way, to the *trapiche*. Zara wasn't there. Then the women stayed behind, and the men piled on to La Povva with the coffin. There were so many of them that they hung from the barred sides as they did at the times of *molienda*. The *compadre* who had brought me Napoleon and helped at the hospital came for me and drove me to Mendoza Fría to the church.

The priest was supposed to be ready to come to the cemetery on the hill beyond Mendoza, but he wasn't.

'You never thought you'd be coming to a nest of vipers,' the *compadre* said and pushed me towards the door of his pick-up truck. 'You've seen what happens when you don't throw your weight around, so go on, *musiua*, get that son of a bitch of a priest out here to do his bit. He's smaller than you, you can bring him out by the throat if it's the only way. Go on.'

Only the day before, I had vowed to myself to take charge, in the name of El Capino who had died of neglect, and of Antonio Moreno who deserved any help he could get, and on behalf of the *gente*, who were helpless in ways beyond my own helplessness. Once or twice, when Antonio had come to the *trapiche* and caught me unawares, his comment on my tears had been by way of advice, 'Trouble and pain come from the outside, life is too short to nurture them from within.' Whenever he came up with anything, he always followed it immediately by a 'Well, so say I, but what would I know?'

I was timid, shy and absurdly passive. I was also pregnant, upset and more tired than I could ever remember having been. I had hoped to start being assertive and strong after the funeral and after a couple of nights' sleep. However, as the *compadre* motioned me to enter the church, I knew that I would have to start from the moment I pushed open its heavy carved doors.

In the 1970s and for many decades before, Venezuela had been officially deemed as a country without vocation. Fewer Venezuelans joined the priesthood proportionately than from anywhere else. All Venezuelans, with the exception of a small colony of Germans in the Colonia Tovar, were nominally Roman Catholics, but they were not devout. The church was somewhere you went for christenings, weddings, funerals and anniversaries. The priests were mostly Spanish. In the Andes, with a largely scattered rural population, few priests could be bothered to traipse over the hills in the heat and rain to tend their flocks. An Andean parish was a penance suffered, more often than not, with an ill grace by a foreign priest who had no sympathy with or understanding of the peasants he occasionally dealt with. In the wealthy families, the women occasionally went to church, the men only ever for family occasions. In the Terán family, the woman paid lip service to the Church, while the men prided themselves on their third-generation atheism. All the children were brought up in a religious tug-of-war.

The priest wasn't in his church, he was in his house beside it. I was ushered in by a nervous, ill-clad servant. He was eating. I informed him as curtly as I could that he was late for the funeral. He told me, in his lisping Spanish, and without bothering to look up from his dish of scrambled eggs, that he would come when he was ready. Sheepishly, I returned to the waiting truck. As I began to explain to the *compadre* that he was finishing his breakfast and was on his way, he shook his grey, balding head slowly from side to side, and lifted his hand to his throat and squeezed it, widening his eyes to me to show that I had not done my job.

I went back in, back down the aisle and through the side door of the church that led to the priest's house. His head was still bent over his dish of eggs. The servant was flustered, she excused herself, 'She pushed past me, I don't know anything, she didn't knock.'

The priest looked up for the first time. He narrowed his eyes and I narrowed mine. He started to say something which I interrupted, 'There are five men out there who will drag you out by the throat if you don't come with me immediately.'

He stared in a bored way.

'They're armed,' I added.

He was unmoved.

'This funeral is for the Teráns,' I told him. 'They are out there, you'll have to deal with them.'

At the name Terán, he blinked several times. His predecessor had been chased around this very church and beaten with a stick by one of the Teráns. He had obviously been warned not to mess with them.

'It's a *peón* kid,' he said.

'Yes, the *peón* kid of the foreman of Don Jaime Terán's *hacienda*. I am the Doña and I have instructions to drag you out by the throat if need be. It's me or them; are you coming?'

He looked up at me and seemed to take in my full height

for the first time. He failed to see that I was no more capable of grabbing him by the throat than I was of keeping the hands behind my back from trembling. At that moment my *compadre*'s voice hollered menacingly through the building, '*Musuia!*'

The priest rose and followed me. I emerged on the steps of the church with my first battle won. I learnt later that the priest often kept the funeral cortége waiting for hours in the hot sun until he deigned to emerge and hurry through the service. There was a varying scale of pay for the varying funeral rites. The peasants always took the quick service, the cheapest one. He made no bones about being by the graveside for his fee alone. His interest in an afterlife seemed to be limited to his fervent wish to spend his own anywhere other than in Mendoza Fría. As he sidled up to the small waiting grave, the *compadre* whispered in his ear, 'Show some respect or I'll break your fingers.' Then he cleared his throat and stood with his head bowed, waiting for the priest to recover his composure and say the final sacrament.

It was a sorry affair in a graveyard scattered with the plain wooden crosses and unmarked mounds of dozens of other dead. Some of the graves had wire or plastic flowers beside them, most of them were covered by goose grass and other weeds. Some of the graves had black and white photographs of their occupants. The photos stared out with dead faces. For most of the peasants, this photograph would be the only one ever taken. Photography was linked for ever with death. Capino, too, had been photographed in the morgue so the only image that remained of him was in vaudeville make-up.

The funeral took five minutes, then the priest demanded his fee and stomped off. Antonio thanked me for having made the service longer. I was still stunned by how quick it had been.

'How long does it usually take?'

'He can rattle it off in half that time . . . It's a shame, isn't it to be sent off by a louse like that who probably pisses on his sleeves when he urinates? It would have seemed more fitting to have buried Capino under my bamboo tree. I've never understood what the Church has to do with the likes of me.'

When the grave was ready, we left. I had taken a wreath of jasmine and oleanders to lay on the grave. Then I returned to the *hacienda*, ready to start a new life.

I wrote a great many letters and made endless lists and resolutions and then nothing happened for days and days.

15

IN MY LETTERS to Joanna, I asked for an endless miscellany of things, including:

> My books, plus an old blanket if you have one to spare. Second-hand: Blake, Dylan Thomas – poetry only, any edition. And some, plenty of, woollens. Vetzyme, Stress, Vitamin A and D drops, worm tablets, ballet shoes, 500 aspirin, Chlorydyn, Cascara Evacuant or equivalent (well packed so as not to spill over everything).

A friend called Pedro was due to sail from England and had offered to take a trunk for me.

Seeing no immediate way to make inroads into the poverty and injustice of the *hacienda*, I took a few minor decisive steps. The first was to employ the old goat-herd, Natividad, to help me water the garden and to fuss around my rose, oleander and hibiscus cuttings with me. This gave him a regular salary for a regular job involving nothing too arduous for his almost crippled hands to cope with. Every morning at seven o'clock he announced his presence in advance as he wheezed along the track to the house. I told Antonio Moreno that whenever he needed me to do anything he had to come and ask, whether it was work or illness; I wanted to help. He nodded and smiled, thanked me and then didn't come for several weeks.

I traipsed up the hill to visit him and Zara several times. Zara seemed to be locked in a shroud of shock and hardly spoke. Antonio was twice not at home and twice he was, sitting on his porch with a milk tin of hibiscus on either side of him and drunk. He apologised for his drunkenness, shrugged and bowed his head. I couldn't really do anything on the *hacienda* without him, so I had no choice but to return home and wait.

Coromoto also tailed off her visits from the time of Capino's death. She no longer came every day, skipping two or three for every one that she came.

Jaime came and went like a phantom, visiting the house and the *trapiche*, usually in the early evening for an hour or so. Sometimes he sat on the cathedral bench on the porch with the dogs at his feet and told them about how the *hacienda* used to be. I would sit and listen. If I said anything, he clammed up. If I sat as silently as Napoleon, he'd talk about his grandfather, Don Rodolfo, who had had the *trapiche* chimney built and bought the Squire sugar-crusher, which lay dismantled on the top deck of the factory with its five giant cog wheels sunk on the far side in weeds. It was Don Rodolfo who had built the dynamo, Don Rodolfo who had brought electricity to Valera and Don Rodolfo who had invented a system for boiling sugar so it spilled from one tray to the next under its own steam without having to be ladled laboriously from tray to tray. It was a system used all over the Caribbean, all over Venezuela. Don Rodolfo had been a great man. There were no photographs of him after his jaw had been shot away in the massacre, but he had, it was said, been extraordinarily hand-some. He had been betrayed by his wife. Her own brothers had led the ambush in which he had been wounded. She had done it to save the lives of their two young sons, the only two male Terán children to be spared in the Herodian massacre. When her brothers arrived, she had taken her youngest child from Don Rodolfo's lap and drawn away; thus proving that she knew of his intended assassination.

After Don Rodolfo had returned from New York, together with his platinum jaw and his beagle hound, he never spoke to his wife again. Every day, she was escorted on donkey-back by two of his servants to spend the day on the *hacienda* with the children, and every afternoon, at four o'clock, she was led back to her family. His silence towards her was unrelenting. He died having neither forgiven her nor spoken to her again.

The story of Don Rodolfo and his silence to Doña Amalia, his wife, was Jaime's favourite story. Inevitably, within the silence of our own household, I drew comparisons between them and us.

'And that', he would tell the inattentive Ross and Megan, 'was how a serious man behaved to his wife. And Don Rodolfo was a serious man.'

In the Andes, the highest accolade a man could have was to be 'serious', *serio*: it incorporated everything that was manly and strong and had little to do with being thoughtful, sober, earnest or sedate. A serious man left no enemies behind him, conquered fear, respected blood ties and inspired fear in others. I was more bemused by, than afraid of, the man I had married.

In my letters to Joanna, I went to great pains to disguise the fact that Jaime and I were estranged. I included him in my goings on and mentioned any activity of his on the *hacienda* as though it were a regular occurrence. I wrote as much as I could about the dogs, since they were something that we shared. I also sent her endless details of my garden.

It had always been my dream to have a beautiful garden. In Clapham, as a small child, despite living in a second-floor flat and having no right to a small triangle of earth to the right of the main entrance, I had wheedled the tending of this small patch from our neighbours. It was to have been a herb garden. I spent my very meagre pocket money on seeds for it. I brought cuttings of sage and thyme and rosemary from visits to friends with 'proper' gardens. It was a triangle doomed to failure. Cars coming in and out of the adjacent car park failed to recognise its aesthetic potential and drove over it. By the time I was ten, it was reduced to a row of herbs with their backs to the red-brick wall and a bed of six-inch nails to protect them. The nails sank into the earth more willingly than any of the roots of my cuttings; and both my revenge and gardening were singularly ineffective.

So much of a subtropical landscape is a garden in itself that from day one at the *trapiche* I made grandiose plans for landscaping around the banana palms, lilies and mango trees, adding ornamental plants to create beds and shrubberies and, dearest to my heart, a herb garden. Whatever I planted, the beagles dug up. Sometimes, they ploughed over my seed-beds, and sometimes they allowed the seeds to germinate and grow into spindly seedlings before their digging and scattering began. Rose cuttings were a particular challenge to them. Beside the onslaught of my own dogs, the weeds and insects proliferated at a speed I had never dreamt of. When it rained, everything rotted, then, with the dry season, everything wilted and died. I was stubbornly determined to persist with this garden despite all the evidence that I was fighting a losing battle.

Joanna also loved gardens. We had often spent our Sundays visiting the English ones that were open to the public and we were regular visitors to Kew. Telling her how well my garden was coming along was like telling her how well my marriage was. She was too far away to know any different and the simulacrum of well-being endowed my hopes with a semblance of truth. When before Christmas I wrote:

> I have planted about fifteen rose stems which are now 12 rose bushes on the rise. 40 small pink roses were given to us last week. I planted an orange tree yesterday and five Trinitarias (Pride of Barbados) a beautiful climbing shrub/tree which flowers all year. 2 elderberry branches that are now little trees. Jasmine and all sorts

it was true. What I didn't say was that for every rose stem that took, some thirty must have been dug up by the dogs and thrown away. Planting anything was the triumph of hope over experience. The orange tree was barricaded inside its own picket fence. The trinitarias were bunkered under barbed wire and the most noticeable aspect of the garden was a jungle of weeds. The child I was carrying was something else I could share with Joanna and did.

> Be thinking, and let me know of girls' names that you like. I have found a lovely one: Iseult – ancient Irish. I'm not quite sure how to pronounce it. For a boy we have Alexander and Balthazar either or both.

Jaime and I had discussed children's names in Italy and I knew that Alexander or Balthazar were a mutual choice. I didn't mention that now that a baby was finally due, in the first week of April, it too had become a non-subject. Only when Jaime arrived on the *hacienda* with one of his innumerable cousins did my domestic life assume what might be described as normality. Since these were rare occasions, I came to prefer my solitude. There was something surreal about slipping in and out of the role of wife merely for the sake of an audience.

Santa Rita,
January 1st, 1973

Dear Joanna,

Happy New Year! How was Christmas? I have two of your letters here unanswered, you sound rather depressed; are you? . . . Three weeks ago, I was preparing a little nosh of *farfalle* with chicken and garlic when I slipped in a puddle and fell, sitting with an enormous crash on the stone floor of the kitchen. A few minutes later, the contractions began and a lot of pain, etc., etc. That's what God does to garlic eaters. I have spent ten days completely immobile in Valera and then in bed here at home with pills and medicines. I got up a couple of days ago and today I am on my feet and fine. The baby seems fine as well and is growing obscenely fast and plays cricket most of the day. I was planning to phone you all on Xmas day, but of course, I was flat on my back here.

As to names, I like Iseult, so there! Even if you do think of 'Celtic dawn choruses' or whatever your objection was (and there are worse connotations with other names). Secondly, nobody knows how to pronounce my names here anyway (or any names come to that). And due to the fact that I am una *musiua* (foreigner) if I called her Carmen, they would call it Carmaiyne.

Jaime does enjoy working on the estate but has a lot of rheumatism/arthritis? Much more than in Europe. Did you ever try that new Danish cure? Minalka? Something to do with vitamins, I believe.

The baby is due at the beginning of April 5th–12th, such a drag working out the exact date, I keep losing count, sometimes it's the fifth, sometimes the twelfth. C'est la vie! Have you read *Papillon*, Henri Charrière?

Our new Persian puss has just sat down on the pad and is heaving all over me. She is lovely, long-haired, white, with blue eyes. All the animals are well – hens are rather bedraggled by frequent onslaughts of Ross and Megan.

As to your operation (on the other foot) would you be able to come out earlier if you had all that time convalescing?

Don't miss next week's thrilling instalment.

I had a letter last week from the customs at Maracaibo. The books Gillie sent me are being held there until I go and fish them out personally. This I cannot do. Four–five hour journey and the doctor does not even let me go to Valera. My visa expired two months ago, so I legally have no right to be here. I have decided to not accept the package and demand that they return to sender forthwith. I cannot think why they have not let it through, all the other books arrived safely.

Following morning:

How are your relations? I am sorry to hear you would end them now. My unwanted opinion is that real friendship is such a rare thing that one should not spurn it lightly. Almost everybody's waiting for one to turn one's back – preying. When someone loves you, why do the same? Only say this because you yourself said you were v. involved.

Could you not get used to infrequent meetings? Don't bother to tell me it's none of my business; I know it's not.

Are you still looking forward to coming?

Jaime has gone out.

I am awaiting Rose (our new maid) 25ish, short, slippers around in rubber slippers (plastic shoes are bad for one's eyesight!), sleeps in the sitting room (other rooms have ghosts, ditto the *trapiche*) makes good coffee, very good coffee.

After morning dispensary.

I don't think clearly any more, perhaps I'm going moron . . .

What was the matter with Bosie?

Old Persian proverb:

When a word burns your tongue, swallow it.

I am disgruntled, I shall have a bath.

Next day.

Time to send the letter. We have just operated on all the puppies' dew claws. I feel utterly sick. All over now.

Write soon,

Love to everyone . . .

My sense of time (never one of my strong points) drifts from that last letter on. I began to juggle events, shifting them backwards and forwards to suit my mother's increasing bouts of depression and her precarious state of health. She needed to have a hysterectomy, she wrote about it to me often. Also, the last serious love affair she was to have had turned sour. Knowing this, I altered my news. I remember falling very soon after Dr Briceño had told me I was pregnant. I was alone and it was afternoon, thus it was before the time when I employed Natividad or he could have gone for help. It was my sister-in-law, cruising the valley in her white Corvette, who chanced by and saved me.

Of all the seven years that I spent on the *hacienda*, only the sequence of events around the death of El Capino is blurred. I don't know whether he died on 30 January as I wrote to Joanna, or whether it was earlier, or whether I fell before or after.

16

THE COMBINATION OF El Capino's death and my own short sojourn at the local hospital settled in my mind where I would have my child. I determined not to return to Valera. Meanwhile, every morning for a couple of hours I ran a makeshift dispensary from my house. With the help of Coromoto, and by scouting for patients myself from door to door, I encouraged a number of people, particularly children, to come down for free medicines and vitamin pills. I got my supplies from Joanna in England, from a doctor cousin in Caracas, and from Dr Briceño, who drove up from Valera to visit me several times a week for a few minutes. By means of a few simple cures and purges, I gained the confidence of an increasing number of *la gente*. The more skin diseases, infections and ailments I cured, the more confident I became in my diagnoses and treatments.

Luckily, at first, all the cases that came to me were ones I could deal with or, at least, improve. I wrote to Joanna about my dispensary and hinted that I might, later, be called upon to assist at births. She sent me a book on midwifery. I studied it and made up my mind to deliver my own child, not through

156

courage but through fear of returning to Valera. I knew that Dr Briceño was a wonderful doctor, but I had seen where he worked and what happened there to the unprotected. I felt I couldn't count on Jaime to look out for me; perhaps he would, and perhaps he wouldn't. Everyone else would assume he would, and somewhere in that misunderstanding my child and I might die of neglect, septicaemia or any of the other awesome conditions described in my medical books.

Santa Rita,
19th Feb

Dear Joanna

How are you today? The trunk arrived, with the package, everything was lovely – especially the sleeping bag, blankets and books. I have begun to knit from the patterns you sent me. You shall see when you come.

The baby's room is now ready and very pretty, red and white with bamboo cane roof and Japanese lantern and big window looking on to the stream and back garden.

The puppies are gorgeous. The runt is called Flora because she is so pretty and delicate. Help me think of two other names if you can.

Our car has been *accidentado* for the last several weeks. I *am* glad you like your work. Have you new friends? How are your guts? Your Bosie?

All news,
Lots of love
Lisaveta

> *Dusk dust turn*
> *Hounds whine*
> *Strange mounds moulding.*

157

Can they see the furnace
Shifting? 'Your love rode away
On a fast steed'
The river drowns
Words, only weird sounds
Tease these walls:
A clutter of spring? Of hooves?
  Screech cockerel crow
Flood upon drought
Your sweetheart has fled
To a less bitter mouth
Till dusk turn night.

A succession of maids came and tested their ineptitude against my own. With each one, I learnt a little more about the place, its ways and tastes. And with each one I learnt to distinguish better the line that divides kindness from weakness. They taught me to soak black beans overnight in bicarbonated soda water and then to cook them for the four hours they needed to soften. They taught me how to make the *guisos* or sauces that were then added. All *guisos* revolved around tomato, onion, garlic and fresh coriander simmered in an orange oil coloured with the seeds of the onoto plant. They showed me how to toast the onoto and to gather it from the hills. They taught me, or tried to teach me, how to make *arepas*. They showed me how to make chilli fritters. I tried to show them how to make a few simple recipes of my own, but found that the only ones that met with any success were jams and chutneys. No one ever mastered their preparation in my kitchen, but they ate them by the jar with a spoon and could often be placated on difficult days by a jam-making session.

I learnt how to wash clothes properly by beating them

against a stone and then scrubbing them with almond soap. They showed me how to make soap out of a mottled leaf that exuded, when crushed, a quantity of slime. They showed me how to deal with visitors correctly. This was an area over which we often fell out. The hierarchy of the *hacienda* was very strict. Every man had his place and station, his wife and children took their cue from him. I was happy to fuss over some, less happy to snub the others. Through my guinea-pig maids, I learnt how to sift through the complex social strata of the neighbourhood and, gradually, how to gain some confidence and respect from the local women.

My trunks were a source of curiosity to all and sundry. Given the chance, all the women wanted to dive into them and rummage through their wondrous and puzzling contents. I had jumped from isolation to acceptance. One of the most difficult things I had to master on the *hacienda* was how to create a line over which no one should pass. It wasn't a matter of forbidding access to my private possessions, it was constructing an aura around myself which in itself would stop anyone from even asking to do such a thing. I had married the automatic right to obedience and consideration, but it seemed more and more during the months after Capino died and before my confinement, that respect was something earned individually.

Almost daily people came to me with their troubles, ailments and quarrels. These quarrels were endless. Several times women came to me with a request to throw a neighbouring family off the *hacienda*. Half the time the imbroglios were a fabric of lies. The tension and animosity in the hills were huge. The children, men and women fought verbally, physically and also in underhand, clandestine ways. Envy and distrust were present in most of the compounds. By getting to know the *gente* through their wives, I learnt of Borgian intrigues played out in a minor key and, through them, I discovered how much strength and wisdom Antonio Moreno must have owned to have been able to hold the *hacienda* together for forty years of his reign.

Every word I spoke, no matter how insignificant, was relayed back across the hills. Everything I did was monitored and analysed, commented on and approved or disapproved. I learnt not to take simple questions at their face value, and not to betray any confidences in my answers.

Old Natividad came to me one evening after work, shuffling along the porch abjectly. He said, 'My daughter, Maria, wants to come home. She is pregnant again and big with it, her time must be nearly due. She brings shame on her mother and me and shame on the *hacienda*. I cannot take her back without your permission. Can she come home?'

I knew how hard it was for both Natividad and his wife, Josefa, to cope with their half-witted, enamoured daughter. I knew from other sources, that the man she continually ran off with was a ne'er do well who was unpopular on the *hacienda*. He was, as Antonio Moreno had told me, 'Unfortunately, one of the best *trapicheros* between Valera and Timotes, a really skilled end-ladler who can tell, intuitively, when the sugar reaches its "point". But for that, I would have turned him off myself, years ago. He has wreaked havoc in Natividad's household and he never pays a *locha* towards the upkeep of his kids. You've probably heard, Doña,' Antonio said smiling wryly, 'he prefers his donkey to any woman on earth. If he could marry the donkey, he would.'

I gave my permission and Natividad shuffled off, muttering, 'Poor Josefa, ai ai ai! Poor Josefa'.

*

Certain moments stood out from the others over the arc of the years. That meeting with Natividad was one of them. Sometimes, an incident provided an irrefutable truth, a piece of evidence that summed up the injustice or absurdity of the social system. On the *hacienda* the social system was so tight it was like a garrotte. It could be learnt like a text and then seen in practice, following step by step exactly what the social law dictated. To be a nineteen-year-old girl, ignorant of life, and to be approached by a man of eighty, whose wisdom had been tested and proved by his mere survival, was, in itself, incongruous. To be asked for permission for this old man to take his own daughter back to live with him in the house he had built struck me instantly with its wrongness. After he left, and after his wheezing had disappeared into the diminishing light, I wondered what would have happened if I had said 'No'. With one word, I could not only have humiliated and hurt both Natividad and his wife, I could have condemned their daughter to a probable death.

I had made grandiose plans about how to improve the *hacienda*, how to improve the lot of all the *gente* there. The 'What ifs' of that evening stayed by me as a welcome warning to what would happen if my attention strayed, if I neglected even little things, let stray words escape unthought of from my mouth. My mother-in-law had been very clear in her instructions on how to deal with *la gente*.

Doña Antonieta had been the Doña on the estate from 1935 to 1962 before leaving for the city. She said, 'Don't let anybody get close to you, keep your distance at all times. You have to impose your authority and if anybody so much as answers you back, turn them off. Never give them food, never give them money, you can give them some medicines but they don't need much, most of what they say are inventions to make you feel sorry for them. They are as happy as pigs in a mud pit up there, that's what they like; and don't ever go into any of their huts because they're full of infection. And', she warned me, 'be careful who you shake hands with, most of them can just bow to you. It isn't healthy to touch their skin. Of course, if you get the children and scrub them down for about three weeks and give them some very sharp purging, then they "do" as servants, but never give an inch, Lisaveta, never relax your power or they'll tear it away from you, mark my words.'

It was largely in reaction to such advice as this that I began my own lax domestic administration of my maids. Nieves, the first, was a failure; Rosa, the second, was marginally better. She didn't ask to leave, but after two months, I found her another place and asked her to. During the one short *molienda* that occurred during her sojourn with me, the *trapicheros* asked *en masse* to have her removed from the vicinity of the *trapiche*. Rosa, it emerged, had a weakness for *trapicheros* and was willing, and able, to take on the entire team and the reserve. On day one, this had seemed like an unexpected luxury; by day two, it was a dangerous disruption.

Work in a sugar factory is highly skilled, and the *trapicheros* knew to their cost what a momentary lapse of concentration could cost. Antonio said that every feeder worth his salt had to lose a thumb to complete his apprenticeship.

'It's the only way', he explained, 'of stopping them from losing an arm or going through to the chest. Half the one-armed men you see around have had that arm crushed in the sugar-crusher's rollers. They work on cogs, you see, they can't stop just like that. It takes precise skill to feed the sticks of cane into the crusher. You've seen the speed it has to go in at to be productive. Eight hours on and four hours' sleep for days and days on end. There's always a moment when the feeder's attention slips. It's only after a thumb's been chewed and the rollers stopped in time that a man realises what's at stake. I've seen dozens of deaths in *trapiches* in this valley, and I tell you, if a feeder comes here to Santa Rita and wants to work in the *molienda*, if he hasn't lost a thumb I won't take him. I tell you when one of the *trapicheros* falls sick, it's a tragedy. Take that piece of shit (excuse the expression, Doña) El Bobo, who won't leave Natividad's daughter alone, I'd like to have run him off and sent him a gift of diarrhoea of nails, but good *trapicheros* are hard to find.'

Then there were the ladlers, all handling boiling sugar, all risking splash burns minute by minute, while underneath them two stokers replenished the furnaces. Under the vats and trays of boiling sugar brick kilns were fuelled continuously with the dessicated *vagasse*, sprayed liberally with kerosene to increase the combustion. Again a moment's inattention, and a fire could spread to the mountain of inflammable *vagasse* beside the furnace. So when Rose roamed the *trapiche* beckoning workers to her willing arms, a state of general alarm ensued.

A tearful and protesting Rosa was sent packing back to Mendoza Fría and I was advised to listen to no more wheedling from foreign girls. Coromoto, who bitterly resented any girl other than herself from approaching my domain was quick to say, 'I told you so.' But Coromoto, at nine, still seemed too young to be working full time despite the local precedents in child labour. Besides which, I felt that Zara needed Coromoto more than ever after Capino died. I promised Coromoto that one day she should come and be my maid and my right hand. Meanwhile, she would have to accept that a number of trials and errors would be passing through my house.

Maria, the next one, lasted three days. She cried almost continually to go home. On day two, I took her back. Her mother thanked me and said that within the hour Maria would return to me and not to wait. Within the hour, a thoroughly thrashed Maria came limping back down the track. She settled into the back room that I had prepared for whoever would be living in, beside the coming baby's room. There she curled up in a heap on the floor on a bamboo mat and wept inconsolably. Nothing I said or did seemed to rouse or even reach her. The next day, she begged me to take her home and said she would rather die of a beating at her mother's hands than die far away from homesickness. Once again, I lumbered across the hills to her house, using Ross and Megan to pull me on their leads in a way that harnessed their zeal to my reluctant hill-climbing admirably.

I gave her a little money and told her mother she was not to beat the girl after I left. I said I would be back the next day to check. Her mother, a withered, hard-worn, slovenly woman with nine small children of whom the twelve-year-old Maria was the second, dug her toe in the guano'd floor of her smoky kitchen and informed me defiantly that I could turn her off but I couldn't stop her from beating her daughter.

'What would happen, Doña, if all my children refused to work? Are we to starve? You can see for yourself the state my husband's in, he's got air on the brain and is fit for next to nothing but giving me another belly. Am I to tell him there's nothing to eat when he gets in from wandering and staring? Am I to tell the babies to stop crying when they're hungry? Look at them, Doña, there's no food in the pot. Maria has to work. She should have been working years ago. She has to. If you can't train her, who would have been kind to her, then she'll go to where they'll beat her into staying. But she'll send her wages home, and the children will eat. That's the way it is, Doña, with all respect.'

It took me a long time to walk home from Maria's house. She lived on a part of the estate called El Hatico, in the remains of what had once been a grand Spanish colonial house. All that was left now were two rooms and endless low walls from the rambling ruin. Bits of the yard of her compound were still littered with beautiful floor tiles caked in mud and guano, but still, here and there, discernible for what they were. Even as a ruin, the place had an air of grandeur about it. I had heard stories that the basis of the Terán fortune had once come from under these tiles where a floor of gold had been hidden away by the last of the Labastidas. The idea that there was still hidden treasure under the old floors of El Hatico persisted. Generations of workers had randomly dug out the floor, discarding the precious tiles in the hopes of finding more of the mythical gold. Far around the house, pits and craters had been dug, some so long ago they had filled with trees, others, more recent, left mounds like termites' nests piled up in and beyond the compound.

Because the house of El Hatico, reduced as it was now to a peasant dwelling, had brick walls and a tiled roof and the remnants of the hand-painted ceramics littering its yard, I had assumed that Maria and her family were better off than the other workers. I knew that Eladio, her father, had water on the brain and was unable to work. I had seen his great gangling frame as he wandered daily across the hills staring into the sky with his watery hazel eyes with a look of such expectancy on his face that I invariably looked up too to see what he had seen. And I knew that his small son, El Mudo, a handsome child with a mop of curly brown hair always trotted by his side. El Mudo was the dumb boy whom Coromoto insisted could talk if he chose to.

Maria's mother, also called Maria, was much criticised by the other estate women for being slovenly. Everyone on the *hacienda* was scrupulously clean. Everyone bathed once or twice a day despite the absence of running water to their huts. The children were ragged and they often had lice, but they too, were scrubbed more than once daily, their hair was washed regularly with the slimy leaf-soap and their clothes were washed every day, beaten and scrubbed and also boiled in cinder water. Of all the women on the *hacienda*, only Maria d'Eladio failed to keep her person, her children and her house clean and tidy. She was forgiven many things, including her sharp tongue, but never her lack of hygiene.

Several of the families were better off than others. At the top of the league were those, like La Ciega, who kept an illicit still and made rot-gut rum for the workers far and wide. Then there were the *medianeros*, those who planted out estate land for themselves and divided the profits with the *padrón*. Then, also, any family lucky enough to have brought their children up to working age and who could count on seven or eight salaries instead of one, was that many times better off than those who had to rely on just one weekly wage coming in to feed a swarm of younger mouths. The skilled earned more than the unskilled, the naturally healthy were better off than the sick.

Seeing Maria d'Eladio's with its pantiled roof and its well, its three outbuildings and its pillared porch, I had assumed, wrongly, that the squalor she had reduced it to was chosen rather than enforced. When I got to know her better, I realised that her apparent laziness was chronic depression. Meanwhile, I had blundered. As I picked my way through the green alley-ways between the fields of sugar-cane, I knew that I couldn't just go home, chastened and wiser. I didn't know how to reply to her when she defied me, but I knew, from Antonio, that I must never allow such a situation to occur. To do so was to undermine not only my position but his own. My mother-in-law would have had no qualms about turning the entire family off the estate. I knew that I couldn't let that happen, not least because the fault was not hers but mine. I wished myself away to no avail. Long before I reached the *trapiche*, word would have spread to curious neighbours that my authority had been defied. Whenever I visited anyone, a second visit always followed mine, to check what I had said and done, to pick over the meeting. It was March, it was hot, so hot that I felt like fainting. I took the long way home to avoid meeting anyone else. When I reached the orchard of La Casa Grande, I paused in its shade. To one side of me were the sentinel palm trees planted at the birth of every male Terán. If my child, due now in only four weeks' time, were a boy, a new palm would join them. To the left, the abandoned stables built by my father-in-law for the forty mules that once carried the cane to the *trapiche* looked ghostly in their veil of goose grass.

The Casa Grande was also empty. 'Los Pollos de Eladio' had finally vacated it some months before. I walked along its long wide corridor and up the cantilevered green marble stair-case that led to the master bedroom suite. I stood in its wide loggia and stared out across the *hacienda*, down the valley of the Momboy, filtered through the leaves of a giant avocado tree. Clumps of dead orchids still clung to its branches, rotting evidence of my father-in-law's hobby. From there, I climbed back down the stairs, noting the sheer drop on the edge of both the stairs and the loggia, from which many accidents (one fatal) had occurred. Below was the big sitting room with its marble floor, its carved doors and its six big shuttered windows. Along the corridor and through the arches were ten more rooms, all cool and graceful, all tiled in terracotta. Under the wooden and pantiled roof, shaded from the direct sun by the pillared loggia that ran around two sides on the ground floor to the courtyard, it was cool and calming. At the other end of the house, there was another staircase. This one was made of wood. It was part of an older house, all that was left when the old Casa Grande was burnt down by a servant with an unguarded candle in the 1920s. The staircase led to two big long rooms, the further of which had a wooden balcony with two french doors leading to it. In one corner of the balcony, giant boring bees had eaten their way through, leaving a gaping hole. I leant on the carved balustrade and surveyed the road, the *trapiche* beyond it, the river and my own little house nestled behind the bamboo. I decided to bring some of my books across, and some of my things, to spend time in the Casa Grande, to drink in some of the cool and calm it exuded so freely. My own house was unbearably hot under its tin roof and the dust and insects were a constant plague. I had never given up hope of moving into the Casa Grande. I knew that Jaime had set his heart against it and I had heard him say both to Antonio and to his cousins that he would rather die than move there. In our estranged state, I felt that he didn't have to live there, I did. What difference would it make to him since he spent most of his time in other people's houses and in bars?

Antonio Moreno had told me, 'When the baby comes, *el padrón* will return to you.'

Antonio seemed to know so much about the past, the present and the future. I felt bad about having let him down, about having created 'a situation'. I thought of Otto, whom I had not seen or heard of since leaving England. I knew only that there had been troubles in Chile. I didn't know if Otto and Elias were dead or alive. I couldn't ask. Joanna had received no news, our coded letters told me so. I missed Otto particularly. In that moment, I missed him even more. He would undoubtedly tell me I was stupid, but would also know what to do.

I went back home and wrote to Joanna. I told her that our chickens had hatched and about the puppies. Then I admitted, in my defeat, that there were moments when I simply couldn't cope.

I keep getting terribly depressed here and quite potty. About once a month I decide to pack my briefcase and go to Norway. It's been going on all year now. Why Norway, I wonder? When we go to Europe again we must spend some time there to get rid of this obsession. It only lasts for a few hours, or a day and then I feel all right again. Silly really.

The cardigan sounds lovely, thank you.

I had an appointment with Antonio for late in the afternoon. I knew that he wanted to speak to me about the *moliendas*. In fact, he had already spoken to me about them. He wanted me to be officially authorised by Jaime to start them, even if Jaime was away. We had had a disaster, earlier, when the cane was cut according to plan, brought to the *trapiche*, the *trapicheros* were assembled, but Jaime had not appeared to give the order for the *molienda* to start. Since he had given Antonio express orders never to start until he was personally present, the sugar content in the cane had dropped considerably while it sat out in the sun, cut and fermenting. Now Antonio had a plan which he wished to unfold formally. If I agreed to take the responsibility, then he would catch *el padrón* on one of his now more frequent visits to the house and gain his consent, embarrassing him into it in front of another party, preferably an older cousin. It all sounded very complicated. I asked him why he hadn't just started the *molienda* on his own authority, he was, after all, the foreman and *capataz*.

He told me, 'Doña, I run this *hacienda*, I have been running it for years. When *el padrón* was in prison, and when he was away, and also when he was in the guerrillas and just out having a good time as well, I ran this estate on my own. But now that *el padrón* has returned from abroad, now that he is nominally the boss, convention forces me to bow to his will. I have to do what he says. If he says wait, I have to wait. If he says start, I have to start. Having given this order, he would lose face to withdraw it. No man can lose face. So only you can help now, you can take his place. We made a loss on that last *molienda*. Santa Rita cannot afford to make a loss. There was a time when Don Cesar and Doña Antonieta were here when the coffers were full and there was money for whatever was needed or wanted. There was money for the family to spend like water. That is no longer the case. There is no reserve. We live from week to week. Unless we have a *molienda* every two weeks, regularly and without fail, the *gente* have to pull their belts in at home and the repairs on the estate fall behind.

'This is your period of grace. From now until the child is born and for at least a month or two afterwards, *el padrón* will be at your beck and call. He will grant you what you ask. All men do. Look at the way every husband runs around finding the impossible because his pregnant wife suddenly craves it. A woman is only ever really in command during the last phase of pregnancy and the first months of that baby's infancy. While it is in your power to keep alive the son and heir, you are important. It is the same up and down the valley.

'Zara is important to me because I love her and she has charmed my old age, but she too is more important when another child is coming or just born. Help yourself, Doña, and help us all, now that you have the chance.'

He had told me all this once, he was coming again to repeat it. When he came, I would own up to having lost face with Maria d'Eladio. Losing face was a terrible thing to do. To make someone else lose face was considered a crime. People fought and killed each other over it. Pride was of paramount importance.

Antonio arrived, punctually after the workmen knocked off at six o'clock. He was hot and tired. We drank *guarapo* syrup on the porch together and I owned up to my bungling. He said, 'The sixty *bolívars* a week that the men earn has changed things here. We used to be like slaves. It's hard for a *peón* to keep his dignity. We have as much pride as any of the Teráns, but circumstances make us eat it and choke on it every day. It's the husk in the corn. Our children have to work. That's all there is, they have to. And they have to obey us. Life is hard. God knows we love our children, they are all we have, but we have to be harsh. No child ever cries uncomforted when they're little, but when they get older, what can we do? If you can bear to come with me tomorrow to Maria's house, I'll sort out the problem. We want you to help us, Doña, but our children are ours.

'Eladio is my *compadre*, El Mudo is my godson. Maria is my *comadre*. I can remember when Eladio was a fine man, as strong as an ox and worth two or three of the other workers put together. Since his accident, he is no use to anyone. He is worse than useless to *comadre* Maria. They're very poor at El Hatico. Zara and I give them what we can, and some of the others help them out. El Mudo works sometimes, but Maria has to go into service or the younger ones will start dying. Later, when all this has blown over, perhaps you'll remember to help them out sometimes with beans and corn.

'The *compadre* Eladio will never recover. He thinks he was knocked down by an eagle. He thinks he can find the eagle who stole his senses, he'll get them back again.

'Everything is balanced here, but the scales so often lie. We get along. If you could get dual control of this *hacienda*, Doña, everyone here is ready to make it work. Pride is a blessing and a curse. It sustains and destroys. You have not been cursed with the petty pride of so many of us. When *el padrón* is here, I believe you could step back without feeling offended, when he is away, you could run things here . . . everything.'

I looked doubtful. The technical side of things was still beyond me and when it came to handling people, I had just shown that I built my own traps and then jumped into them.

'I'll be there for you. I'll be between you and *la gente*, between you and the sugar merchants in Valera. I won't leave you on your own, not for a long while yet, at least. My mother, Florencia, lived to be one hundred and eight. My father, may he rest in peace, was nearly a hundred when he died and he worked until he took his last breath. By the time I'm gone, you'll have mastered all there is to know here. Meanwhile, help me. I have worked all my life here at Santa Rita. Apart from myself and my family, it is a matter of pride to me that this estate returns to its former glory. If *el padrón* can do it, let him, if not, take his place.'

Although Antonio had clearly told me that Maria's mother was technically in the right, he told her that if she ever dared to lecture me again, the consequences would be dire. Although I knew that he had no intention of penalising her in any way, *she* didn't know that. She was afraid. She apologised and I went back to the Casa Grande feeling not only like a tyrant but a sneak.

Antonio left me by the wrought-iron gates to the courtyard.

'Remember what I said about your time of grace, Doña. This house is yours, you should live here.'

17

THE PACT OVER the running of the estate was made and I was given a verbal power of attorney. Then, in the middle of March, Jaime came home and called me out on to the veranda. He announced that he had booked a room at the hospital for me to have the baby. He told me he had asked for an extra bed for himself to stay over there. He said he would send a telegram to Joanna as soon as the child was born. He organised a *molienda*, and supervised it almost in its entirety. He was calm and quiet although unduly nervous, pacing and chewing his finger-nails. He fainted several times during the week.

When Abrán and Antonio returned from Valera with the brown paper bag of money on Saturday morning, he took what he needed and gave me the rest, then left with a parting, 'You pay the workers.'

It was the first time I had ever paid them. Antonio ceremoniously brought a table to the porch, then lined the men up, with the *trapicheros* at the front of the queue because they were exhausted and had to be paid first. Antonio himself always waited until last, disregarding his own tiredness in the interest of adjusting the accounts. Every worker had loans and debts against his pay. They were usually paltry sums, the equivalent of a few pennies for a twist of *chimó* or a few shillings for tabs run up at the local shop. If a man missed an hour for any reason other than serious illness or accident, Antonio docked the time from his daily wage. At the end of paying out, I had over £200 left in *bolivárs*. I asked Antonio if this was usual. He assured me it had been a mediocre *molienda*. I gave Antonio a hefty bonus and stashed the rest of the money away, pondering the future wealth to come my way and wondering how best to spend it.

The last person before Antonio on the payroll was an old toothless man called Alfredo Peña. He was a distant cousin who lived in the slums outside Valera in a mud and tin shack because he had been born on the wrong side of the sheets. Alfredo Peña was an expert on sugar-crushing machinery. He could take apart the most intricate *trapiche* and put it back together again without any apparent effort. He worked with a lentitude that made him the laughing stock not just of the *hacienda* but of the entire neighbourhood. He also spoke more slowly than anyone I have ever met before or after. Between each word, he left a long, infuriating pause, as though he had fallen asleep mid-sentence. He ate lunch with me every day. It was part of his contract that he always eat with the family instead of with the other workers. He had a great chip on his shoulder about the ill-usage he had received at the hands of most of the Teráns.

I was not fond of Alfredo Peña. For the first seven or eight weeks that he was cleaning the dismounted Squire *trapiche* and servicing the smaller one we had in use, I found our lunches interminably boring. He either spoke of cogs and rollers, or of his shabby treatment at the hands of his grand cousins or of the evils of soap. Alfredo Peña was convinced that soap was the cause of all known diseases. It washed away the natural oils and should never, ever, be applied to the skin. Every day, he inspected my rudimentary bathroom, saw the soap (often tucked discreetly away) and then launched into a two-hour diatribe about the dangers of detergents. What someone else might say in a minute, Alfredo Peña would draw out into eight or ten. Increasingly, I found myself wanting to fall asleep as soon as he started talking. He told me several times that it meant a great deal to him to be lunching with the Señora of Don Jaime Terán and how good Jaime had been to him in the past.

Within a week of starting work, Alfredo Peña borrowed the white Hillman van that had become our second car. He had arranged to be picked up by Jaime and driven home, but when his cousin didn't turn up, he assured me that he would drive himself back the twenty minutes it would take him to get home and return the car the following morning. Half an hour after he had left, Antonio Moreno came flapping down the hill.

'Where's the car?'

I told him Alfredo Peña had borrowed it, and Antonio buried his head in his hands.

'Ai ai ai!'

'What's the matter?'

'Didn't you know about Alfredo and cars?'

'He's a mechanic.'

'He's death to a car. You'll never see that van again.'

'Of course we will. He lives in the *barrio*, we can go and get it.'

'You could trace Alfredo Peña's entire life through the cars he's wrecked and the crashes he's survived. It's a miracle he survives, and it's a miracle he crashes. Everyone on the road knows him. They see Alfredo Peña and they just pull over.

He's *chocho*, you know, senile when it comes to driving, he has been since he was a boy.'

Sure enough, a cut and bruised Alfredo Peña reported for work next day, apologising profusely for having smashed the car.

'Who knows how it happened?' he drawled. 'One minute I was reciting T. S. Eliot, then there was a line I couldn't quite remember . . . I was searching for it and then, there I was in a ditch and everybody was shouting at me again . . . extraordinary,' he said and shook his grey head so that his lank hair danced from side to side.

I had long since given up listening to Alfredo Peña. It was enough to know that he had smashed the car (that I was beginning, tentatively to drive) without being bored by his rambling explanations of how and why. Yet the mention of T. S. Eliot caught my attention. Alfredo told me that he had 'The Wasteland' and 'The Four Quartets' at home.

'In Spanish?'

'In cristiano, the originals, by T. S. Eliot, you probably don't know anything about him, you see, they are books.'

From that moment on I forgave him his slowness, his greasy hair, his lunchtime dribbling, his toothless mouth, his endless lecturing, and got to know him better. Although he flatly refused to recognise the concept of translation, and proved obtuse and sometimes maddening in discussions, Alfredo Peña, in that literary wilderness, hoarded books. He loved them. He dipped them in kerosene and read them, over and over, until great chunks were committed to memory. His apparently asinine mumblings as he worked, were actually slow recitations of poetry and sayings. He had grappled from illiteracy to a certain erudition, alone and unaided in the slum where he lived.

He had two sons, Hannibal and Hasdrubal. The latter, an

ethereally beautiful boy, lived strapped to a rocking chair. He had suffered from severe meningitis aged two and never progressed beyond that mental age. At six, he had tipped a kerosene cooker over himself and burnt 50 per cent of his body, but not his face. From the time he recovered, to protect him from further damage Hasdrubal had been strapped to a rocking chair which he rocked incessantly. Alfredo Peña worked to feed his children, to replace Hasdrubal's rockers and to buy books.

Santa Rita

Dear Joanna

Today 21st March – first day of Spring. I hope it feels like Spring there.

I have been taking photos to send you, but they are not yet developed. Here is the first instalment taken by a friend. No. 1. taken immediately outside the patio, on the left, by the stream between the two rose bushes is Napoleon, he is a domesticated turkey vulture, very charming and coy. Because he has one wing temporarily clipped he strides around the garden opening his wings and then flapping them closed behind his back, his head hunched between his shoulders. He follows one like a dog, and eats (raw meat) only from our hands and disdains to eat alone.

No. 2. Napoleon sulking; and very pregnant me trying to get him to look up for a photo.

No. 3. Puppy in the upper part of the *trapiche*. In the background you can just see a spoke of the waterwheel. The floor is littered with sugar-cane. N.B. *Trapiche* means sugar-crusher, but is also used to mean place where sugar is crushed.

No. 4. Is a view of Santa Rita. To the left (off the picture) is the big house, to the right, the estate continues for a good deal more as one approaches Mendoza Fría. The main road runs through the sugar-canes (the light greenness) and to the front, the River Momboy runs hidden by trees and overgrowth.

The hill in the background really begins where the photo ends and it takes many hours to get up it.

No. 5. Santa Rita, to the right is the Big House, the foremost slope is the same as in no. 4, the other slopes seem to go on for ever in the background. What looks like grass on either side of the road is sugar-cane. As you can gather, most of the lands on the estate are hills and valleys. Nobody has ever actually measured the estate, it just has boundaries.

We have not had a *molienda* for weeks which is why the trickle [of money to Joanna] no longer flows, but Jaime reckons that within two weeks we shall be solvent again. We are remaking the last two ovens of the furnace and remounting the copper tanks on top. We have gone 6 weeks living on saved money and are only £150 in debt, which is very good considering that wages alone are £100 per week plus expenses on the estate, plus extra expenses, in special bricks for the furnaces at 14 shillings per brick!! Each *molienda* produces from £250 to £450, half of which goes in expenses (wages etc.) half profit. We have enough cane now to harvest every fifteen days until the end of the year.

The french beans and *caraotas* that are planted with the new cane are doing well, and the price of *panela* (the sugar we make here) is on the rise.

The rainy season began late, about ten days ago.

The garden is looking *much* better and I spend most of the day gardening now, pruning and planting. I am trying to get it more or less into shape before you come.

I am doing lots of knitting: 5 pairs bootees, 2 pairs mitts, a cardigan (raglan), leggings and I am now making a coat.

I read in the papers about a probable general strike, and the bombs. Thank goodness you live where you do: there is not much risk of an IRA attack on Clapham South.

As I was saying, long ago, I would like you to bring with you:

A few decent wooden toys.

1 pr of wellington boots size 6½ *not* clumpy, but *elegant* (if you can imagine an elegant Wellie).

Aspirin, chlorodyne, 'Stress' (for dogs).

Seeds for growing herbs (not sage, rosemary or oregano).

Yourself.

If you have excess luggage, do not worry, I doubt if you will have because the allowance is quite generous.

For V. mosquitoey areas I use long woollen socks.

Bring sunglasses – absolutely essential.

Bring a sunhat if you like (from the shell shop outside Foyle's?).

Bring lots of underclothes, summer dresses, skirts and shirts.

Alcira, our maid, washes and irons daily so you will not need too many heaps of clothes.

You will arrive in the middle of the dry season – lucky old you. It will be interesting to see if you like the heat. I, personally cannot bear it.

As you see, I have got down to drivel again.

One last thing, please find out how does one pronounce 'Iseult'?

What did you think of the poem I sent you? You did not say.

Cat had kittens yesterday.

The books arrived, did I tell you?

Excuse this rather incoherent letter, I have flu and a sinus and am not thinking very clearly at all.

Love to everyone.

Alcira, the latest in a string of maids, was the first girl to work in the order I was whittling out of my domestic chaos. I instigated a routine and strict, clear instructions about what she should do and when. Miraculously, it worked. She didn't give notice, I didn't fire her and no marauding cousins came to *sonsacar* her from my service. She disliked Alfredo Peña but forbore to show it to his face. She feared and disliked Napoleon, but realised after a few tentative kicks that if anyone had to leave, it wouldn't be him. Alcira even managed to find a way round Coromoto, inviting her in to help, appealing to the younger girl for advice, flattering her in such a way that Coromoto grudgingly consented to drop the guerrilla warfare she had carried out against the other maids. Together we walked the dogs, made chutney and took picnics into the orange grove on the hill.

Hda Santa Rita
23rd April 1973

Dear Joanna,

I last wrote to you ages ago, but there has been a local postal strike *plus* a broken-down car – hence incommunicado.

What news? I have not heard from you for an equally long time probably for the same reason.

Please confirm your arrival date *20th JUNE* 1973 CARA-CAS (Maicatia). Are you really going in August? Could you not stay until September?

Please count on £75 in May, i.e. next month towards your fare.

When will you be going into hospital? and when will you be coming out? How do I write to you then?

By the time you get this letter the baby will probably be already born. Due tomorrow now.

Winter set in here last week. Winter as opposed to summer, i.e. the rainy season, much belated. It is rather like an English November, dull and drizzly with mist and frequent downpours – a very pleasant change.

In honour of your arrival we have begun to organise our house. So far we have (Ramón Rivas has) completely rewired the house: electric light throughout (with *switches* to turn on and off) wire netting in several windows, a roof for the dog pen. Mended rooves and lots of other things.

I am writing in bed with your big green blanket on top and the crashing din of rain thundering down on to the corrugated iron on top. The girls are cleaning up the dining room, dishes and dogs (very comfy arrangement for me!).

I shall give you your birthday present when you come (I have not forgotten).

Do write to me from time to time, I am not getting letters nowadays (or so it seems, or so it is). You will be here in 8 weeks now.

Lots and lots of love,
Lisaveta

Two weeks, exactly, after the last *molienda*, the next one started, as the next one would, two weeks later still, and then the next and the next with a regularity that in itself became monotonous, carrying on through the next several years. The cane was cut from certain fields, loaded on to La Povva and trundled to the *trapiche*. Then the feeder fed it through the roller blades of the cane-crusher, turned by cogs that were turned by the waterwheel. As the grey juice trickled down a channel into the first copper vat, it began to heat up. It was then ladled into the next copper vats, each of which was the size of three bath tubs put together and twice as deep. By the third tray, the sugar had begun to boil; from there it bubbled into another tray and on downhill to several more (the *mayor a menor* system devised by Don Rodolfo) until it reached a great round cauldron where the *puntero* left it until it reached its *punto* or point. After that, while the furnaces raged underneath the trays and vats and the cauldron, it was ladled into wooden trays into which a divider was sunk to break up the cooling sugar into twenty-four blocks each of exactly one kilo. These trays were then levelled with the flat of a machete and set to one side, to cool properly. Once cold enough to be prized out of their trays, they were packed and stacked and wrapped.

Relays of small children carrying billycans crossed the bridge to the *trapiche*, hurrying on their way in to deliver their food still warm; dawdling on the way back to make the most of their unaccustomed freedom. On the last day, the twenty-four kilo packs of *panela* sugar were stacked on to La Povva and taken into Valera to sell. The string for the packaging and the lye for the sugar were purchased from a sugar merchant at the edge of the main market square in Valera. The sugar was then sold to him, with the price of the string and lye deducted from the total. His shop was a bare, square storeroom, with a plastic chair, an old wooden table and a calendar with naked girls entwined by snakes. The calendar was several years out of date and fixed on the month of February. The sugar merchant had a cast in one eye, he was short and brown and always sweaty in his khaki shirt and trousers. He took his tally of the sugar, made his calculations, haggled, agreed (always reluctantly) on a price which he claimed would immediately put him out of business, and then sidled into the back of his shop, re-emerging with a used brown paper bag and a wad of bank notes. Week by week and year by year, despite his claims that each deal would cripple him, he continued to thrive on the marketplace. He never had a shortage of money in his back room. The biggest *molienda* I ever sold was for £1,800 which in those days, and there, was a small fortune, but he still had the cash to hand to pay for it. He was a middleman. He disliked me on sight. It offended him when I went, later, to sell the sugar myself. He hated handing money to a woman. He always told me I was a disgrace to my sex to be bothering my head with business. The final sum to be paid was never a round figure because of the deductions for string and lye. In all the years I dealt with him, he never once gave me the correct amount of money. It was a fortnightly test he set me. The big wad of notes would be out by some varying amount each time. He didn't believe that women could count. It irritated and then finally amused him that I always caught him out. It came to be a game we played in what was otherwise a cut-throat transaction. The middlemen made over 100 per cent profit on our sugar.

The baby was several weeks overdue. Somebody told me that jumping induced a birth, so I jumped. Someone else told me that mopping floors vigorously was a sure way to break the waters. I mopped our new concrete floors for hours every day. I ran up and down the *camino real* with Napoleon flapping behind me. I climbed up the hill behind our house and stripped the mango tree of its green mangoes, jumping down from its branches. Apart from getting very tired, nothing happened. I spent the last two weeks of my confinement on my own with Alcira and Coromoto. Alfredo Peña was sick with bronchitis and stayed away. Jaime, who had, as Antonio Moreno told me he would, been disarmingly attentive, had grown tired of waiting. His initial impatience turned to anger, and once again, he went away, returning in the small hours with a curt, 'Have you had it yet?'

My earlier rebellious plan to deliver the baby myself on the *hacienda* was beginning to look like a distant necessity. If I went into labour at night, Alcira would never go out to get help, not even to as far as the *trapiche* to loosen the wheel. Fear of El Coco made her quite clear on that point. She told me something that I was to hear repeated over and over again from many different mouths, 'I'd do anything for you, Doña, but not that.'

My resolution for the home delivery stayed firm until 3 May, when I stopped feeling the baby moving inside me. I was now sure that I was a good ten months' pregnant. When the twins arrived to check on me in the morning, I asked them to drive me into town. When they asked me where Jaime was, I had to admit that I didn't know. They were so upset when they learnt that I had been spending the last few weeks on my own, they made me promise solemnly to come and find them or to send for them if I ever needed help again. They took me to see Dr Briceño, who assured me the baby was well, but agreed that I had been carrying it for quite long enough. He arranged to induce the birth the following day.

Then the twins, Mimita and Mimella cruised around Valera looking for Jaime. After six or seven abortive calls, they located him. He arranged to meet us back at the *hacienda* later in the day. Rather than stay on the *hacienda* meanwhile, they took me back to their house. Their father, Don Felipe Neri, sat on the L-shaped veranda, crippled from a road accident. On one side of his chair he had a glass of whisky, on the other a glass of brandy, which he drank alternately to keep his blood pressure level, or so he claimed.

I had heard a great deal of gossip about Don Felipe Neri Terán; he was said to be a tyrant, and his wife Elia, was said to be a saint. Every ten or twenty minutes he rang a bell and a servant called Lucy Grey rushed to tend him. I never saw his tyranny, it was always hearsay, but his sons and daughters, servants and neighbours were all visibly afraid of him. Upon arrival, he showed me an old-fashioned sweet-shop jar full of snakes' heads, all of which had been caught in the cane-fields of his *hacienda*. He also told me how to catch a snake by making a noose on the end of a cord and by means of a slip knot, luring it in and then tightening it until the snake could be safely carried away.

'You have to stay really still and quiet, though, *Musiua*, or it'll get away.'

After this lesson, he let me past him to the main part of the house. He was like a toll gate, exacting conversation from all who came and went.

We played Ludo and gin rummy and drank papaya milk-shakes and ate hot dogs with tomato sauce, listened to pop music (the twins were both hooked on a song called 'Puppy Love', the lyrics of which they insisted I translate). Then, having been thoroughly blessed by their mother, Doña Elia and told I could and must return any time I wanted, I was driven home to where Jaime was waiting patiently for life to go on. He took me back to Valera, to the hospital. In London, Joanna was having a hysterectomy.

Central Hospital, Valera
Fri. 4th May, 5.30 a.m.

Dear Joanna,

How are you?

I take this opportunity of dawn and bird chattering to let you know that all is well and we think of you a lot. How was your operation? I imagine you are nearly well again already.

In a couple of hours they are going to induce the baby.

Happy birthday for Sunday.

Happy mothering Sunday if I do not get out of here before then. I am reading *Murphy*.

When will you be at 6 Cavendish Gardens again so as to be able to send your £75 directly? It is already put aside for you.

How is The South London? This hosp. is, so far so good (in the private paying section). Only unpleasant when the two parts meet – as yesterday when for general examination I was sent to undress and *all* the cubicles were swimming with shit and vomit. A bit nasty! One just had to step over it and take one's clothes and hold them with one hand and the X-ray plates with the other and struggle, God knows how, into a funny green rag coat? with all possible skill and ingenuity.

We are already painting the house in your honour and making bookcases and curtains, doors and windows.

I shall write again as soon as possible

187

    Lots of love,
      Lisaveta
      Jaime (NB) original signature
    P.S. love to anyone who may want it.

Dr Briceño came at seven p.m. and told me that I would have to have a Caesarean section which he would perform personally. He told me not to worry and to get some sleep. I was worried, and I couldn't sleep. At seven a.m., they prepared me for theatre. I had had several operations as a child, so I knew the procedure. In Valera, it was rougher but similar. At eight o'clock, two male nurses in white wheeled me away. Instead of going straight into theatre, there was a delay of two and a half hours during which, instead of wheeling me back to my private room, they left me in the public labour ward. I had never seen a baby being born before, I saw half a dozen then. I had been given my pre-med anaesthetic, so I was drowsy, which lent the whole episode a surreal overtone. There were some fifteen or twenty women and girls all in various stages of advanced labour and all either screaming or wailing. One nurse and one doctor sauntered through from time to time; neither seemed in the least bit concerned for the ward of agonised peasant women. I remember the girl next to me. She was so close I could have reached out and touched her. She was very dark and fat and drenched in sweat. She kept screaming herself into a faint. When the doctor came past her one time, she called out, 'Doctor, please help me, I'm dying. Help me, I can't bear this pain.'

The doctor said, 'I bet you could bear it when half the neighbourhood was sticking it in you, you silly bitch,' and walked on.

The cries continued, multiplied, backed by sobs and choking. The girl next to me gave birth at nine forty-five by the clock on the wall in front of me. The nurse arrived in time to help the last of the baby out of her. It was wrinkly and pale grey under the blood. I could only see the women in front of me clearly (too clearly). I watched head after head emerge from between their tortured legs, sometimes with and sometimes without the assistance of the doctor. Time passed so slowly on that ward, and the noise was so unbearable, it felt as though I would be there for ever. I had given up hoping for a reprieve when my two stewards returned and wheeled me away to the operating theatre.

My anaesthetic was to be by lumbar puncture. There was a woman not far from where I lay who had been given a lumbar puncture in the wrong place and had shrivelled up to less than half her former size over the twelve years of vegetation that had followed the failed attempt. The twins had once offered to take me to see her, she was a local curiosity. I had heard endless stories about lumbar punctures that had gone wrong in Valera. A favourite topic of discussion was failed operations and failed anaesthetics; the town was littered with comatose guinea pigs from what must have been that very operating theatre. I tried to express my qualms but was too inarticulate. The anaesthetist had four gos at jabbing into my spine and missed on each time. The twins had told me that one miss was enough to become a vegetable. After his fourth stab, the anaesthetist said crossly, 'Well, I can't find the right place, does any one else want to have a try?'

Someone else did have a try and failed.

Dr Briceño was cross and told them to stop it. Then he ordered a general anaesthetic. I was turned over, and strapped down with sticking plaster round my arms. I didn't know that it is usual practice to have a countdown between the anaesthetist and the surgeon in such cases and that the knife must enter the flesh at the exact moment that the anaesthetic takes effect. I trusted Dr Briceño as far as I trusted anyone, but I didn't really trust anyone there. My nerves were rattled by the labour ward. When he lunged at me and my baby with his knife, I was convinced that I was the victim of an elaborate murder plot. I saw him not as my surgeon but as my assassin and screamed.

The operation was successful, and I didn't feel a thing; but for years, I would have nightmares of a kind man gone mad stabbing into me.

As from the Hda Santa Rita, etc.
Thursday, 10th May 1973

Dear Joanna,

How are you? How was your operation? You will be here very soon now.

Iseult is doing well . . . I am very well now too and I think we shall all be going home this weekend.

In my last letter I said the doctor was going to induce the birth, but he later decided not to because it seemed possible that the umbilical cord was either caught round her neck or round her foot. So, the following morning, 5th, I donned my gown and cap and bootees and was wheeled off at seven a.m. for a Caesarean section. Dr Briceño performed the operation personally. The cord was wound round one of her feet several times. Only hitch was that she (being overdue) and being born feet first to disentangle her, breathed in the fluid from my womb and thus filled her lungs. She spent two days in an incubator with oxygen and pumps to clear her lungs and Briceño brought in 5 child specialists to attend her. She is now completely well.

You must have spent your birthday in hospital. I hope people went to visit you. How do you do for visitors there?

You said only one name, but we put 'Joanna' after you, I'm sure you will not object.

I am going to have a little sleep now, write soon, get well quickly. Happy Mother's Day next Sunday.

> With lots of love
> Lisaveta

Iseult spent five days in intensive care: she was not expected to live. As soon as she could be moved, the doctors suggested she would be better off at home away from the infections of the hospital. They warned me that if she caught so much as a cold, she would not survive it. No one was to go near her, no maids, no friends and no relations.

'Guard her with your life,' the chief paediatrician said. 'To let her have contact with anyone else will cost her hers.' Her room was sterilised, everything around her was sterilised, I wore a mask around her and rubbed myself endlessly with pure alcohol.

When a baby is born in the Andes, it is customary for the mother and child to enclose themselves in a darkened room, surrounded only by women, and to observe a strict diet and a number of closely observed rites. A woman should not bathe, *la gente* said, for forty days and no red meat should be eaten. No spices or vegetables should be eaten, no air or daylight should touch either mother or child. Babies were swaddled and then cocooned in blankets, regardless of the heat. When they were finally taken out, or, if they were forced to leave their quarantine, they were half-smothered to do so. It was believed that the slightest breach of this quarantine was to give an immediate foot-hold to the evil eye. The evil eye preyed, particularly, on new-born babies. The mother, contaminated by the birth and in a state of exhaustion, was forced into bed, where, half-starved by the diet and lack of air, she obligingly developed a weakness that made the presence of the other women an absolute necessity.

A number of women came forward, both in the capacity of friends, family and servants, to guide me through the perilous waters of the quarantine. They assured me that if a baby could survive its first forty days, it was over its greatest danger. Over the years, it was never possible to get the women of the estate to break with this tradition. For them it was enough to see with their own eyes how many babies died in their first few days and weeks of infancy. They wanted no further proof of the infallibility of their ways. Rows of garlic teeth were balanced around the entrance to both the house, the room and around the cot. Nothing was more effective for scaring off the evil eye than garlic. Then orange seeds called *pepas de San Pedro* were strung on thread and dangled around the cot, and round the baby's right wrist. Certain aromatic herbs that were a mixture of the bitter and the sweet were burnt on the threshold to the room. So, according to the women of the *hacienda* and some of the Mendozeros, I should enclose myself in a darkened airless room, take to my bed and stay there for forty days while they took care of Iseult. Not to do so, would be, they warned, fatal.

Meanwhile, the more enlightened women, the cousins from Valera told me that I didn't have to be in the dark, but I shouldn't let in too much light, I shouldn't go outside. I didn't have to stay in bed for forty days, fifteen would be quite sufficient. I should bathe, but not with soap, and not too often, soap and even water were debilitating in my condition. I shouldn't, of course, eat any meat for forty days, or flavour my food at all, and most important of all, I couldn't possibly breastfeed the baby. 'Only animals and peasants breastfeed,' they told me. 'It is a disgusting and barbarous custom left over from the days of savagery.' They brought me dozens of tins of Reina Del Campo baby milk and dozens of plastic bottles, rubber teats and three sterilising units.

I told the more enlightened cousins that I was going to breastfeed my child and that in Europe it had long been discovered that bottle-feeding was bad and breastfeeding good. I told them it was common practice. They raised their eyebrows and noted down this further evidence of the dreadful place I came from. They forbade me to try. My mother-in-law was summoned from Caracas to use her authority with me. I was told in no uncertain terms that the family had been very lenient to me, they had overlooked my obvious ineptitude at commanding others, they had forgiven me for the lack of grace and taste I displayed both in my dress and the absurd way that I insisted on wearing my hair, long or short. I had gone out of my way to shame them and make them look ridiculous. I hobnobbed with the peasants, and gave the estate children decent clothes when they were perfectly happy to wear their own rags. I was obviously a dreadful wife or my husband would not be driven to spend most of his time taking refuge in other people's houses. But they, *en masse*, were going to prevent me from being a dreadful mother to this child whom I had borne (unfortunately a girl and not a boy, but I was young and could try again, and meanwhile, Iseult was the most direct heir to the old Teráns) and who belonged not to me, but to them, the family. Who did I think I was to defy the family?

They said they didn't know how I had attracted the notice of Jaime, they had racked their brains to discover it, but I had, and I had been lucky enough to be taken into the most exclusive clan in Latin America and probably in the world. It was bad enough that I insisted on living in a miserable mud hut like a peasant, but I was not going to bring up *la niña* Iseult like one. She would be given decent God-fearing powdered milk from a decent plastic sterilised bottle, and that, they informed, me, was that.

It was always enough for Doña Antonieta to say one thing for her son to dig his heels in and say another, and vice versa. Most unexpectedly, Jaime, who had not once stood up for me in all the time I had been in Venezuela, told them unceremoniously to mind their own business and leave me alone. They left, in high dudgeon, warning me that I was wantonly killing my daughter.

I was to take Iseult directly from the intensive care unit to a car (which reeked of disinfectant in her honour), then straight to the *hacienda*. Once there, no one was to see or touch her. Although I and the doctors had informed the waiting family that this was to be the case, they didn't really believe it. So we left the central hospital in a convoy of cars.

My failure to share the baby was taken very ill. The women argued with me through my padlocked door. I didn't want their diets or their superstitions, their amulets or their incantations, but I would have gladly shared her for the benefit of their experience. I had no idea how to handle a baby and learnt my way nervously. Luckily, she was quiet and easy and I had no problems but for the stream of irate visitors who picketed my yard. Once the twins and my sister-in-law finally grasped that they too should be excluded from handling Iseult, they were helpful and kind, ferrying what I needed from the shops to my self-imposed imprisonment. Coromoto came several times daily to wheedle at my door. I held Iseult up for her to see through the window as I had done to others, keeping their distance, but she wouldn't accept her exclusion. Alcira boiled nappies and cooked meals. She was scandalised and frightened that I defied the quarantine diet, she crossed herself over and over, muttering as she cooked, that whatever happened, it was nothing to do with her. I was inundated with presents.

I counted the days until Joanna arrived. She was due out on 20 June. The baby did not die as the doctors had predicted she might and as the family *gente* had insisted she would. The *moliendas* continued, announcing their start with the crashing of the great waterwheel and the opening of the sluice gates, swelling the reasonably fast stream by the house into a treacherous millrace. After each *molienda* ended, and the shouts, laughter and voices from the *trapiche* were gone, the lingering smell of lemon juice and trementine wafted down from the copper vats, which were scrubbed out with half-lemons to keep them clean and shining ready for the next boiling up.

Hacienda Santa Rita
5th June 1973

Dear Joanna,

I have not written to you for what seems like ages.
How is life in the English countryside?

Iseult, whom we call Iséult is well and seems happy.

Lisaveta is no better than well and in a year-old stupor and at the same stage of inertia as before.

1 'The smother of an ex-lover'

2 'Like a volcano erupting over a land that no longer worships its lava'

Being the only words I have composed in the last six months or more: and they are not very brilliant.

Founder's Day, school, buns and bloomers, too long away to be real somehow.

Your room is now well under way. It is, at present, being painted.

Iseult does not cry at all, except every 3–5 hours for a feed. Please go and see *El Ultimo Tango en Paris*, with Marlon Brando and Maria Schneider. Be sure to see it. It has been banned all over South America and we want to know why.

My mother's visit was delayed, she was convalescent and had to postpone her trip by a month. It was a dreary month sliced into twice by a sugar harvest. It was interrupted occasionally by Iseult's waking hours. But, while she slept, I felt depressed. I was afraid of losing her and, although her health seemed to be good and she gained strength daily, I felt overwhelmed by feelings of inadequacy. I had had to suspend my daily dispensing of creams and unguents, pills and linctuses, to keep the risk of infection away. Antonio Moreno, a great respecter of the quarantine, kept away. Men were unwelcome visitors to any house after a child was born. I felt the little territory I had gained slip away. Napoleon was disconsolate and becoming severely maladjusted, venting his rages on everyone and everything. He was jealous of the baby. He knew exactly where Iseult was; he flew up at the wire-meshed window, colliding with the shutters, in a daily protest. He was taciturn with me and took refuge in the company of Leila, the white Persian cat. They slept together, black and white, she curled, he huddled. As though to show the extent of their friendship, Leila even began to look like Napoleon. She developed mange on her neck and the long silky fur fell out, leaving her neck bare from chin to chest. She had a thin, ungainly neck like a chicken. It was red and raw and then scabbed, recreating the wrinkles on Napoleon's own bare grey neck. Old Natividad, unwilling to bear the consequences of breaking the taboo of my quarantine, stayed away. When I summoned him, he sent a small girl down to explain that he was ill. I didn't know if he was really ill or just pretending, but I sent him four aspirin in a twist of brown paper and wished him well.

Jaime hovered around the house. Bearing in mind Antonio's advice, I tackled the subject of the Casa Grande. For once, Antonio Moreno's wisdom failed. The Casa Grande was out of the question. Yes, it was empty, but no, we couldn't move there. The mention of it became another taboo. Not wanting to invoke another estrangement on the eve of Joanna's arrival, I let the matter drop.

Santa Rita
28th June 1973

Dear Joanna

Thank you for your two letters. How are you? I received your plans, passage and flights, it all sounds all right. Iseult is well and smiles and laughs and gurgles, drinks orange juice and honey.

Jaime very rarely smiles or laughs or gurgles with me now, and gets cross about everything and grumpy. I think it is just a phase he is going through. I hope so. I have never felt more like Norway than at present. A bit depressed and depressing.

I am frantically battling with our garden/jungle. It is overgrown *again*! Please do not be disappointed when you come to find a heaving mass in front of the house, hence garden. This is the tropics: weeds grow six foot high with roots six foot under.

I am going to hack away at the garden again with the help of 80-year-old Benito who waters it daily but is worse than useless for other things here, so slow, slow, slow.

    Love to everyone, love Lisaveta
Don't forget the shortbread.
Don't forget me.

Benito Mendoza, the old man who had come to see me a year before, turned up quite unexpectedly one afternoon, defied the quaratine that kept all men away from my house and announced, 'Here I am, Doña, I'm back. You sent for me and I've come and I won't leave any more.'

I was delighted to see him, although I certainly hadn't sent for him – he hadn't been living on the *hacienda* in the interim and I wouldn't have known where to send. Benito was thin and wiry with skin the colour of tamarind where his hands and face and feet had burnt, but surprisingly white on his thin spindly legs when he rolled up his trousers, which he did often, being fastidious in his own way. He was permanently drunk. Antonio claimed that Benito was preserved in spirits. Despite his age, a mysterious quantity – over eighty and under ninety – he had no wrinkles. His small, round brown eyes were quick and alert, though the whites were reddened by the *aguardiente* rum he drank. The faint aura of spirits that haloed him and his bloodshot eyes were two signs of his inebriation which he carried with great dignity and poise. He always walked and moved very slowly, as though uncertain whether he could otherwise keep his balance. Benito was to become my closest companion. He had outlived his entire family, bar one, a daughter who lived in the *páramo* and who wanted nothing more to do with the old man. She had just turned him out, though he didn't say so. She would not have him back, though he would never admit it. He was lonely and together we passed the nights of many years to come sitting on the old cathedral bench while he told me about the past and I listened.

18

JOANNA CAME TO stay, arriving at the end of July, for six weeks. Through her eyes, I saw again the loveliness of bougainvillaeas cascading down the hillside, of the waxen and cloyingly heady frangipani flowers. I saw the novelty of poinsettia trees growing like weeds with their red leaves clashing in the undergrowth. I saw how beautiful the bluebirds were when they circled the *hacienda*, and how cheerful the noisy squawks of parrots could be in their harlequin formations. I tasted again the sweetness of dwarf bananas warm from the tree and breakfasts of scooped-out paw-paws.

My little house had never looked prettier, and though Joanna was shocked to see the traces of its former poverty and squalor, its tin roof and what was still a pounded mud floor in the sitting room, I saw the improvements in it and grew to like it more. Seeing the *hacienda* through her eyes, I saw it as a tourist might, with admiration, and not as one bound in its timeless cobwebs. She told me how desolate she had been when I had sailed away, and how hard the intervening year had been, but, she said, seeing the transformation in myself, she felt she could now accept the separation better. She had never known me be anything other than shy and timid. She liked what she saw. Besides which, the *hacienda* made her happy in a way that I had not seen in her before.

After the euphoria of the first few days wore off, she found the poverty of *la gente* distressing. Sitting out under a mango tree in the beating sun, we made lists of things for her to send; things for me to do and for her to do. She insisted that I start a school and that I put my dispensary on a more permanent footing. She saw ways of improving the little things of day to day: new wellington boots for Antonio Moreno, who suffered from rheumatism, a warm jacket for Benito, easily washable blankets for the estate babies to help stave off the nightly chills. She suggested better and more varied purges and how to trick the women into giving vitamin C to their children. Citrus fruit was not eaten by *la gente* on the grounds that it curdled the blood. Most compounds had a lemon tree and maybe an orange tree too, but the fruit was allowed to fall and rot on the ground. Only the lemons were gathered to scrub out the *trapiche*'s copper vats. She pointed out that most of the children were suffering from protein deficiency. Together we went over their diets and tried to work out ways, within the narrow precepts of what was and was not taboo, to enrich particularly the children's protein intake. I would have to win over enough mothers to allow their children a better diet. Once, by example, the others saw the improvement in the children's health, they too would follow suit.

Apart from the pity that the poverty aroused in her, and the giant hairy spiders which inspired her with terror, and her squeamishness when one of the workers came to the house with a big machete gash in his arm and needed suturing and binding up, Joanna enjoyed her stay.

Iseult, now nearly three months old, was deemed by her

paediatrician to be able to get out and about so long as it was within reason. So we went to the *páramo* to see the *frailegónes* growing on the cold rocks, weaving round steep mountain roads past strips of topsoil laboriously carried into dips in the stone, in which straggling rows of barley, oats and potatoes were grown. Around the market town of Timotes, there was an intensive tract of market gardening, strip-farmed by peasants with the long beaked noses of the Timotocuican Indians. They were sombre and gaunt, wrapped in their Andean ruana blankets, with their cheeks stained purple by their staple diet of potatoes in their skins, and by the biting wind that was the legacy of the *páramo*. We dined at the houses of several cousins and friends.

After my own reception, I was afraid that Joanna would be snubbed by the family or disrespected in some way. They had all said such nasty things about my family and my dubious origins that I was constantly alert for any hint of rudeness to her. I need not have been, for she was welcomed with open arms. Whatever it is that divides a lady from a mere woman in the Andes, Joanna had it, instinctively. Nobody made snide remarks to her. Her height and bearing were autocratic, her manner authoritarian in the way that headmistresses are, even when they are offduty. Joanna was the headmistress of a large Remand Home for delinquent girls; she was used to being in command, and it showed. Had she had none of these attributes, she would still have been welcomed, not because she was my mother but because she was fair with an unequivocal whiteness that set off her red hair. Red hair was top of the colour chart, it was desired beyond any other. Joanna became known as 'the lady with the lovely hair'. Even on the *hacienda*, where the women wondered what kind of mother could send her daughter out alone and unprotected to a land where to be without family was a social disgrace, they forgave her for her colouring and for the haughtiness she had never known she possessed. *La gente* sent their own daughters out through want. My lack of family had been a stigma that implied a background of circumstances as dire as their own. Even Don Jaime, it was noted, was courtly to 'the lady with the lovely hair'.

For five weeks, the tropical idyll was sustained. Iseult thrived, Joanna was content and the household spun out a simulacrum of domestic harmony. Within days of arriving, Joanna fell in love with the Casa Grande, I tried to keep her away from it so as to avoid the obvious question of why I did not inhabit its empty halls. However, her appetite had been whetted by the sight of its graceful courtyard and enclosing wrought-iron railings and she insisted on being shown around. Over the weeks of her holiday, she refused to accept that I should live in what was ultimately a damp, insect-infested dell under a tin roof when such a lovely edifice was standing empty within beckoning distance of my wicket gate. I made her promise not to say anything about it. Reluctantly, she kept her peace until her final week when, filled with the *bonhomie* of Bacardi rum and lulled into a sense of being able to speak her mind regardless, she chided Jaime for forcing Iseult and myself to live as we did out of mere caprice. She actually asked quite nicely, making the question half in jest.

The five-week charade had been almost perfect. It ended abruptly as the *padrón* crashed his fist on to the table with such force that it cracked, and, with his face contorted into his old grimace, he left. He was gone for three days. He returned, taciturn and monosyllabic, kept out of our way and finally reverted to complete silence. Joanna was frightened, she was always frightened by anger or violence. She wanted to know what was the matter with his face? What had she said? What had she done? Where had he gone? I was sorry that she had seen the fabric of my marriage had threadbare places. She wanted me to confide in her, but I felt that there was too much to confide. She wasn't strong enough, or so I thought, to know that anything other than a sudden rupture had occurred. I kept calm, and seeing that I was unperturbed by the incident, she eventually let it pass. She left, tearfully, at the beginning of September to return to her London flat and her teaching post, her Siamese cat Bosie, and her maladjusted girls.

After she left, the house emptied in her wake. Alcira, my maid of many months, quit summarily after bearing the brunt of Jaime's rage one afternoon. In her place, Coromoto came for five hours a day to help me with Iseult and the chores. Then Jaime left and I was back where I'd begun. Benito Mendoza, in an excess of rum, fell from the window of the sugar-packing room into the millrace and nearly killed himself. He was taken to hospital and then released to the care of one of the workers whose mother had once been married to old Benito's son. Napoleon, who in the past had kept me company so well, was no longer with me. His jealousy of Iseult drove him into daily frenzies. He tore her clothes and nappies from the line and shredded them. He threw himself against the door of her room. Then, one morning, I awoke at dawn to hear a strange tapping over my head. I looked up just in time to see Napoleon finish boring the hole he had been making in the baked clay and bamboo wall above Iseult's cot. He had widened the hole. He stuck his head through and craned his long scraggy neck towards her sleeping face. The look in his eye was transparent. I sensed that he would kill her if he could. His beak and talons were strong enough, he had already shown both his intelligence and his vindictiveness. The furious eye that roved round my room, defying me and then fixated on the baby, was out for revenge.

I had let him go reluctantly. He had been my friend; even now his jealousy was a form of loyalty. I had received several ultimatums about him in the past. A number of women, including my mother-in-law, had vowed that unless Napoleon left the premises, they would never visit me again. So he had been not just a pet, but a protector. When Doña Antonieta said, 'Me or him,' I had chosen Napoleon. I would have chosen him over almost anything but this. Antonio Moreno and Abrán took him in a sack to the abattoir some forty miles away at Mototán. There, among hundreds of other vultures hovering over the river and its cargo of offal, they had released him. After Joanna left, and Alcira, and even Benito Mendoza, I missed him.

Although it was still nominally the dry season, the *hacienda* was battered by torrential rains. The storms swept up and down the valley and the River Momboy flooded three times in as many weeks. On the first occasion it rumbled and growled as it headed down the valley, smothering everything in mud, tearing up every plant in the garden except for the mature fruit trees and the bamboo. It flattened the banana palms and filled the bamboo and the porch with debris. It filled the courtyard deep with mud and the higher back rooms with a wash of sludge, and it deposited a dead, bloated pig in the kitchen.

It is a standing joke when dealing with Latin Americans that nothing gets done today that can be put off until tomorrow. *Mañana, mañana* is the rule of thumb. *Mañana* doesn't mean tomorrow in the sense that other nations use it, it means not now – at some undefinable point in the future – or never. There is a slowness about the passing of time, a monotony.

Over the spread of the seven years that I spent in the Andes, the days dragged into months and years often with a relentless nothingness crushed by the roller blades of routine. The cog wheels of the elements undid what the people with their ant-like toil had done. Storms, floods, earthquakes, fires and disease ruled over the hills and valleys with an imcomprehensible tyranny. The uncertainty of life swung like random blades cutting the people down without any warning. Life had to be lived for the day, the future was always too unsure. It gave the peasants a fine sense of humour, it brought a satisfaction of its own, despite their drudgery. Merely staying alive was an achievement, surviving for another day was cheating destiny. I had grown used to the slow pace, to the almost dreamy dragging of the days. I had seen how death came and visited shacks in the night, marking someone out to be carried down the hill on the following day. Disaster happened quickly, with a swiftness that never let one see whence it had come. When things went wrong, they spiralled down in a precipitous headlong race in which a malign fate seemed to push and shove.

After Joanna left, once again I changed. A chain of events took their course and, far from being in control, I became as helpless to alter them as a boulder rolled down by a grossly swollen river can stop its flood. After the first inundation and the dead pig, the river subsided leaving its carpet of foul-smelling sludge. Within hours, the rain ceased and a plague of flies invaded the *hacienda*. There had always been flies, they were an ongoing nuisance all over the valley. They buzzed and settled everywhere. All food had to be covered, cups and plates, and pots and pans, everything had to be kept away from flies. They were carriers of disease, they had dirty feet.

They spread the many epidemics of gastroenteritis that ravaged the *hacienda*.

Despite dousing the floors and walls with creosote and boiling everything in the house that could be boiled, there were flies all over the house. The estate children were going down with the virus like ninepins; in one week, I used up what I had thought would be a year's supply of suitable drugs: my entire stock of liolofilised milk solids and two tins of black tea.

Iseult had begun to cough, to eat less, to fret. The twins, Mimita and Mimella, had taken me under their wing. They cruised in and out of the *hacienda* every other day, bringing my letters, if any, from Mendoza Fría, and ferried me backwards and forwards to the paediatrician in Valera who gave Iseult her weekly bill of health. They came after the first flood and took me and the baby to their house to sleep. They helped to disinfect the house after the flood mud had been shovelled out by the workers. They took me to the doctor's next day, when Iseult went down with a tummy bug. They took me again next day when instead of getting better, she was worse. They took me to the pharmacy to get the antibiotics for her. At nine o'clock each morning they called together down the track, 'Musiua y Musuiuita, qué tal?' If I needed them, I had only to say.

One night the fever rose and my four-month-old baby coughed herself sick over and over again. At nine o'clock I was ready to take a lift straight back to the doctor. He diagnosed pharyngitis and prescribed a more specific antibiotic, a febrifuge, and sent me home with the assurance that everything would be all right. I paid him my fifty *bolivárs* and left feeling infinitely relieved. The twins stayed with me that night to give me moral support while I dosed the baby up with her new antibiotics. She quietened and slept, her fever fell and late in the morning the twins went home to sleep.

As luck would have it, Antonio Moreno and Abrán, the only two workers who could drive had gone to Barquisimeto to collect some machinery for the tractor. They had taken La Povva, much against everyone's advice (since it was scarcely roadworthy). The only other car on the *hacienda*, the Hillman van, had been smashed to a standstill by Alfredo Peña.

It began to rain again mid-morning, and then it rained all day. By four o'clock, the rain had settled into a fine drizzle. By four o'clock, something had gone extremely wrong. The peaceful sleep that Iseult had been enjoying all day began to resemble some kind of coma. She was breathing with increasing difficulty and her skin was distinctly blue. From my scant medical reading, I knew she should be in hospital. As each breath rasped, shook and rattled out of her, I knew there was no *mañana* for what I had to do. I had to weigh taking a sick feverish baby out into the rain and mist, or wait in the dry for her to expire in my arms.

I thought I had only to get to the road and one of the passing trucks or jeeps would give me a lift to Valera. People didn't go out in the rain if they could help it, no one would take a baby out in the rain. To be by the roadside with a baby in my arms, I felt, would, in itself be enough to show that there was an emergency at Santa Rita. Trucks passed: three, four, five, then many more. I signalled for them to stop. They drove on. Twice I was sure I had recognised a driver, saw them approach, prepared to jump in as they slowed, but they too drove on. Precious minutes had gone by, the bundle in my arms was struggling to breathe with less and less success. I could have stood on the edge of the road all night and through the following day with its deep V-shaped concrete ditches either side to drain the flood waters away. No one would have stopped for me. They couldn't, 'Qué dirán?' What would people say if anyone picked up *la Doña de* Jaime? What would people say when they saw me riding in a strange car? If I was on the edge of the road in tears, there had obviously been a row or a fight, no one would get involved, to do so was to risk their life. So the rain came down and the cars sped by and I set off to walk, not in the direction of Valera and the hospital I needed to get to, but to Mendoza and San Isidro where the twins lived. It was a thirty-minute walk, Valera would have taken me nearly two hours.

There were certain shrines in the vicinity to which people made promises in cases of illness: there was the child Jesus of Escuque, said to perform miracles. When a baby got sick, the family promised to visit the plaster statue at Escuque if the baby could live. There was the doctor, José Gregorio Hernandez whose memory cured beyond the power, so people said, of any living doctor. Venezuela was trying to get Dr José Gregorio Hernandez canonised in Rome, lists of his miracles passed from mouth to mouth. As I walked along the tarmac road, I longed to be able by some act of faith to save the child in my shawl. Instead, I made the promises to myself: if she lived, I would never more worry my heart over vain and idle things, I would use my time better, do more, be altogether less self-absorbed. If she lived, I would do anything.

Somewhere, in the flattened cane-fields beside the river, lay a dead carcass of some size. The sickly-sweet smell of decay was in the air and the vultures were circling overhead. It seemed that they circled me, in particular, waiting for the prey in my arms, biding their time impatiently. I prayed to Napoleon not to lead them down to the child he had so wanted to destroy. The rain was driving against me; it grew harder, forcing me to bow my head. I was wet through, but Iseult was still dry. I held over her one of the gaberdine squares that Joanna had equipped me with when I came out. She had said they would be essential. As I passed the steep escarpment a mile and a half beyond the Casa Grande, I heard a cockerel crow from Abrán's yard. He lived back from the road with his mother, the *comadre* Matilde as she was known to one and all, his wife and three children. Had he been there, he would have helped. A hundred yards past his compound the road was traversed by a small aquaduct. Under its meagre shelter, I rearranged Iseult's wrappings. Her fever was rising again, sharply, her efforts to breathe had become less marked. I could not rouse her.

On either side of the road, set back, there were huts and shacks. I knew that from each of them, I would be observed. They were, perhaps, too far away for anyone to see that I was carrying the child Iseult with me, but I myself was recognisable. I was watched. I was always watched, so why, I thought, was there no one to watch over me? There was no one in the hills or in the valley who could help me. The passing cars could have helped, they could have got me to the hospital in time to save her, but they wouldn't. I hated them all for their refusal to help. I hated the ones who sped past and the ones who slowed. Every few minutes, as another engine neared me, I tried to flag it down. I knew I couldn't just run into the road and try to block their path, I would have been run down. The world divided itself into two classes: people from good families and peasants. The former drove and had cars, the latter didn't. In good families, so called, each member of the family had a car. It was quite usual to see seven or eight trucks and Jeeps and Cadillacs by every house. At the twins' house, in San Isidro, there were never less than ten cars. All I had to do was get there and get back down to Valera; it didn't seem so much to do or ask, but it was raining and time was running out. It seemed that nothing could feel worse than the desolation I felt then as I tramped along the road that *la gente* regarded as a curse.

Despite all the other perils of the place, more people died on the roads in Venezuela than from anything else. The rich died in car crashes, the poor were run over. The deep ditches either side of the road were where the injured crawled to die. I thought, if she dies on me here, I'll lie down in the ditch. It was just more than an hour since I had left the *trapiche*, Iseult was hardly breathing at all now, and she was blue. I massaged her chest as I walked, more to have something to do than through any real hope that it would help her.

Where the road forked, just below Mendoza Fría, to the left, up the steep hill of San Isidro, the twins pulled into sight and screeched to a halt beside me. I had been crying too hard to talk any more, other than to say she was dying. We were minutes away from their house. The entrance to their domain was down a steep drive at the point where the River Momboy runs closest to the road. Along its bank, Don Felipe Neri's *chimó* factory spread out in a succession of brick buildings and squat brick chimneys. It was always busy there. Don Felipe Neri had seven children and seven house servants and thirty workmen milling round his yards. Doña Elia had a kind heart and found employment for men in the factory and women in the house who might not otherwise have been employable. The ratio of maimed, deformed and freak workers was very high. It lent an air of the circus to their establishment. As the twins' pick-up truck swooped down the drive, two dwarves were bustling in the yard, hovering on the far side of the invisible demarcation line past which no workers were allowed to pass. Don Felipe Neri, immobile in his chair on the front porch, made the rules; his wife, Doña Elia, via a back door that opened behind the forbidden line, gave out money, food and medicines, advice and help, unbeknown to her ungiving husband.

Doña Elia was an expert on medical matters, she knew all the good doctors in Valera, the specialists and who to turn to in an emergency. She took one look at Iseult, her youngest cousin, and agreed that time was of the essence – she was dying. Our turnaround was almost immediate and Mimella (who prided herself on being the sensible one of the twins) drove at breakneck speed to the private clinic where the new paediatrician was to be found. Everyone, rich and poor, called this clinic 'La Guillotina'. Its reputation was for taking in living patients and dispatching them swiftly to their maker. For this service, the private clinic charged exorbitant prices. So the poor were saved the dubious privilege of ever going there. I never did know what the clinic was really called, it was just 'the Guillotine'. When Doña Elia advised us to go there, she said, 'Get her to the Guillotine.'

The twins knew the clinic well, their father had been there after his crash. They ordered me to run after them, which I did, with the child Iseult in my arms. In the consulting room, four plump women in pink frilly blouses and highlighted hair were sitting with identical flowery plastic baby bags on a chair beside them. Each was attended by an Indian girl, each holding, or struggling to hold, grotesquely overweight babies. The girls were dressed in striped cotton dresses with starched white collars, their glossy black hair tied back neatly. As we barged in, they looked up and began to ask questions. One of them, a cousin I had never seen before, stood up and came into the consulting room with us. The doctor was busy with another child. Mimella took charge and explained. The doctor unceremoniously lifted the small boy on the examining table into his mother's lap and attended to Iseult. She had laryngitis, pharyngitis and double pneumonia. He knew the twins (he had delivered them) and he told Mimita to get two nurses, another doctor, an oxygen tent and a drip. Mimita left and within ten minutes we were all in a hospital room with two beds and a cot, an insulin drip was put into Iseult's arm. The sleeve of the hand-embroidered gown she was wearing lay roughly cut on the floor beside the nurse's feet. The oxygen tent proved difficult to put up, bits of it were missing, and the ice it needed to work had run out in the clinic.

By the evening, the infection was beginning to respond to the powerful antibiotics dripped through the insulin, and the tent was up and working, encasing most of the cot.

The nurses spent most of their time in conclave in a glass-walled office. There was one such office for each floor. There were a lot of nurses, but they did not perform the duties I thought usual to their calling. *I* was expected to control the various dials on the oxygen tent, to keep it well supplied with ice, to take the baby's temperature, to clean and bathe her and change both her and the bags of insulin as they ran out on the drip. I knew from my own time in hospital that if a bubble of air got into a vein, then the patient died. For the seven days and nights that I stayed in the hospital, I didn't dare sleep for more than a few snatched minutes at a time, and then only when the twins were present to keep vigil in my place. Any change in breathing, pulse or general appearance was up to me to note and then inform the doctor. There was an electrical buzzer by the cot to use in case of emergency, and all these buzzers (one for each room) were connected to the nurses' booth. When they rang, a light came on in the glass wall around them. They had a television in their booth. They spent the day watching soap operas imported from Brazil and dubbed. The buzzing of their patients was an interruption in the ups and downs of the screen melodramas. I noticed that they often switched off the buzzers, the better to enjoy their soaps. Every four hours, every eight hours and every twelve hours, the nurses took it in turns to administer drugs into Iseult's drip. They were rarely punctual; it was up to me, as it was up to every other bedside watcher, to remind them of the time.

So many relations came to see Iseult while she lay recovering in the Guillotine that I had to ask the doctor to clear them from the room. They came to see how she was, to bring presents, and then, having got that bit of the visit over, they gossiped and exchanged news in the shrill noisy way of the country. Everyone talked at once, talking over, shouting down. These were woman of what was called in Spanish 'el High', they were members of high society, they were not used to being banished from rooms even if they were sickrooms. So they stood outside, piqued and critical and with voices no less shrill, though muffled by a closed door. I heard more than one proclaim that this illness served me right and went to show that I had been wrong to ever set myself apart. *They* didn't bring *their* children up on *haciendas*, *they* didn't live in shacks. ('Have you seen it? There's a dirt floor, and no bathroom in the whole place!' 'I heard there was plumbing now.' 'No, just a sort of public lavatory of the kind you'd get in a bar, you know the ones where everyone shits in the basin and washes their feet in the bidet. I went up just to look and I pretended to need to go, but when I saw it, I tell you, no wonder the poor baby's sick.' 'They should take it away from her.' 'There are plenty of people who could bring a child of Jaime's up. It's a disgrace.' 'Is it true she fed her herself?' Choruses of 'No,' 'You don't say so,' 'I don't believe you.' 'I swear by my mother and the Virgin, she refused to use bottles.' 'Well, no wonder then! What did she expect?')

Until I went to the Guillotine, I thought I had finally integrated rather well with the local families. I had the entrée to many houses. I played gin rummy and drank milk-shakes, I copied down recipes and took note of their housewifely tips. I listened politely to their advice about how to deal with servants. I even took pains to dress a little more like them. On top of everything else, it was a revelation to discover how deep-rooted the dislike and distrust of me were. How they rejoiced at Jaime's infidelities (details of which I also learnt from them). I didn't feel in any way it served me right that my only child should be suffering as she was, but it certainly served me well to know who were my friends and who my enemies. The friends were few. In the face of such outspoken opposition, it took a lot of courage to defend me. I noted everyone who did and let the others gossip on like a chorus of evil spirits on my doorstep.

The men who came were kinder. The general assumption in the district of Valera was that within the two-tier class system, every man had a right to make love to every woman if he could. The men and boys of every household used the maids for sex. If they were caught red-handed, the maid in question was fired. If the girl got pregnant, then she was also fired, usually with a couple of weeks' wages to help her out, but often with nothing more than a thrashing. Peasant men were not allowed to make advances to the rich or even to notice them as sexual beings. Within any network of family and friends (and friends were almost always distantly related), the men made advances to the women. In theory daughters and wives within the family were sexually taboo, in practice this was not the case. Rebuffing the sexual advances, and often harassment, of Jaime's family had come to be a matter of course. Like bees to a honeypot, they kept coming round.

When a woman 'fell', it was usually more as a trophy to her seducer than as anything else. Then the kiss and tell began. The men boasted of their conquests to each other, carefully keeping the infidelity secret from the father, brother or husband in question. After one 'fall', further conquests were easy, the next cousin threatened to tell if he too didn't get a share. If a brother, husband or father found out, whoever was named responsible was summarily shot, or, since it went against the grain to kill a cousin, the seduced woman was. Men who were soft and not serious, sometimes merely turned their wives out to fend for themselves, taking all children away from them and forbidding any further access. The disgraced woman then had to leave the neighbourhood. There was little leniency, though, as far as I could observe. The men who didn't make advances were few and far between. It was never possible to relax around them, or to drop my guard. The very few men friends I had who didn't try to manoeuvre me into corners, whisper obscenities or grab, were doubly valued for their tact and discretion. The others were no more respecters of place than they were of person. Twice I had to fight my way out of the tiny bathroom at the clinic in the few days that I was resident there.

Don Felipe Neri Terán had five daughters and two sons. As in any Andean family, each son was worth the five daughters put together in the yes of his parents. The elder, Eliseo, was a notorious Don Juan. He had a fortune to spend, fast cars and all the girls that his blond, green-eyed looks could want. He spent as much time attending to his person and his fair drooping moustache as he did to any of them, and, in a place of idle ways, he was singled out as being the most idle of all. He spent more than the average amount of time cruising the valley and picking up girls and more than the average amount of time drinking in roadside bars and dancing. He had given me more than the average amount of bother when I first became the target for every roving male. Every meeting involved a routine proposal and a routine refusal, but beyond his superficial vanity, he had inherited his mother's heart and had a streak of kindness in him that he showed in helping out on the *hacienda* in little ways. He often came with the twins to see me at Santa Rita, and he also came several times to see how Iseult was faring at the Guillotine.

By the fifth day of her stay, she was doing well, so well that she would be able to go home soon. The only thing I had at the clinic that I wouldn't have at my sister-in-law's house in Valera, was the oxygen tent, and this was no longer in use. While I was at the Guillotine, the little house had once again been flooded. Eliseo had gone to inspect the damage. He had promised to return. I had spent the morning on my own, interrupted only by the paediatrician who came twice daily to monitor Iseult's progress. At twelve o'clock, a nurse came by and injected one of the antibiotics into the drip. She was as surly as most of the other nurses had been. There was no question about vocation or caring there, nursing was a job that paid better than domestic service. Any girl capable of scraping through the simple exam could be one. I had noticed at the General Hospital when I came round from my Caesarean section that there was no question of kindness with the job and few nurses would take any patient so much as a glass of water (you had to bring your own, something I hadn't realised then). Any request whatsoever from either patients or watchers was met by a curt, 'I'm not your servant, you know.'

At two o'clock, the same or another sulky colleague was supposed to administer a different antibiotic. By ten past two she still hadn't been. I went out and down the wide corridor to the glass booth and tapped on the window. Nothing, in the whole clinic, annoyed the nurses more than this, but since they had switched off their bells, it was the only way of penetrating their gum-chewing television spells. There were six of them in the glass box, the television was blaring and they steadfastly refused to notice me. The door to the booth was kept locked (it was where a trolley of medicine was kept and they argued that they locked themselves in for drug security). I rattled the door. I could see they had seen me, but they were not going to look up. They would take their time, as they always did, and at some point in the next twenty minutes one of them would come shuffling along in her white shoes.

The room next to Iseult's was empty. A man had died of a stroke there two days before. On the other side, a middle-aged man was racked by dysentery. He was new. He moaned loudly for hours on end. At two-thirty, the nurse arrived and added Iseult's medicine to her drip. By three-thirty Iseult had lost all interest in anything other than the effort to breathe. Her back arched and her face contorted after each inhalation. I pressed my buzzer and kept it pressed. Very quickly her breathing became more tortured and more violent and the pale blue that had begun to creep over her darkened. I opened my door and called for help. No one came. Far away down the end of the corridor, I saw the booth full of nurses and ran to it. I didn't tap this time, I hammered on the glass and I kept hammering until they responded. I made them come with me, then I made them go for the doctor – the paediatrician or any doctor. The oxygen tent, still sitting in my room, was without oxygen. They left and I stayed. They promised to keep my buzzer on. Between each breath, Iseult passed out, rallied and struggled again. Her colour was alarmingly wrong. No one came, minutes ticked by, no response came from the buzzer. I was holding her up because she seemed to find it easier to gulp air upright. One hand was still strapped to a board and drip. I undid the plaster, pulled out the needle, picked her up again and ran along the corridor to the nurses. As I ran out, Eliseo Terán sauntered along in the opposite direction. I told him what was happening and that no doctor had arrived, and that there was no working oxygen tent. Since leaving the room, Iseult had not drawn breath. As I spoke, she went completely limp, limp and blue. I had been taking her pulse almost continually. Her pulse had stopped.

We had reached the nurses' booth. Eliseo strode past it.

'Come with me, Musiua,' he said. 'Hurry!'

I had stopped beyond the glass box and held the baby tightly to me.

'Musiua!' Eliseo shouted. He had reached the end of the corridor.

'She's dead,' I told him, and my voice which is usually so quiet, resounded down the corridor. Eliseo began to kick a door. He threw himself at it in a great rage. I couldn't move. He smashed in the door.

'Musiua,' he said, 'run, trust me, I know what I'm doing, this is the oxygen cupboard. Quick.'

He put the hose of a giant oxygen cylinder straight into her mouth, pushed it in and as it hissed, she choked. As he was doing it for the second time, the doctor arrived. She had died and Eliseo had brought her back to life.

She had had heart failure. Most of the Teráns die young of congenital heart disease. It seemed, for some hours, that Iseult had inherited the taint of four hundred years of inbreeding. She had been checked over carefully at birth for any of the tell-tale signs of the too frequently repeated genes. Her eyes were both blue, not lined on the right by half an iris of another colour. She had the right number of fingers and toes, she had all her vital and non-vital organs (unlike several others of the family crop). Now it seemed that she had inherited the worst weakness of all. The weak heart that, when apparent so young, scythed down the children before their seventh year.

Only the doctor was not convinced. He finally made one of the nurses confess. A dose of Lomotil intended for the dysenteric man next door had been added, by mistake, to Iseult's drip.

A month later, she was fit and well. I stayed in Valera while she convalesced. There seemed to be no lasting ill-effect. The doctor summoned Jaime and told him that if he took Iseult back to the *trapiche*, she would die. She was frail, she had been born delicate and after the pneumonia and the 'incident' as he called it, she must not live in the unhealthy atmosphere of the *trapiche* by the damp of the Momboy. We had to move into the Casa Grande. Those were his orders. He said, 'I'm telling you this, and I'm telling all your family. Then it's up to you to see what you do about it.'

19

Dear Joanna,

We have moved into the Big House and are redecorating etc. little by little.

I have not written for so long because Iseult has been very ill. She is quite better now, though still convalescing. She had bronchitis and spent 7 days in the hospital in Valera.

I have been meaning to write for ages but was waiting for her to recover.

Next day. I am rather dopey. There is so much to say that I hardly say anything.

I am waiting for the twins to pass by to get a lift into Valera – a face ache – sinus? I can scarcely think for it.

I am trying to persuade Jaime of the necessity of a holiday in England. Keep your fingers crossed for January.

Forgive the time of not writing, when we got out of hosp. I had 7 days and nights without sleep (Venezuelan

custom of mothers nursing sick children: good and bad)
and got home to the Big House to find I had no servants.

Coromoto helps a bit. Angela is coming tomorrow and
another very pleasant young girl is coming on the 15th to
live in.

The dogs are fine, driving me mad – but fine. I now
have four ducks in the garden. My face aches and it has
stopped raining.

    Lots of love,
    Lisaveta

The 'very pleasant girl' was called Mary. She stayed with
me for the next four years. Within days of arriving, she complained she was lonely, took off to the hills and returned on
the following day with her little sister Alba. Alba was seven
and rarely spoke except to say, regardless of whatever the
question or request, 'I don't know about Mary,' thus ridding
herself of any responsibility for any of her own actions and
heaping life and all its cares on to her sister's shoulders. Alba
had the patience of a sloth, she would play with Iseult for
hours on end, crawling around after her without ever showing signs of irritation. She was placid to a degree. She seemed
to be immune to praise or rebukes. She never betrayed any
emotion. She helped her sister assiduously and suffered
numerous illnesses and accidents with the stoicism of one well
past her years. Mary was always more pleased with the presents Alba got than Alba ever seemed to be herself. Mary was
a good-looking girl; she was fifteen when she started working
for me. She was tall by Venezuelan standards and darker
than most of *la gente*. She had very thick black hair, big
almond-shaped eyes and chiselled features. Unlike Alba, she
was open in her manner and communicative, cheerful and

easily pleased. Alba was fair-skinned but always sallow, her hair was thin and straggly and she had the look (not entirely uncommon in Venezuela) of a toad that has been squashed by a stone. Her face was wide and scrunched and her mouth disproportionately wide. The only thing that ever brought it to a grin was when she was asked to kill a chicken. Despite her otherwise gentle nature, Alba loved killing chickens. It became her special job because she was also exceptionally good at it. She caught her victim with the minimum amount of fuss and then held it on to a big flat stone outside the henhouse. With another hefty stone, she broke its neck. As the stone crashed down, she always muttered 'Visto!' in grim triumph.

Benito Mendoza also moved with me to the Big House. He had been camping in the sugar-packing room of the *trapiche*. When we moved, I offered him one of the many rooms, but he insisted he liked to live on his own and chose a thin stone room adjoining the henhouse. It was little more than a shed, but he assured me that it was what he wanted.

November-mid?
Ilda Santa Rita,
Mendoza Fría,
Estado Trujillo

Dear Joanna,

I forgot to post my last letter so I sent you a telegram. Did you get it?

My face-ache turns out to be neuritis.

Iseult is very well, thank you for the photos.

I am planning to go to England next year in Jan or Feb. Maybe Mimita Terán (twin) will come with me.

No papers or books as yet.

How much money do you think I need to cover a six-week journey?

Fares for myself and Iseult by air.

Write soon,

Lots of love, Lizzie.

The longer I stayed on the *hacienda*, the more I became swallowed up by it. It was like the medicinal plants I had taken to studying, it could both kill and cure. It was like the boa constrictors the workmen found sometimes in the sugar-cane fields. It wrapped itself around a passing stranger, it squeezed and crushed until it had broken every single bone, then it slimed over its prey and engorged it, bit by bit, until no trace was left except for a transitory bulge. Eventually, that too would go and nothing would be left but the beautiful, powerful snake, waiting lazily for its next meal to wander by.

I became very aware of losing my own language. Apart from my letters to Joanna and my occasional poems, I neither spoke nor heard English spoken. When Iseult was born and the two of us were cloistered away, I spoke English to her. Once the house filled with maids, they took my speaking English as a personal insult at best, and as the casting of sinister spells at worst. So I spoke Spanish even to my daughter. The Spanish of the Venezuelan Andes is elaborate and archaic. Andeans look down on the rest of the country and the rest of Venezuela looks down on Andeans. The Spanish of the *hacienda* was full of pure Latin and Arabic words. It was formal to a degree, it was courtly. I loved its florid forms and its melodic incantatory style. It was endlessly rich in intricate double and triple meanings; it was consciously subtle. Speech was not a thing learnt once a child had mastered it, it was carefully perfected. An illiterate, like Benito Mendoza or

Antonio Moreno, often spoke poetry. It was not the poetry that I worried at in my study: it was infinitely more masterly. As an aspiring writer, I learnt a great deal from the high Spanish that I heard there. Yet I was afraid to write in Spanish, although I felt entirely bi-lingual. If I wrote in Spanish, I thought I might lose my own language altogether.

After I moved to the Casa Grande, both the house and the estate ran so smoothly for a while that the sensation of being swallowed up by it made me claw back a little bit of my previous identity. As a child, my family had always called me 'Lizzie'. It was my name. My father sometimes called me Lisaveta, but I only saw him for a day or so at a time every few years, so it never really felt like my name. It was Jaime who, on meeting me, took against my name. He said it sounded like a cat's name and did I have any other? I told him 'Lisaveta', which he liked better (I discovered later because there was already a Lisaveta Terán). From that moment, he changed my name. He and Otto and Elias then changed it once again, to 'Veta'. In Venezuela, the letter V and the letter B are both pronounced as B. Thus Venezuela is pronounced Benezuela and thus Veta became Beta (pronounced better).

One of the many legacies I took from my time in Venezuela was to be a workaholic. When I emerged there from the apathetic cocoon in which I had lived the first eighteen years of my life, I was left with an abundance of energy and the need for very little sleep. Both these conditions served me well. There was always a prodigious amount to do. No matter how much I did, though, it was never enough. I was driven by the desire to do better. Not many people called me by my name. To *la gente* I was 'la Doña', to most other people, I was 'la musiua'. But those who did use my name – like Eliseo Terán and his mother Elia – used it often. Spanish is a language of

much repetition; as it is spoken in the Andes, it is more repe-
titious still. On days when things were not going well, the urge
to do better was inside me. I have always been resistant to
being told what to do. I like to do things for myself.
Sometimes, I felt my name like a goad: better better better.

We had giant red ants on the *hacienda*. They were called
bachacos. If they came into the garden, marching in a trail
hundreds of metres long and ten centimetres wide, they
stripped every leaf off every plant and shrub. They turned the
hibiscus, jasmine and oleanders into skeletons, they stripped
the roses down to their thorny stems, they took every leaf off
every herb in the garden and then they marched back to their
giant labyrinthine nests. They came without warning and laid
everything waste. They came frequently. Dealing with the
bachacos was an ongoing battle. When we moved to the Casa
Grande, under the shade of its existing orchard Benito and I
began to plant out black polythene bags with avocado seeds.
Every time the *bachacos* came, they stripped off every leaf. I
could describe my life entirely from the ups and downs, the
victories and the defeats, of the *bachaco* war.

Together with Benito, I lay kerosene trails into their nests
and burnt them out. They found ways of moving their sur-
vivors to new hidden sites. We bought chemical bombs that
exuded poisonous gas on a slow release. We used gunpowder
and detonators. We spent entire days searching for their secret
nests.

The *hacienda* was like a piece of quartz with many facets.
Each facet was different from the next. Sometimes little bits of
it glittered, sometimes it seemed like a jewel and sometimes it
felt like the hard rock it was, grazing my knuckles as I banged
them against its ungiving face. It could have swallowed up all
of me. I felt it would if I didn't hold something back. If there

was nothing left of me, I would have nothing left to give. I began to write again. I wrote a lot of poetry. I rewrote the story I had written down at the *trapiche*, based on my days spent in Bologna. I wrote a story about the green boy. My writing became more important to me than it had ever been before. I didn't just talk about it any more, I did it. And, as a token rebellion against the all-engulfing estate, I changed my name back to Lizzie on my letters out.

20

MOST OF THE man-hours on the *hacienda* were taken up with sugar-cane and sugar. The planting, weeding, cutting and processing of the cane were carried out all through the year. After every *molienda* stumps of sugar-cane were replanted. At any given time, there was always cane at different stages in its growth. When it flowered, the long grey feathers it produced scattered a fluff like thistledown across the valley. It grew so tall that the lanes between it towered over my head as I walked between them. It was watered by a network of irrigation ditches with sluices. These ditches had to be regularly maintained. The only official holidays on the *hacienda* were Christmas and the New Year.

There were numerous other holidays, each bound by law to be marked by the showing of the Venezuelan national flag, but these were so many, they broke into the year. Antonio Moreno was loath to observe them. The National Guard in their green army Jeeps and trucks patrolled the valley enforcing, among other things, the observance of national holidays and the displaying of flags. The National Guard were unanimously hated. In rural areas, they pressganged for the army, dragging the boys from the fields and packing them off for their two years' obligatory military service. Because the country was so corrupt, the rich bribed their way out of this military service, while the poor were pressganged into theirs. The boys who left for the army didn't come back. Children were always posted along the escarpment by the road to give the signal when an army Jeep was sighted. Upon this signal, everyone under the age of forty ran into the hills.

On an average day, between fifteen and twenty workmen would be taken on to work. *Moliendas* were different and employed far more men. Sometimes anything from five to ten men would be sent away, having not been chosen for the day. The workers used to line up outside the railings of the Casa Grande for this ritual at five-thirty every morning, Monday to Saturday. Since the wages were so low and their standard of living so poor, it seemed to me that no one should be sent away without work if they came for it.

When we moved into the Casa Grande, Antonio Moreno was true to his word about easing me into managing the *hacienda*. Since Iseult was an early riser, I was usually up and about by five-thirty when the line of workers came to be selected for the day. He asked me if I wanted to choose the men, with his assistance, as my father-in-law had once done before me. I had noted the injustice of the rollcalls and was anxious to improve the workers' lot by offering full employment. Day after day the men came and stood in line, bleary-eyed with sleep. And day by day, I chose them all. However, each day, more men and boys appeared, until, at one point, we were employing some sixty of them. Each morning, Antonio told me gently that we only needed ten or twelve or however many were required for the day's tasks, but each day I defied him, taking on everyone who reported for duty.

About three weeks after this began, a group of workers hung around the stables after I had paid them off one Saturday lunchtime. Antonio Moreno was with them. They seemed to be having an argument. One of the men kept walking back towards the Casa Grande and then changing his mind and shuffling dejectedly back to the group, who promptly pushed him out again. Eventually the entire group came back to the house and stood in the courtyard. They were all looking very uncomfortable, hanging their heads lower than usual. I was used to being not looked in the eye, it is not the way of *la gente* to do so.

'Look, Doña,' one of them finally said, 'if you need us, we are here for you. You know you have only to ask and we'd do anything for you. We'd die for you if need be, but could you please stop picking us all out for work every day, Doña.'

Another one took up where his brother had left off, 'Life's hard enough as it is without slogging in a damp ditch every day or breaking our backs weeding. I haven't got the cane hair out of my skin for I don't know how long, Doña, and my back is killing me.'

Antonio explained to me later what he had been trying to make clear for weeks: he only needed a certain number of men, the others came out of courtesy. They took it in turns to bulk out the rollcall, but the last thing they wanted was for all to be chosen. They worked to keep the wolf from the door, not because they enjoyed it. Once their cooking pots were full, they were content to tend their own bean and yucca plots, to play with their babies, to see their families, to lie in their hammocks and play dominoes. If I needed them, it was their duty to come forward, if they needed me, it was mine to help them. If anyone on the *hacienda* died, it was I who must buy the coffin and pay for the funeral; if they were ill, the medicines were on me. In return for their labour, I gave them security, but it wasn't part of that semi-feudal pact that I work them all into early graves.

'Why didn't you tell me before?'

'I tried, Doña.'

'Any time I put my foot in it, tell me. I want you to guide me, but I also want you to tell me when I go wrong.'

'I can't do that, Doña, I'm too old. I can tell you what's right, I can advise you, but I can't criticise what you do.'

'You could try.'

He shook his head.

'Please, Antonio, what's the point of doing something wrong for years just for the sake of it?'

He shook his head again.

'If you took away the structure that holds this up,' he said, waving his arm to the hills behind him, 'there'd be nothing left but confusion . . . You thought I was wrong to turn the men away, you thought I was being unfair. Did you tell me? No! . . . Well, it's the same for me.'

When Antonio had problems or complaints, he clammed up and hovered around me with his thin lips pursed until I guessed what was up. It often took me weeks to read his mind. For instance, I'd been in the Casa Grande for nearly a year before I discovered that the *trapicheros* were supposed to have substantial meals provided for them by their employer, by me.

This seemed to be the perfect occasion to improve the local diet, deficient as it was in several vitamins and first-class protein. Three days was enough to realise that the nourishing meals being sent across to the *trapiche* were being spurned in favour of surreptitious billycans, which re-emerged on the second day. Everyone wanted what they'd always had: black beans four times a week and chickpeas twice, salt fish, *mojo*, chicken necks, offal and sardines, *arepas*, dips and chillis.

I cooked for three or four *moliendas* single-handed, catering twice daily for twenty-three, and then I hired a cook. My first cook, Leonor was a loan from the twins' mother, Doña Elia. She came for three months during one of Iseult's many illnesses, together with her four-year-old son, Adriano. Leonor was so efficient, she was intimidating. She wanted the kitchen entirely to herself. She had a way of giggling behind her hand that made her seem mild and even slow-witted. Under this camouflage, she hid a strong mind, set, in my house, on brooking no interference with her chosen domain. She sulked if I so much as made myself a pot of tea. She rose at four-thirty and then, throughout the day, she served exclusively what she approved of. The *trapicheros* were delighted, Leonor catered exactly to their tastes. She also insisted on catering for mine.

Whenever I went visiting off the *hacienda*, if someone really wanted to go out of their way to entertain me, they made me cups of tea. This, word had it, was what English people drank for pleasure. Not tea as in medicine, but tea served with milk and sugar. Bitter black tea was usually bought in a powder. It tasted bitter, but then, since it was only used as a medicine, it was meant to. For me hostesses prepared this with milk. A teaspoonful of powdered tea was put into an electric blender with two heaped tablespoonsful of powdered milk and one heaped tablespoonful of sugar, two cups of boiling water were then added and the concoction was beaten to a froth. This beverage was then served to me. The first time I tasted it I gagged, but was too polite or too shy to alter the recipe. So the formula was handed around and cups of thick steaming 'English tea' awaited me for several years wherever I chanced to call. Doña Elia had given Leonor strict instructions about how to make tea, and to serve it at frequent intervals. In lieu of a blender, she beat up my froth with an egg whisk and refused to accept that the ensuing tepid cream was not my favourite beverage.

Meanwhile, the household expanded. Mary and Alba returned home one Sunday and brought back another sister with them. This one, Lorena, was only four. She was as dark as Mary, with big lustrous black eyes and thick wavy hair which she wore short. She was lively and inquisitive, affectionate and eager to help. She was so young, it took a lot of time and ingenuity to find things for Lorena to do. She didn't want to just tag along and play, she wanted to make herself useful and she wanted her work formally inspected and admired every few minutes. It was Lorena's job to count the dogs in the dog run, to give the chickens their elevenses, to polish the spare dogs' collars, to dust the highchair before it was disinfected each day, to wash the dolls' clothes and the like. She took all her jobs very seriously and carried them out so well that after the first year I got the impression little Lorena could have probably run the house quite well on her own if she had to. I tried very hard not to have favourites, but Lorena was, undoubtedly, my favourite estate girl, and Coromoto's unbelievably taciturn younger brother, Goyo, was my favourite boy.

With Coromoto coming daily to the big house, his brother dead and no one but the baby and a much older Antonio José, Goyo got bored and lonely at home and took to spending most of his days with us. Though four years older than Iseult, he became her closest friend. When she was a baby, he would stand, pot-bellied with his chin buried in his chest, looking grumpy in the yard.

Coromoto would chide him, 'What are you waiting for, Goyo?' and he'd reply gruffly, 'For the child Iseult to grow.'

At one end of the scale were the children, joined from time to time by sick children who needed nursing and who stayed or convalesced at the Casa Grande, and sometimes by girls too young and delicate to be sent out to work elsewhere, who joined the troop to satisfy their parents' need for their wage.

Some I taught to read and write, others I only managed to confuse. I taught them to sew and I tried to teach them to knit. Coromoto was the only one to master knitting, though. I taught them to iron and clean, to make jam and arrange flowers, to garden and the basic rules of first aid and hygiene. I never succeeded in teaching any of them not to fear El Coco, the Bogey Man. Nor did I manage to wean them from their lifelong habit of soaking clothes. Their clothes, my clothes, the tea-towels, towels, sheets and tablecloths would disappear, only to be found soaking in a bowl or bucket of suds. These bowls would then be tucked out of sight; the more I was against them, the harder they were to find. In the heat the suds went sour in a matter of hours; from one day to the next they went off completely and then rotted and eventually stank. All the girls did it, even Lorena; just as everyone who came into my courtyard garden tore a leaf off one of the plants. I noticed that even visitors from as far away as Caracas always did this. Every time they passed a growing thing, they tore a little piece of it away. The toll on the garden was noticeable.

It was the custom to cultivate ferns and hang them in the chicken-wire baskets on the porch. My ferns rarely lived longer than six months, which was the time it took Mary and Coromoto to strip them as bare as though the *bachacos* had been at them. Even Benito Mendoza, who spent his days pottering round the orchard planting avocado seeds and tending to the potted saplings never settled down to an evening's reminiscing

234

without first tearing a piece off the night-flowering jasmine that grew on the trellis between the pillars.

At the other end of the scale of domestic staff were the geriatrics. Benito took precedence over all the others and guarded his position jealously, bossing the other old men who worked with him in the avocado nursery. He was often joined by Natividad. Then there was old Molinas, a small man bent nearly double who turned up one day and told me that he had once worked on the *hacienda* when he was a boy. He had nowhere to go and moved into a shed beside the stables. Together with Alfredo Peña, they formed what Antonio Moreno called the Broken-Mouthed Brigade.

Once a week, for lunch, they were joined by another old man called Gonzalez. He looked older than any of them. He was painfully thin and shook constantly in a steady quiver. He wasn't from Mendoza, he was from Trujillo. Once a week, he was given a lift to Valera. The first few times he came, I found I couldn't understand anything he said. I thought he was drunk. I fed him because the laws of hospitality dictated that everyone who came to my gates had to be fed, but I had no idea who he was or what he wanted. One day he showed me a frayed and crumpled slip of paper which was a medical certificate to testify to the fact that he was not drunk but ill. Slowly, I learnt to decipher his speech. He had been a common criminal with an uncommon skill for playing Tapas, a game played with three beer-bottle lids. Something was placed under one of the lids, which were then shuffled on a flat surface; whoever guessed under which lid the thing was hidden won money. Despite his trembling, Gonzalez could still play his Tapas trick, which was his only way of earning a living. Because his condition and appearance were so off-putting, he rarely got close enough to anyone to show them, but when he did, he was good. As a boy of eighteen, he had been put in jail for fighting. While in prison, he had been used as a human guinea-pig. An experiment was under way in the prison to create a vaccine for encephalitis. For the purposes of research, Gonzalez had been injected with equine encephalitis virus. It had partially destroyed his nervous system and damaged his brain. With no compensation, he had been turned out of the jail and left to fend for himself. For the next ten years, he was in and out of prison. On one of his visits he had shared a cell with, among others, Jaime, who was in Trujillo jail as a political prisoner. They were, as I saw from the medical certificate he carried, the same age: thirty-eight. Gonzalez didn't look a day under eighty. Sometimes he didn't come by for months at a stretch. When he returned, he explained that he was often beaten up on his peregrinations. He looked like a hopeless old drunk and he was treated like one. With no one to protect him, he was a figure of fun to be kicked around the marketplace. He carried the medical certificate for the National Guard, who often had to scrape him up. I offered him a home on the *hacienda*, which he refused. He said he was a city man and found it hard to breathe away from a market square. When Iseult was four, he disappeared.

By the end of my first year at the Casa Grande, we had a red pick-up truck, an old Dodge, a Jeep, the Hillman and a Toyota lorry as well as La Povva. Abrán, Matilde's son, became the official estate driver. He acted as my chauffeur, ferried in supplies, drove out the sugar and also carried the avocado crop to Caracas. He became Antonio Moreno's right-hand man and an indispensable member of the rapidly expanding estate.

The price of sugar had begun to fluctuate wildly. Although

on the ups the *hacienda* made a great deal of money, on the downs there were worrying gaps in the budget. I needed to make some capital investment in the *hacienda* to make it more productive. I talked the matter over with a few of the cousins who, I knew, also had big estates. They all pointed out that banks would not be the answer. There was scarcely a bank in the state which my husband hadn't been accused of robbing in his day; which wasn't the best credential for taking out a loan. As it was, we were keeping all the money that came in from the *moliendas* and the annual avocado harvest in a dressing room, so as not to have the embarrassment of being turned down for a bank account in Valera.

The best solution seemed to be to diversify with a short-term cash crop. This quick profit could then be ploughed back into avocados. The avocado groves were the most lucrative part of the estate. They brought in as much as all the sugar put together. Avocados were easy to grow but hard to put into production. Ours was the only avocado plantation in the state of Trujillo which had not succumbed to the deadly root fungus that attacked other avocado trees. Nobody knew how or why the *Phytophthora cinnamomi*, which could and did destroy entire estates overnight, had never struck at Santa Rita. Because of this root fungus, the price of avocados was unnaturally high. Our old trees were mostly of the varieties Winslowson, Trapp and Nellan, with the first predominating. It was the most commercially popular kind. Each avocado, conveniently, tended to weigh exactly one kilo.

I joined the Californian Avocado Society and from them I received the latest news and views on the root fungus that was wiping out not only the Venezuelan but all avocados. They said that avocados grafted on to a rootstock of the variety Fuerte were most resistant to the disease, which still had no known cure. We had plans to plant out 5,000 new trees. Although the adult avocados took care of themselves and produced a crop so valuable it was as though they laid golden eggs, the first four years of the trees' life until they fruited were expensive and difficult. Money had to be spent for no immediate return. Meanwhile fields had to be tilled, fertilised and planted. The seeds had to be pared and grown into saplings. The saplings then had to be individually grafted, allowed to convalesce from the operation and then transplanted. Unlike the sugar-cane, which grew like a weed, the young avocados had to be watered.

The sun on the *hacienda* was too hot for the young trees, which needed shade for at least two years. To get round this, we planted coffee in between them. I derived endless pleasure from walking through each newly planted orchard. Used as I was to the slow growth of trees in England, I found the progress of our orchards on Santa Rita miraculous. Antonio Moreno and Abrán were used to beans and corn and sugar-cane and were worried by the waiting. Every time a new tree died, they saw it as an omen for the beginning of the end. Yet two in three of the trees were surviving, which more than satisfied me.

Eliseo Terán, in the only real commercial venture of his life, had lost a small fortune on an avocado estate in a place called Caja Seca by Lake Maracaibo some two hours away, where the lagoon bit in closest to the Andes. They had died with the fruit on the trees after eight years. Eliseo came regularly to supervise the new plantings and to predict their eventual failure. With the movement towards avocados, Jaime regained his interest in the *hacienda*. Avocados were his pet subject.

He spent entire days grafting and paring. Most of what I

learnt about the avocados, I learnt from him. It was the only topic that drew him out of his silence. So, although we didn't have much of a marriage, we shared a common hobby. We could meet on neutral ground in the seed-beds and we could even walk together across the *hacienda* to the newly planted trees. His father had also loved avocados, it was he who had planted out the existing groves. Because there were seventeen different varieties already matured, the avocado harvest stretched across four months, supplying the market in Caracas when the prices were at their highest. So, we not only ate avocados daily for six months of the year, we lived off their profit, fed them to our pigs and hens, gave them away as much-valued presents, and even found some harmony between us, thanks to them.

For two years, Jaime's enthusiasm for the avocados waxed and waned. When it was there, it knew no bounds, when it was not, he would forget them almost entirely and disappear, as was his wont, for weeks on end. The grafts and saplings did not take kindly to such sporadic passion. I had learnt to graft the fresh shield buds of one variety on to the root stock of the Fuerte saplings, but my success rate was very low. Grafting avocados is more than a skill, it requires a good hand and a natural affinity for the plants. I didn't have it. Fortunately Antonio José did. He had been practising grafting in secret and came one day with Antonio Moreno, the proud father, to show his early prodigy. Antonio José, still in his teens, became foreman of the avocado planters. His wages tripled, he learnt to drive and he became enamoured of avocados, waiting eagerly for the Californian Avocado Society's bulletins to learn from me more about his chosen crop.

To finance our green dream, we grew green beans and tomatoes, cucumbers and lettuces, cabbages and carrots. The carrots were burnt out overnight by a fungus called *candelilla*. The cabbages also proved to be a dismal failure and rotted at their base. We had planted them in a field directly in front of the Casa Grande's orchard and the smell of rotting brassicas was for many weeks like the stench of decomposing meat. Our first tomato crop also failed when Jaime, overcome by the Labastida in him, ordered Antonio Moreno to plough it up a week before it was ready to be harvested. The green beans, however, were a big success. Abrán took them, crated, by the lorryload to sell in the highland market of Timotes. They grew from start to finish in five weeks. We staggered their planting and enjoyed their profit. With the pretext of supervising their sale in the upland market town in person from time to time, I made many round trips to the *páramo*. In order to sell them while they were still fresh and crisp, Abrán had to set off at half-past three in the morning. Every time I went with him, despite the early hour, I felt as though I were playing truant. Much as I loved the *hacienda*, the more involved I became in it and its people, the more I needed to escape, even for a few hours, but preferably for a few days, to anywhere else so long as it wasn't Valera.

21

CHRISTMAS IN VENEZUELA is called La Noche Buena (the good night) and it is taken very seriously. Unlike the Christmases I had known as a child with their religious overtones even in our non-religious family, decorations and a giving and receiving of presents incorporating a Christmas dinner of roast turkey and Christmas pudding, La Noche Buena is a time exclusively for drinking, eating and greeting, in that order. For most of *la gente*, it was the one time of the year when meat was eaten in any quantity. Every household kept a small pig, which was fattened up through the year on slops expressly to be slaughtered on the morning of 24 December.

Scalding vats circulated from compound to compound and the hills echoed with the shrieking and squealing of slaughtered pigs. Every single part of the pig, except for the eyes and the teeth, was then used. Because of the climate, fresh meat went off within the day, which was a great incentive to binge on the fresh pork. What could not be eaten straight away was salted and kept to be eked out over the next month. The pigs were not big like English pigs; they were, full-grown, about a third or a quarter of the size and stayed relatively lean no matter how forcefully they were fattened. Each household also set aside some of the meat to sell, which they did from covered buckets along the edge of the road. Anyone from the town wanting fresh pork for their Christmas recipe knew that this would be happening and sent out for it.

The first year I was at the Casa Grande, although I had my own chickens and ducks, I didn't have my own pig to slaughter and so bought in our meat. I knew that the traditional, and indeed, only food eaten at Christmas was *ayacas*. The *ayaca*, eaten only once a year, is a rich, spicy stuffing wrapped in maize paste and then wrapped in a smoked banana leaf, tied round with banana fibre and boiled for four hours. Benito Mendoza had promised to be my teacher and assistant in the making of these *ayacas*.

It was the custom to keep maids working over Christmas and then allow them home for two days after the festivities were over. I knew from *la gente* that this was one of the usages they most resented in their servitude. In gratitude for the smooth running of my household since my move, I sent the girls who worked for me home all armed with bundles of food, meat, spices, raisins, star apples, capers and eggs to spend the holidays with their families. Each had a new cotton dress and a new pair of *cotiza* slippers as a Christmas present. The house felt suddenly very lonely without them.

Benito ran over the list of ingredients I had already bought for the *ayacas*. I had gleaned the ingredients from several other sources, but they all differed slightly. *Ayacas*, it seemed, varied from family to family. Everyone insisted that theirs were best. In a round of Christmas visits, drinks were toasted and downed, followed by an obligatory *ayaca*. Judgement was always asked for as the gastronomic bomb was consumed. Benito insisted that he knew exactly how to make them. My first doubts appeared in the morning when his recipe varied noticeably each time we repeated it together. He listed the ingredients, and I wrote them down, then I read them back to him, he quibbled, added and subtracted certain things, and then started again. Eventually, we seemed to have thrashed out a definitive recipe and he took off towards the hill to gather banana leaves for the wrapping. He was gone until mid-afternoon.

He staggered back full of Christmas spirit, with a negligible bundle of banana leaves straggling under one arm. He then proceeded to lay and light a small fire for the smoking of his trophies. This he did to the accompaniment of several *gaitas*. One of the surprises on the *hacienda* had been to discover that there was no local music, no folk songs, no Andean flutes or pipes or drums. The one musical instrument that was played was a four-stringed guitar called a *cuatro*. This was not, as I had imagined, strummed in the evenings by masterful hands for the entertainment of friends and family. Only two men out of all the *gente* played the *cuatro* and both of them did so indifferently and so rarely as to make no mark at all. Singing was limited to a handful of nursery rhymes or to snatches of pop songs crackled through the transistor radios that Antonio and Ramón Rivas, Abrán and a couple of other families owned. Owning a transistor radio was a status symbol. The price of batteries tended to prohibit its use. Christmas was not only a time for eating meat, it was also a time for adding batteries to the family budget and the radio transmitted the traditional songs which came from the distant plains of Venezuela known as Los Llanos. There, the cowboys lived out on vast estates, spending months at a time on the lonely savannas with only Ceibu hump-backed cattle for company. It was these cowboy gauchos who had devised the *gaita*, which was a mixture of satire and social commentary. New *gaitas* were invented and repeated every year for Christmas. These were repeated by word of mouth and by the radio until, in a bastardised form, they reached the *hacienda*, where, after a year of musical repression, the peasants half-sang and half-chanted the somewhat tuneless songs, whose meanings were largely incomprehensible to them. If anyone actually managed to decipher a line or verse, word travelled round the *hacienda* with almost the same excitement as at a murder.

It always seemed to me, as a music lover, that it was a great deprivation visited upon *la gente* that they had no music. I asked endlessly whether it had always been so, and they assured me it had. They were a community of story-tellers but not of songs. Yet, on the few occasions when I happened to spend time away with any of the workers, such as on trips away with Antonio Moreno or Abrán, in their cups, they would sit entranced in roadside bars and listen to the crooning of Mexican songs as though drinking them in. It made them instantly moody and pensive, inducing a state of maudlin yearning. Or so it seemed. Meanwhile, Christmas brought a truce in their musicless lives, reintroducing the fast patter of the *gaitas*.

Benito Mendoza was singing his garbled version of one as he grappled with what was (and shouldn't have been) a sizeable bonfire. As he swayed over it, the first green banana leaves were burnt to cinders. When I drew his attention to this, he smiled drunkenly and assured me that he had everything under control. Twilight found us in a state of confusion in the Casa Grande. Benito, fortified by innumerable tots of rum from the quarter-litre bottle he kept in his back pocket and replenished from stocks he kept hidden all over the outhouses and grounds, was sitting propped against the wall on a chair. He had passed the point where he kept telling me everything was *perfecto* and under control and was intent now merely on not falling off his chair. In this, he was not entirely successful.

Iseult, who woke early and slept early, was asleep in her room. The dogs, now numbering twelve, were sleuthing imaginary hares in their compound. There were Ross and Megan, the original pair of beagles, their four puppies grown now to full size, a bitch on heat that someone had dumped to be mated, three uninvited pedigree dogs who were spending Christmas in the compound, Melissa, a Siberian Husky who had been given to me by someone who had liked her as a puppy and then grown bored with her sleigh-pulling ways, and a completely mad Dalmatian whose myriad neuroses had been bequeathed to me.

The *ayaca* collaboration was not doing well. The neatly shaped packages that I had been led to expect were proving hard to achieve. The smallest were the size of a misshapen tea-cup, the biggest were the size of fat salmon trout. My efforts to rouse the comatose Benito were no help: if I shook him gently, he didn't stir, if I shook him harder, he fell off his chair. Having started, I felt honour-bound to keep packing and wrapping. The quantities were supposed to be sufficient to make twenty-four *ayacas* – by three o'clock in the morning, I had made sixty and was still packing. I hadn't enough pots to cope with my production. When the first of them was ready, it was a greasy, saltless, soggy mess. I had anticipated serving this national dish to streams of Christmas visitors together with the jugs of eggnog I had waiting in the fridge. As it was, Christmas was a lonely time when it was assumed that I would be too busy with everyone else to need to be invited anywhere. The custom was that everyone circulated from house to house, got drunk and staggered on.

I spent that Noche Bueno on my own accompanied by the snoring Benito.

Next day, 25 December, which would have been Christmas to me in England, I too did the rounds of Mendoza Fría and Valera, eating other people's *ayacas*, which were delicious and quite unlike my own.

On Boxing day, Otto's younger brother José arrived unannounced on the *hacienda*. José was a geologist by profession. I had known him first in London and then in Oxford, where we had become close friends. Like his brother, he had been involved in politics since he was a boy. During the time of La Guerrilla, the fighting that convulsed Venezuela in the 1960s, José had been shot in the stomach and smuggled out of the country to Cuba. Later he had gone to Russia, where for seven years he studied geology at the Lomonosov University in Moscow. From Moscow he had met up with Otto in London, and then, a year before I sailed for Venezuela, José had returned.

When we passed through Caracas in 1972, José hadn't been there. I had hoped to see him during my first year. In fact, before leaving, I had counted on it. He enhanced the quality of life and was a natural protector of the weak. It had been my vague plan to shelter under his wing.

He first came to the *hacienda* in the late summer of 1973. Joanna had just returned to England. I already knew from Joanna that Chile was on the brink of collapse and war was imminent. Neither she nor I knew if Otto was still there, but I assumed he was. José arrived, rumbling down the track of the *trapiche* in a bright yellow Jeep. He was driving, and two friends sat squeezed beside him. When the back doors of the Jeep were opened, another six passengers tumbled out, looking dazed and drunken. José never travelled alone. He was a dedicated extrovert. Otto called his brother's companions the 'travelling zoo' or 'the band'. 'José and the band are on their way,' 'José and the zoo are coming!'

He took hold of me and hugged me until I could hardly breathe. I had so many questions to ask him, so much to say that the words jumbled. Before I could straighten out a single coherent phrase, he said, 'I can't talk in front of this lot, I was just passing through the Andes and I dropped by. I came to give you three kisses and to say I'll be back here any day. I'm going to be working in Mérida, it's only three and a half hours away.'

He paused and I tried to interrupt him, 'As to the Boss,' he continued, 'nobody knows. It's looking bad down south, very bad. Where's the *Cuchiflina?*'

Cuchiflina was an affectionate diminutive for a small child. I told him she was sleeping. He went through to see her, kissed her, kissed me and then left. He had stayed for less than five minutes. I tried to persuade him to stay. He said, 'I have to go, we're late. My mother is unwell in Caracas, but, I'll be back soon. I'll come and find you. Don't worry.'

José had a way of making everything seem all right. It was impossible to be cross with him. Because of the long silence since last seeing Otto and Elias, I had imagined them both dead. Although José's news of them was not, on the surface, good, it gave me hope where none had been before. Now that he had re-established contact, however briefly, I had hopes too of renewing our friendship. Too much happened in the rest of the year for me to feel other than fleeting sadness that he had not kept his promise and returned to see me.

From my occasional trips to the drive-in cinema in Valera, I had discovered a new source of news. Before the feature, there was a newsreel. From this, I learnt that there had been a *coup* in Chile, that Salvador Allende was dead, that thousands of foreigners had died in the *coup* and that the country was now under the right-wing dictatorship of General Pinochet. I also learnt that a woman called Chilo, who had been Otto's mistress when I first met him in London, had escaped from Chile, been flown to Venezuela and was in prison.

For six months before Christmas, there were general elections in Venezuela. The entire country was convulsed by the electoral campaigning. Jeeps with loudspeakers paraded up and down the valley, urging either 'Vote for Rafael Caldera, vote Copei,' or 'Vote for Carlos Andrés Perez, vote Adeco.' Copei and Adeco were the two warring parties. When I arrived, the government had been in the hands of Copei under the guidance of Rafael Caldera, who had declared an amnesty for left-wing insurgents and brought about a pacification of the country. It was under this pacification that Jaime had been able to return. Although the older people harked back to the days of the dictatorship of Perez Jimenez, Caldera had managed to subdue a country supposedly torn by political strife without resorting to the methods of terror used by the previous government.

Venezuela was still a police state. There were still road blocks every thirty kilometres along the roads. People were still wary of speaking their minds or mentioning the leaders of the socialist uprising, but it was poverty rather than police brutality that harassed the peasants.

However, the levels of corruption ran high. When Copei was in power all government posts and all big contracts were given almost exclusively to Copeyanos. When Adeco came to power, every office was cleared out, every public work begun by the rival party was abandoned and all posts and contracts went to Adecos. Since the constitution insisted on a general election every four years at least (and, as a protection against dictatorship, no president being able to repeat his term of office) this meant general chaos was the order of the day. Every household was either Adeco or Copeyano to the last member of staff. The two parties, though, as far as I could see, almost identical in their outlook, were deadly rivals. The vested interests in a changeover were huge. A family's fortune could be made or broken depending on who came into power. Vast sums of money were spent on propaganda. Everyone was bombarded with it.

There were so many candidates and so many parties other than the two main ones running for power that it was virtually impossible to know who was who. A voting sheet, devised for the illiterate, could have over fifty grinning faces looking up expectantly from the page. There was universal suffrage and not to vote was a criminal offence. To cast your vote you just pressed your thumb on to a pad of indelible ink, then placed a thumb print on the face of the chosen candidate. The ballot was supposed to be secret, but this was palpably not the case. On a *hacienda*, for instance, all the workers of age were expected to vote for whoever their *padrón* supported. Not to do so was enough to get them turned off the estate.

Under Caldera, a gentler form of socialism had been allowed to group and become politically active. It was hoped that their party, the MAS (Movimento al Socialismo) would win enough votes to gain representatives in the government. The MAS also campaigned vigorously, although they had none of the funds that the big parties had. However, they had a very important card in their hand: their leader, Dr Rafael Rangel was, in profile, identical to the aspiring Venezuelan saint Dr José Gregorio Hernandez. Voting for one, it was implied, was tantamount to voting for the other. This didn't bring in the peasant landslide they had been hoping for, but it did secure them some seats in the new Adeco government, led by Carlos Andrés Perez.

The new president and Don Felipe Neri Terán were old buddies. I believe Don Felipe Neri contributed more than generously to the election campaign. As a sign of respect, just before the election, on his way through the Andes, Carlos Andrés Perez paid a whirlwind visit to Mendoza Fría to visit Don Felipe Neri. I knew from Mimita and others that Carlos Andrés Perez was hated not only by his rival Copeyanos, but more generally because he had been at the head of the hated secret police at the most bloody time of torturing and disappearances during La Guerrilla.

I was playing gin rummy one afternoon with Mimita and Doña Elia, waiting for the other twin to return from Valera with some medicines I needed, when a host of heavily armed secret police swept into the house and began rather roughly to search it. This visit, it seemed, had not been entirely unexpected, but no one had known quite when it would occur. The whole house leapt into frenzied excitement, preparing suitable refreshments for the future president. Not wanting anything to do with him, nor the embarrassment of having either to gravely insult the household I was in by insulting a fellow guest or the moral dilemma of having to shake hands with the unrepentant torturer of some of my friends, I prepared to leave. For security reasons, I was not allowed to. Don Felipe's house was in a dell, and was particularly unsafe in that anyone from a passing car could lob a bomb down the steep slope to the river and blow the house up. So I stayed, lurking in the girls' bedroom. Perez arrived in a long cavalcade of bullet-proof cars and Jeeps. His security men leapt about the house and grounds as though they had ants in their boots. He stayed for over an hour, sitting on the porch with his host. Through the green mesh of mosquito netting in the girls' room, I noted that he too looked like a toad squashed by a heavy stone. He was very full of himself. He was only weeks away from gaining power over what was, at that time, one of the richest countries in the world. Despite the poverty of the peasants who made up over 80 per cent of the country, Venezuela was rich in petrol dollars beyond the dreams of even the greediest politicians.

In January 1974, when José came to see me for the second time, he once again arrived with an assortment of passengers. For the next two days, we had a party. Parties in Venezuela start whenever they start, and end when the last of the revellers has collapsed in a drunken stupor. In a land of hardened drinkers, this usually took a party into its second day. Depending on the level of drunk and disorderly behaviour, parties were graded. A really good one was called an *abraza poceta* (a lavatory bowl hugger). José was a connoisseur of *abraza pocetas*, and brought the first such to Santa Rita in my time.

He told me that Otto and Elias had been caught in the crossfire of the *coup* in Santiago de Chile, taken refuge in an embassy, been flown out to Mexico and then had spent some months in Peru. Now Otto, alone, was *en route* for Venezuela. José also told me that his job in Mérida had come through, and he was teaching there in the Faculty of Science. After the party, he sent out for a case of beer which he took as the hair of the dog. Then he waited an extra day to see if Jaime would return, gave up and went on his way.

After that, José became a regular visitor to the *hacienda*. He came once or twice a month, usually with a crew of colleagues, students, fellow canvassers for MAS, which he threw

251

his charisma into campaigning for, or girlfriends. It was increasingly difficult for me to steal time out of the days to attend to friends, so José took to visiting by night. He would pick me up at around eleven o'clock and drive into the hill towns of Jajó or Escuque, there to while away some hours in talk, drinks and grilled chicken before dropping me back on the *hacienda*, at any time in the morning so long as it was before the five-thirty rollcall to select the workers.

Every hour of the day was taken up by the *hacienda*, from dawn till nearly ten o'clock at night. After all the medicines had been dispensed and the sick who came to the house dealt with, there were accounts to do, dogs to tend to, the girls' daily wrangles to be sorted out. In between and never far away, there was Iseult. From nine o'clock to ten o'clock, whenever I could, I spent an hour listening to old Benito. Then, after he had tottered off to bed in his shed, I sat in the wooden room with the wooden balcony with a hole in it at the top of the house and wrote. I wrote poetry and stories, letters and lists. And sometimes, when my face ached more than usual or the infection that had crept into my kidneys the previous summer and refused to go away, got the better of me, I moped. When letters from Joanna got through to me, the comfort of her ongoing love and support made everything easier. When they didn't, I often fell prey to depression.

Santa Rita, Mendoza Fría,
Edo. Trujillo,
Venezuela.
12th January 1974

Dear Joanna,
    Happy New Year! How are you? I have had no news now for more than a month. Are you all right? Did you

receive Christmas cards? I have not written since Xmas because poor Iseult has been unwell. It turns out (diagnosed yesterday) that she has amoebiasis (from the dogs!). It is bad enough, but I feel so relieved that it is nothing worse.

Your presents arrived on 6th January. They are lovely. I think everything is here except half a hobby horse.

I have sown all the seeds you sent me and they are already nearly half an inch high. The new garden is getting on much better than the old one.

Another lot of your newspapers arrived last week (November's). I go twice a week to Mendoza looking for letters, but 'el coronel no tiene a quien le escriba'.

Leila has had five kittens, not as pretty as herself, but passable. People here were very bucked to get Christmas cards from you (except for us, though I suppose you did send us one and it has just been delayed).

The general elections are finally over, although the blistered propaganda remains.

Tell me a day and time when you are at home in February and I shall nick 50 *bolivárs* out of our mutual drawer and phone you. Nick from the estate, that is, because I have the money in my hands. I shall finish now because Iseult will wake up any minute. She is very anaemic as well.

Do write something, anything, everything,
   Lots of love,
     Lizzie

Dear Joanna,

What's up?

I have had no news, no replies to my letters, no letters to reply to, only newspapers and an empty envelope from Gillie.

Here is a new address:

Apartado 32

Distrito Valera, Estado Trujillo, Venezuela.

I shall telephone/radio this week to give you this address just in case this letter does not reach you either.

I so much miss your letters and news, please write.

Iseult is very well and crawling all over the house. We are doing up a room for her and one for you next to it.

I just seem to keep writing the same old letter and posting it and nothing happens.

I was very sure of going to England this Spring. But last week I 'had it out' with J. and he has changed (??). So I shall wait till after you come and see if I go back with you in September.

Are things awful there at present? The papers say the most alarming things: fuel 3-days a week, Ireland, IRA; what is happening to you all? Do tell me.

When are you going to buy your ticket to Caracas? Let me know in time to send you part of it.

For God's sake (or anybody's) write to me. Have you got problems too? Then tell me. You sounded so sad before, are you?

We now have a magnolia tree in our garden.

Write to me.

PLEASE
   with love and hope to hear from you very soon,
   Lizzie

For every letter that scraped through the postal system, five or six went missing. For a while, all mail to the *hacienda* stopped getting through at all. Whether or not this was the action of fate or the censor, I don't know. I suspected the latter because an increasing number of empty envelopes arrived. Joanna sent me newspapers by a special book post, and these got through, never sooner than six weeks to three months after they were sent, but still they kept me in touch with the world beyond the *hacienda*. Since time stood still and had done, it sometimes seemed, for the last hundred years, it didn't matter that the newspapers arrived out of date.

When I was sixteen, and cramming for my Cambridge entrance exams in London, my English tutor had been a poet called Jonah Howard Jones. We had become friends, and while I was wandering around Italy before my time in Venezuela, we had written regularly to each other. I had promised to continue to do so. I wrote to him more openly than I did to my mother. Having lost his address in the *trapiche* floods, I sent my letter to him in a sealed envelope to her and asked her to forward it. Joanna was the most upright person I have ever known. After her first visit to the *hacienda*, I took pains to conceal from her the depth of and frequency of my depression. After she died in 1981, I was shocked to find a photocopy of the letter that I sent to Jonah via her. It would have been very much against her principles to have opened and read the letter, to have done so showed how secretly concerned she must have been from reading between the lines of my missives to her.

Dear Jonah,

I have waited this long to find a beginning, somewhere to start from, but finding none (my mind stutters since I have come here) I shall just say, please write, again and again.

I want to tell you so much, that nothing comes. First impressions as a tourist, scenery, roads and mountains, endless family – apparently friendly – apparently.

Second impressions of life on a semi-feudal estate: a year of solitary. Only one poem in all that year:

> *Home-hell*
> *Valley or hole,*
> *Under the ponderous shadow of the wheel,*
> *Shunting smiles upon its brim,*
> *Sun-sunk, rough-weathering*
> *Beam and rim.*
> *Sadness trickles from my finger tips*
> *In drops and clots*
> *Until the earth is thick in it,*
> *Yet nothing grows.*
> *Mountains enfold my shell,*
> *Born too old and worn*
> *To croak a harvest song or Spring.*
> *Relentless dawn*
> *Shoves through the land*
> *Where thawed hands are sown.*
> *Shove-shunt what you will*
> *The soil corpse is still*
> *And nothing grows.*

A depression, a daughter, another depression, which pattern would have become tedious had not I come out of it feeling well, and though not particularly happy, able to be so and to write again after a year and a half of silence.

End of sob story.

Write soon,

with love

Lisa

22

UNDER MY WOODEN study in the Casa Grande, there was a triple arched hall. This opened out at one end to a further triple arch and two more communicating halls. At the other end, it gave on to a low hill slope and the road. There was an iron balustrade across the open arch with a gate in the middle leading down to a flight of steps. These steps proved an irresistible attraction to the maids. They spent every spare moment of their time sitting on them and surveying the road. The Casa Grande was a gossip's paradise, it had almost as many french doors and exits as windows, thus enabling its occupants to slip in or out of the house from any one of its four sides, and it commanded views across the four compass points. The great advantage that it had over any other dwelling, though, for purposes of surveillance, was its direct command over both the road and the *trapiche*. Because of the lie of the hills, the road was invisible from almost everywhere else on the *hacienda*. Most of the time, if you didn't know it was there slicing the estate in half, it would be hard to believe in it. At the time it was built, as part of the Pan-American Highway under the dictator Perez Jimenez, my father-in-law had been governor of the state of Trujillo and had planned the road's passage through his estate at this strategic point especially to service both the big house and the *trapiche*.

Mary and her sisters never tired of watching it. It gave them a head start on news of all visitors. They knew before anyone else who came and went and in which direction they were heading. They kept the *trapicheros* under constant surveillance. When Mary was busy, she posted Lorena to keep her informed of their every movement. Coromoto was the same. She said it made her feel comfortable to know everything that was going on.

There were four tramps on the road who passed at irregular intervals, and one who was as reliable as a calendar. When women or girls were cast out, they turned to prostitution. Valera had a street called La Calle Vargas, which was its red light zone. Beyond Valera, on the road to the thermal springs of Mototán, there was a more upmarket brothel called El Arco Iris, which was run by a woman called La Rusa who claimed to have been a Russian ballerina. When a man became destitute, or went mad, he became a tramp.

The natural instinct of all the girls was to hurl insults and stones at the tramps as they passed by. It was very difficult to teach them not to do this. I don't think any of them, except perhaps Lorena, ever lost the desire to taunt the vagrants, they merely curbed the habit to avoid my displeasure.

There was Culo Negro, as he was universally and disparagingly known, who hobbled along the highway bowed down by a sack of stones that he carried on his back. This sack was so heavy that he could hardly walk. Unlike *la gente*, Culo Negro, far from fearing to go on the road, feared to leave it. Whenever he neared the house, he began to yell to attract attention. He always wolfed down whatever food was given to him, but he steadfastly refused to climb up the steep bank to receive it. He would not even meet me half-way, preferring to go hungry than to stray from the black asphalt that was his home. He was paranoid about people wanting to steal his sack. His skin was ingrained with dirt so as to make him almost black. His hair was a matted crust and he stank of his own excrement, which was what had presumably given him his nickname. Neither Antonio Moreno, Benito nor any of the other workers knew where he came from or what had driven him to the road. All the workers unanimously despised him, and if he was unlucky enough to be snailpacing along when La Povva passed by with its cargo of young boys clinging to its sides, the children would drop down to abuse and tease him, grabbing his sack and making him cry.

The second tramp was a middle-aged man with a mild manner who climbed the slope to the house about once a fort-night and respectfully asked for any old *arepas* that might be lying about. He was given beans and whatever else was going in the kitchen in a brown paper poke. He always thanked me or the cook most politely and then went on his way.

The third tramp was a young man in his early twenties. He was fair-skinned and dark-haired and he walked like an athlete in training. His arms swung and sliced rhythmically by his sides and he walked at a tremendous pace. He always carried a piece of towel or cloth around his neck, which every now and again he would rub, as though drying his neck after a shower. The back of his neck was chafed raw. He talked to himself as he hurried along. Listening to him, he seemed to be talking to someone else, promising things to a wife or girl-friend like, 'I'm coming, don't worry, I'm nearly there.'

His eyes were feverishly bright and he was so thin, his joints stuck out. It was very difficult for him to accept any food. When it was offered, he would look startled and then offended by the interruption, hardly pausing. He was known as 'Ya Vengo' locally, which means, 'I'm just coming.' Ya Vengo had murdered his wife in a fit of jealousy and lost his mind in his remorse. He refused to believe what he had done, and lived in a state of constant expectation of seeing her again. Apparently, he had stabbed her to death immediately after he had finished taking a shower. It was said that she had called to him to hurry up before the murder occurred.

The fourth tramp, Crístobal, was the strangest of all. Nobody teased Crístobal. Nobody dared. He was at least six foot tall, one-legged and walked with a long staff. His hair was white and curly and stood out so far around his head that in the sunlight it looked like a halo. He had a handsome face, weatherbeaten and ruddy cheeked. His eyes were the dark blue of a night sky. His habitual expression, under his leonine mane, was fierce. Although his clothes were so ragged they barely covered him, he kept himself clean. The worn cotton trouser of his left leg was tied in a knot. Crístobal never begged and he hardly ever spoke. If anyone came anywhere near him, he waved them off with his staff.

Because he looked so unlike any of *la gente*, mothers frightened their children with Crístobal. They said that he was El Coco, the Bogey Man whom everybody feared. They said that if any child disobeyed, then Crístobal would get them. I had first encountered him when I was newly arrived. He was standing on the bridge to the *trapiche* one morning when I set out to walk the dogs. I said good morning to him as I passed, and he had said good morning back. His manner had been almost courtly as he addressed me as 'dear lady'. It was when we moved to the Casa Grande that I noticed how regularly he came past. Benito told me that Crístobal walked from Valera to Timotes and back. The round trip took him six days, so he traversed the *hacienda* every third day. He was a compulsive walker.

One day when I saw Crístobal approaching in the distance, I asked Coromoto to run down and see if he wanted some food. She said she would rather eat snakes or be whipped to death than go anywhere near him. When I told her that he was harmless and that I had already spoken to him, she looked at me as though I were mad.

'He's really dangerous. He beats people up. No one can get near him.' Then she lowered her voice to a stage whisper, 'They say he's El Coco.'

To prove to her that she had no need for such terror, I clambered down the hill myself and approached him. This time, he didn't return my good day and it was clear that he had no wish to speak or be spoken to. He was lost in thought. The expression of knowing sadness on his intelligent face was disconcerting.

That night I asked Benito Mendoza about Crístobal again. I fully expected him to reply as he had to further questioning about the other tramps, 'Why worry about such rubbish?' Instead, he told me a story about him, that of all his stories I found hardest to believe.

Crístobal was a cousin of the Teráns. He had been born a gentleman on an upland estate. He had lost his mother as a small boy and his father had moved away to the city, leaving Crístobal and the misty estate to the care of his two elder brothers. Crístobal had been a wild boy, given to roaming around the countryside. His brothers objected and tried to beat him into staying at home. The more they punished him, the more he wandered. They felt that their pride was at stake. The family and neighbours were talking, their peasants were too.

Qué dirán? What would they say when a mere boy made a fool of them and defied their authority?

Yet Crístobal continued to run away both from them and from his tutor. He ran into the hills which had comforted him after his mother died. His brothers did everything they could to keep him back. They whipped and weakened him. They locked him naked in his room and fed him only cornbread and milk. Somehow he managed to escape, cover himself and take refuge once again in his roaming. It became a battle of wills. Their father had died and the two young men were left to run the estate for good. They were painfully aware of their youth and of the need to be respected despite it. If Crístobal could escape through a window, then he should be locked up in a windowless room. They jailed him, naked, in their own house. He was plagued by the cold, by insects and his untended, festering sores. The servants told the villagers and the villagers told the boys' family.

The brothers were chided for their cruelty. But they were masters of their own estate, heads of their own family. It was Crístobal and not they who was in the wrong. It was Crístobal who had made them the laughing stock of the neighbourhood, who had brought shame on their name. It was Crístobal who refused to live in a decent house like a decent gentleman. They knew that everyone was talking behind their backs, everyone was saying they couldn't control their brother. Their pride drove them to settle the matter once and for all. It was Crístobal's feet that had offended them, it was his feet that they would punish.

They branded the sole of his right foot with a white-hot cattle iron. The burn festered and brought on a fever. Undeterred, Crístobal made himself a staff and took to the hills, where he was taken in by one of the peasants. But the war was not yet over. His brothers tracked him down, turned the peasant out of his hut and off their estate. There and then, they cut their brother's leg off with an axe, cauterising the wound with the same branding iron. As soon as the stump healed, Crístobal had made a second staff and left the uplands, renouncing his inheritance, his brothers and all his other kin.

Ever since, he had patrolled the valley, monitoring its progress and its decline. His route took him from Valera, the city he had fled to after he finally left home, to Timotes, the town in the *páramo* nearest to his lands. The peasants who had once worked his brothers' estate had followed him, abandoning the chill uplands for the lower lands. Like a curse, the estate failed, the crops withered on their stalks, and one at a time, childless, his brothers died. Before the Highway was built, he had patrolled the old *camino real*; after the new road cut through the valley, he followed that. Since the day of his maiming he had scarcely spoken again. As the years passed, fewer people remembered his story. The family scattered so that even his distant relations ceased to see him vaulting along.

'Some things chafe the memory,' Benito said. 'Some things hurt so much it's easier to forget them.'

Seeing how shocked I was by his story, Benito explained, 'These hills are cruel to us, Doña, you have to be stubborn to survive. When stubbornness and pride wed, they give birth to cruelty. The Teráns are famous for their pride: it has been both their greatness and their undoing. It is like a double-edged machete.'

Every day on the *hacienda* was so long it seemed to stretch life as though on an elastic band which occasionally snapped back. Mostly, though, it was just a slow turning of a wheel. New threads were added to the tapestry of routine and worked in to become a part of the general pattern. A cousin of

Jaime's father came to stay for a week and stayed for two and a half years. He stayed from Monday to Friday of every week, returning home to his wife and children in Barquisimeto at weekends. He proved to be an ideal companion. Luis Daniel was a hydraulic engineer by profession, but his first love was books. He read, recited, declaimed from, and collected literature. He not only shared my passion for certain writers, he introduced me to new and exciting ones like Vicente Huidobro and Pablo de Rocca. He took an interest in my own writing and encouraged me to write more. Because he returned regularly every evening, for the first time since I had arrived in Venezuela my house was neither lonely nor a glorified children's-cum-old people's home. When Jaime was around, he too was happier for the presence of Luis Daniel, who had been a surrogate father to him.

Luis Daniel, like all the older Teráns, was a mine of information about the family history. He told me the same stories that Benito Mendoza had recounted adding in the missing names, dates and places. He told me about General Mario Terán whose face had been corroded by leprosy. General Mario, like Luis Daniel himself had been a hydraulic engineer, but he was also an inventor. He hid the signs of his leprosy behind a screen and no one, including his wife, ever saw him again. Everything he touched was destroyed after he had used it to prevent contagion. He issued his instructions, running his household and his estate and pursuing his inventions, from behind his screen. Over the years, people found this so intriguing, they travelled from far and wide to ask his advice and hear his oracles.

It was Luis Daniel who took me to the sight of the Massacre of the Teráns in the hill town of Escuque. He showed me the magnolia tree that General Rodolfo Terán had planted there upon his return from New York with his platinum jaw to give thanks for his miraculous survival.

He told me about Rosario Terán, Don Felipe Neri's sister, who had fallen in love with one of their peasant workers when she was still a girl and had borne him an illegitimate daughter. He told me how the baby had been taken away from her, and her lover killed before her eyes; and how she had been locked in a set of stocks in a storeroom and half-starved for a year to punish her. He told me how the servants had tried to help her and how she had sung lullabies to the pile of rags that she was allowed to keep with her. He told me how Rosario Terán was still alive, locked away somewhere in a lunatic asylum in which she had been forcibly incarcerated after the year was up. He told me that she wrote to her brother Don Felipe Neri sometimes, begging to be let out and that she was as sane as either of us despite the forty years of her seclusion.

When I asked other members of the family about this story, they denied it, but Mimita showed me one of Rosario's letters retrieved from a wastepaper basket. She wrote twice a year.

Luis Daniel also told me about his own brothers and sisters, scattered across Venezuela. They were Diego, La Bebella, and Ana Enriqueta who was a poet and lived on the Island of Margarita. He urged me to see more of them, to balance the view of the family I was gleaning from La Cañada and from Valera.

The gossips complained that it was wrong of Luis Daniel to take advantage of my hospitality, but he was a rock in the shifting sands and he gave me more than ever I could give him. Half-way through his stay, he started to have his own house built for him in Jajó. When it was almost finished, and he moved there with his wife and their two small children, I was sad to see him go. We often visited him to admire the vast ground-floor library he was building like a temple for his books.

Hacienda Santa Rita
April 16th 1974

Dear Joanna,

How are you?

Forgive my not having written before – I have been writing. I shall send you two new poems soon.

We are up to our eyes in puppies. In two weeks we are going to Caracas to sell them. Wish us luck!

1) Please do come to Caracas and we shall meet you there.

2) Please do send some books by open book post as things do arrive that way.

3) I shall send you a list of things to bring in a couple of weeks when I have some money to cover it.

4) Count on 1000 *bolivárs* towards your fares.

5) All is well here. Iseult is beginning to walk. We have finally taken some photos (they are being developed).

6) Excuse these numbers, it is the only way I can write a letter at the moment without forgetting what I have to say.

Elia and Carmen and Maritza and Luis Daniel and Leonor all send their love.

Rodolfo and Loris are back here in Valera. Rodolfo says that you would like to come to Venezuela for good. Would you? You are very welcome to if you would like it.

Things are different in this house; much more comfortable and happier.

We have a smashing cook-cum-housekeeper called *la comadre* Matilde (she is Jaime's and the twins' ex-nanny) and she is running the house beautifully with three-course meals and everything under control.

Write soon; don't be depressed. Send me news; and send my love to everyone there.

Lots of love,
Lizzie

Rodolfo Terán was Eliseo's brother and Don Felipe Neri's younger son. He went to England to study, befriended Joanna, and then returned. Shortly afterwards, he was killed in a car crash.

The *comadre* Matilde was Abrán the driver's mother. Abrán was her only son, born to her late and she doted on him. The *comadre* Matilde was fat and nearly black and she flapped about like a bird of ill-omen. She was quite exceptionally ugly of face and had a truly massive goitre at her neck, which bulged in a great black growth over her throat. Goitre was very common in the Andes. Far from the sea, there was no iodine in the diet. The rich, like Doña Elia, had their unsightly growths removed, leaving a long scar as though their throats had been slit. Collars were often worn high and pearl chokers were fashionable camouflage. Despite the *comadre* Matilde's ugliness, her waddle and limp where she had been kicked by a cow as a child, and her layers of black aprons worn over a black dress that gave her the appearance of an obese vulture or crow, she was lovely to be around. She cooked with consummate skill and turned out the repetitive recipes in such a way that I acquired a genuine taste for Venezuelan food.

Like me, she had bad kidneys, and she shared her wide knowledge of medicinal plants, brewing up the beards of young maize, barley water, mare's tail and many other cures which helped the ongoing infection that antibiotics alone were not abating. Twice a week, after her work was over, she brewed herself a noxious tea from the poisonous ñongue plant and retired to her room in a half-trance. On Wednesday afternoons she trudged laboriously up the high hill behind the *trapiche* to the old estate of Tempé, the furthest tract of Santa Rita on that side. There, on the near side of Tempé, her only other relation (apart from her son) lived: an old lady called Constancia who was Matilde's aunt. Constancia was, by everybody's reckoning, over a hundred years old and blind. She was tended by an orphan girl. Constancia was impatient to die. Matilde lived in a constant state of impatience to visit her. It was as though she lived for Wednesdays. It was the highlight of her week. She hoarded her wages and gave all the presents I gave her to her aunt. She treated Constancia like a shrine. During the week she talked about her endlessly.

After much urging, I once accompanied Matilde on her weekly trek. It was a four-hour walk each way. The nearer we came to the borders of Tempé, the more excited Matilde got. At one point during the visit, the shrivelled, withered Constancia sent her niece away. She asked me, 'Has she gone?'

I told her she had. The aunt said, 'Thank God for that. I never could stand Matilde. I've been blind for nearly forty years, but I can still remember her ugliness. These visits are a cross I have to bear. If God loves the Virgin, he will take me to him soon and rid me of this curse.'

Matilde often invited me to go back with her to the aunt on Tempé, but I never had the heart to return again. Instead, I stayed and listened to Matilde constructing her entire life around her unwanted visits.

Every month, around the time of the full moon, Matilde's mood changed. Usually she had a strong sense of humour. Little things amused her and kept her happy during the day.

When nothing happened or there were troubles, she contrived to dredge up incidents from our recent shared past and laugh about them, making her fat frame shake so hard she had to sit down to recover. One of her favourite recollections was of when Ramón Rivas put a kilo of plaster of Paris down on the kitchen windowsill and one of the girls put it up on the shelf by mistake. Later, Matilde made *arepas* from the *páramo*, which were kneaded wheatflour and water as opposed to maize. The more she kneaded, the harder the dough became. She added water over and over again, but the dough kept hardening, until she called me to come and witness its bewitching. When she discovered that she had been kneading plaster of Paris, she laughed until she cried. To keep up her spirits, she often carried the story further, imagining what would have happened if she had cooked them, and what would have happened if Benito had eaten them and what he would have said when his three last precious teeth had broken on them and fallen out.

However, once a month, Matilde grew moody and she wandered around the house grumbling and muttering under her breath. This ill-humour lasted until she had retold in every detail the story of the plague of locusts that had brought starvation to the valley in 1905, wiping out, among others, almost her entire family. For two or three days, which sometimes lasted more, Matilde became a prophet of doom. She cornered anyone and everyone, and warned them of the transitory nature of life, the perils of invasion and the pain and hunger of starvation. The girls, in particular, with their finickity tastes (Alba didn't like eggs, Mary didn't eat avocados and Lorena refused to eat salt fish), incensed her. On normal days, she just told them off. 'It's a sin to waste food. It's a crime, you should be thankful that there's food on your plate and eat it. I lived through a famine, I know what I'm talking about.'

But when the moon was full, and her memories of the locusts took hold of her, she made them finish what she served them and the anger in her was too great to be defied. She had spent her entire life moving from house to house along the valley, spreading her gospel, warning people of the need to prepare against the return of a famine that would wipe them all out. She kept a storeroom in my house stocked with tins of milk and oats, coffee and sardines, and she insisted that I bulk-buy my rice and corn so that there were never less than three sacks of each in this cupboard. They gathered weevils, but she didn't care; if the locusts returned, we at Santa Rita would survive.

Most of the workers laughed at Matilde behind her back. Most of them were too young to remember the famine. She saw it as her mission to make them understand. She said, 'The locusts first appeared as a shadow in the sky, they blackened the day, then they descended like an articulated mat, the noise of their wings was deafening. They ate everything in the valley, every leaf and blade of grass. Only the bananas survived and that was what we lived off; first the stewed fruit, and then the skins. The bananas saved us. I owe my life to them.'

When fields were cleared for new avocado groves and coffee, Matilde was alarmed, part of the wild scrub cleared had been banana palms. Her bovine eyes roved across the horizon as though scanning it for the certain arrival of another swarm of locusts, invited by my rash lack of foresight. Change, she said, was evil, God was waiting to punish the land. The more *la gente* strayed from their old simple ways, the sooner his vengeance would come down. Matilde didn't care that no one took her seriously in her prophecies, if she was the only one to have had the veil lifted from her eyes she would keep going until she died, warning.

Unlike most of the *gente*, Matilde was deeply religious. Every hut had a small shrine, usually with a picture of Saint Anthony the patron saint of lost things, and Saint Benito, the national saint who was black and also the patron saint of drinkers. Whenever anyone mislaid anything, they turned their picture of St Anthony on its head and asked him to find it. This he often did. Matilde, however, had more than a small tinsel shrine and a votive candle, she had several crucifixes, a plaster statuette of Christ and one of the Virgin, plaster stat-uettes of St Anthony and St Benito and dozens of black and white cards of the saints. She had a rosary, which she told whenever she was out of sorts. She also had a bible, which she couldn't read but which she held fervently between her splayed black hands. It worried her when I read books. It worried her so much sometimes that I told her they were, in fact, tracts from the Bible. She often interrupted me and asked me to read out bits to her. When I told her that the books were not in Cristiano, she urged me to burn them.

Once, when a bluebottle got into her ear and buzzed her half out of her mind, died and caused a serious infection, I read to her from her battered Spanish Bible. After a handful of verses, Matilde stopped me. She said she liked to imagine its good words rather than hear them. There was something con-fusing about the actual text and it didn't talk specifically about locusts and damnation.

When the passion of her vision abated, waning with the moon, Matilde described the valley as it used to be and talked about herself, her life, Abrán, her aunt and about medicinal cures. I grew very fond of her, of her lumbering frame and I grew so used to her ugliness that it blurred and became almost attractive to my eyes. When visitors came and were taken aback by her, it surprised me. Her kindness, humour, loyalty and generosity did not show on the surface, but they were so close below it that I ceased to notice the alarming size of her goitre. Matilde interpreted life from the signs and portents that she saw daily. She taught me to recognise them, sharing the omens, rolling her protruding eyes theatrically as they manifested themselves. As we grew closer, she believed that she had, at last, found a convert to her message.

Because of her bad kidneys, she sometimes got up in the night and brewed up a potion to ease their pain. She noticed that I too was up and about at night. Sometimes we met in the kitchen. When I explained to her that I was writing about the *hacienda*, about the valley and its past so that other people would know about it, she asked me if I had told of the plague of the locusts. When I told her I had, she sighed gratefully. From then on, she excluded me from her harangues. She would say, 'La Doña understands, she's telling people, she has received the Word.'

Benito, another survivor of the famine, dealt with his memories of it in his own way. He hoarded scraps of food in his shed, both cooked and dry and kept them until the cockroaches and weevils took them away again. He was particularly anxious about his drink. He lived in fear of running out, he kept all the quarter-litre bottles that he bought and found and put a last gulp of *aguardiente* firewater in each one, then hid them. He hid them in his shed, in the stables, under the eaves, in the kennels, in little pits under the avocado trees, in the fork of branches and under stones. Antonio Moreno said that old man Benito feared running out of liquor more than he feared death. Because he was so old, and his short-term memory was failing, Benito often forgot where he had hidden his bottles. A part of every day was spent hunting and scrabbling secretively round the grounds, checking. Every night, when he was drunk, when the quarter-litre he was drinking ran out, Benito would go out and top up from his hidden cache. It was a favourite game of the children to find his stores and relocate them to other hiding places. More hours were spent by Benito checking and searching for his missing bottles than were spent on the avocado seeds he pared and planted.

> *Santa Rita,*
> *Apartado 32,*
> *Valera*
> *19 April 1974*

Dear Joanna,

How are you? We are on fair to middling ground here, almost well.

Please send enclosed forms to kennel club with enclosed £5 and get Export Pedigrees under way. It seems we have actually sold some puppies, £100 each! I hope so.

One of Jaime's cousins is here for a visit this afternoon, very tedious, she gets so much on my wick, I can't even think to write to you.

I am glad you will be here soon, for many reasons, many selfish. I am no longer *involved* with anyone here, occasionally with J. though I am becoming uncaring. A real sob story and a real relief.

Write soon to your dissector of humanity daughter and tell me your news.

> With lots of love,
> Lizzie

23

OTTO RETURNED TO Venezuela. I didn't need to wait for José to come by and tell me the news; I saw it at the drive-in cinema with the twins. Sitting in their pick-up truck with my lap full of hot dogs and Coca-Cola, the newsreel prefaced the film. It said, 'One of Venezuela's most wanted men was arrested today as he disembarked from Curaçao. Osvaldo Barreto is now safely behind bars.' There on the screen I saw the diminutive and heavily sun-tanned Otto as the human rope in a tug-of-war. On the gangplank, security officers pulled him by one arm, while several members of the ship's crew tried to pull him back with the other. He was eventually led away, hand-cuffed and apparently unperturbed.

He was held in the prison of Catia La Mar outside Caracas. He was there for many months. Via José, I got in touch with Otto's girlfriend, Mariana Otero in Caracas. She had been with him in London and in Chile, in Mexico and Peru. I travelled to Caracas with Eliseo Terán, stayed with Mariana in her father's sumptuous villa, and together with her went to visit Otto in prison.

It was scorchingly hot. The prison had a big car park away

from its gates and walls. We parked and joined a long queue of visitors waiting to be checked by the security guards and get in. Mariana had warned me to wear plain clothes that completely covered every inch of my flesh apart from my face. To get to Otto, who was held upstairs in the high-security wing, it would be necessary to pass through the other cells. At the guard post, our identity cards had to be shown. Everyone, by law, had to own and carry a *cedula de identidad*. I had sorted mine out before Iseult was born and my papers were all in order. Most of *la gente* had no papers, not even a birth certificate. The ones who lived nearer the road were officially registered, but the ones who lived in the hills lived in another world.

Because I was a foreigner, the three guards in the booth told me I needed to show my passport as well as my card. This I had left in the car. They insisted I could not go in without it. Mariana and her mother were ushered through, and I was left to get my passport and rejoin the queue at the end again. It took the best part of an hour to get back through. Once in the concrete compound of the jail, I crossed the interminable yard, following the other visitors to a side entrance. There, I was body-searched by a very rough female guard. I then put my clothes back on, loose trousers, shirt and thick, shapeless jacket.

'No jackets are allowed,' my searcher told me. 'You'll have to leave it here.

'I need it,' I said.

'Well, you can't have it. Security. You could be carrying a gun under it.'

'But I'm not, and I need it.'

The jacket was taken roughly from me, 'Either go in or go back, what do we care?'

I needed the jacket because it was what I had worn to comply

276

with Mariana's instructions. Underneath it, I was wearing only a long-sleeved voile shirt. It was virtually transparent, and I had nothing else on underneath. If I went on, I was almost half-naked. If I went back, I wouldn't see Otto. So I went on, into a series of communicating corridors, each guarded by a soldier with a machine-gun who unlocked the next door for me as I showed my pass. The corridors were narrow, and lined by cells whose closest wall was barred from floor to low ceiling. Each cell was crowded with sweaty leering men. They stuck their arms out through the bars, making each passageway a running of the gauntlet, except that it was forbidden to run. By keeping close up against the far wall, I managed to get by so that although their fingers touched me, none of them could actually pull me into the bars. Hall after hall had to be traversed in which, literally, thousands of men were held. Otto had a room on the second floor. It was small and spartan but he had it to himself. Despite the overcrowding in the jail, he was considered too dangerous and subversive to be allowed contact with other prisoners, so his solitude and its relative quiet were a bonus he gratefully enjoyed.

I had been warned that it was better not to talk much as every word spoken in his cell would be sifted over by the secret police.

By throwing myself whole-heartedly into the lives of the *gente*, the work of the *hacienda*, my writing and my motherhood, I had managed to anaesthetise any other feelings or needs in myself. Seeing Otto and being close to him, holding his thin, sun-burnt hand, faded artificially by his imprisonment, I felt a sudden yearning to love and be loved. I sat with him for half an hour, looking up at the pocket handkerchief of sky filtered through a heavy grid, at his few books, and papers, his pile of clothes folded neatly, his narrow bed and his otherwise spartan cell. I felt overwhelmed with confusion. I also felt ashamed that I would get up and go soon, while he would be forced to stay, no one knew for how long. He looked old and frail.

On my way in to Caracas, I had dropped off five puppies to a pet shop where they had already been sold. I was given a cheque for 2,500 *bolivárs* (£250) which a bank told me would take two days to clear. On my way back, I went into the bank to collect the cash. I bade Mariana farewell and set off to spend the day in Caracas before meeting up in the evening with Eliseo. He preferred to drive by night, out of the blinding sun. I had (unwisely as it turned out) spent every penny I had brought with me from the *hacienda*, and was counting on my puppy cash to buy up medicines and supplies to take back with me. When I reached the bank, they told me the cheque was bad. I returned to the pet shop only to find it closed. I had ten hours to kill and nowhere to go. I called up Mariana's house and got no reply. I wandered around the concrete city in the heat and got lost, finding my way, eventually, to the University campus.

When you feel lonely and depressed, there is nothing more alienating than to be surrounded by crowds of happy students. I slunk through the campus and took refuge under a stone bridge. Everywhere I looked, young couples were sitting holding hands and kissing. I had not been to a city for over a year and the contrast with the lost world of the *hacienda* was so great that I felt like a visitor from another planet.

On a card of Jacob van Ruisdael that had been sitting in my bag for several years, I wrote to Joanna:

Joanna,
    A very happy birthday with lots of love.

The Hacienda

Dear Joanna,

How are you all? All of you? Surely cooler than I, here
under a stone bridge, sitting between concrete and slab,
students, university surroundings, somewhat lonely and
alone as usual. And to be different, quite well and happy
and with no desire to leave, but not a penny and very
hungry. No money but a bum cheque in my pocket
very funny! Selling puppies at £50 but the last one was a
bum cheque. Reading *All Quiet on the Western Front* Erich
M. Remarque second time round. I have had no letters for
a while. I fancy . . . I want so many things, so much. And
for it all to find me without my stirring: hence multiple
frustrations. Iseult is well, walking and has had a
birthday – is perhaps too young and bald to reflect on her
mother's immaturity and would-be looseness.

I tried to send you some flowers but found no
Interflora. I would like to go to England but shall bide my
time. I miss London and London's countryside and smog,
sludge and pedestrians. Miss it a lot a lot and family and
friends so much I can hardly bring myself to write at all.
Please write soon and often, same address as usual.

With lots of love, Lizzie

As I grew hotter and hotter and more disconsolate, I mused
on the *hacienda*, missing the companionship of Benito and
Mary, Matilde, Iseult and Antonio, Coromoto and the dogs. I
thought of Napoleon, who had kept me company so well. He
had returned, only the week before, to the bridge by the
trapiche and stood there, huddled, staring down at the little
house now overgrown and abandoned. I had pointed him out

to Antonio, who insisted that it wasn't Napoleon, couldn't be.
It was just a vulture, any vulture from the dozens that circled
over the valley. But I know it was Napoleon because of the
ungainly mend in his leg where I had splinted it badly. I wrote:

Napoleon
Was a turkey vulture
With black wings
Folded on his back
And an eye for
A sore.

Napoleon
Could tear the hide
Off a cow
At the will
Of his grey
Gluttony.

And the sack
Of grizzled scrotum
At his neck
Made people shudder;
But I was in love
With Napoleon.

He gave me
A new creed, and he
Showed me how to kill.
He redefined
The meaning
Of mercy.

The Hacienda

And he taught me
To wait in the dark,
With his black feathers
Belted like distilled
Anger, and a finger-nail
On the nerve

Of the world. And
Napolcon taught me
To stay still,
With that claw
Poised over the
Weak places.

And it was he
Who taught me
How to use
The power of power.
Napoleon with the
Bare head

And his eye,
That was always plainspoken.

Otto was in prison for nearly a year and was finally released thanks to a complicated appeal to the government that claimed the charges against him could only be substantiated by an unofficial and illegal branch of the secret police. He had, in the past, spent many years of his life in prison and claimed that he was an ideal prisoner, calm and polite, amenable and quiet. He settled into his life of solitude, using his time to study and write. Despite this, he had never been sure, from day to day, whether he would be bustled out in the night and 'disappeared'. It was a serious risk and one that took its toll on his nerves. He emerged into his relative freedom and light with what he termed 'galloping neurasthenia'. His telephone was bugged, his apartment was routinely searched and he was watched and followed day and night.

I visited him regularly in Caracas, accompanying the lorry-loads of avocados that Abrán ferried to the capital. The avocados turned brown in the sun once picked, and the precious cargo had to be transported by night. Abrán made the ten-hour drive, dropped the avocados in the market and then retired to sleep for twelve hours before driving back. This gave me an entire day to spend with Otto.

These days could not have been more different from the ones I spent on the *hacienda*. The mornings were spent drinking litres of tea at Otto's flat, talking about literature, life and politics, and occasionally translating texts for him on the work he was writing on Jean-Paul Sartre. Lunch was in a restaurant or cooked by Otto himself with all the precision and care of a military campaign. The afternoons were spent in 'El Chicken Bar,' an Austrian tea-room in a part of Caracas called Sabana Grande. In this bar writers, actors, painters and intellectuals gathered daily to discuss art. It was there that I met Renato Rodriguez, a novelist who had lived for many years in New York and who later translated my short stories into Spanish. There also I met Juan Sanchez, Adriano Gonzalez Leon, David Alizo and a number of other writers. As the afternoon slid into evening, everyone got more and more drunk and the discussions more and more impassioned. At nine o'clock, punctually, and without fail, I took a taxi to my rendezvous and returned to the Andes. Because I always disappeared just as the party was really getting going, they called me Cinderella.

Apart from Otto and Renato, there was no one who read or spoke English. The others had all published books and made their names, and being among writers was comforting. I day-dreamed often of a time when my own work would be published and I would walk into an English version of 'El Chicken' to be hailed as an artist among artists by people whose work I admired and who had also read my own.

When I finally returned to London, it was a grave disappointment to discover that this intellectual café society did not exist. The thought of it had sustained me for many years on the *hacienda*.

Sometimes, because of accident, illness, floods, or the sheer workload of the estate, it was not possible for me to go to Caracas. Then Otto would come out to the *hacienda*. Unlike his brother José, who never stayed for more than a couple of days, Otto came out and stayed for several weeks. He was a great help in finding simple practical ways to solve problems. He was also the only person I could talk to about the bizarre nature of my marriage. Although Jaime had become far gentler in his ways, his rages had become increasingly violent and his actions correspondingly strange.

On one of my trips to Caracas, when Iseult was still a baby and I had taken her to be registered at the British Consulate there, Jaime had the roof removed from the Casa Grande. Fortunately, it was a whirlwind trip, and I returned to find only a quarter of the old tiles taken down. However, it meant that a long corridor and four rooms of the house were open to the elements. The tiles had all been thrown down and smashed. There were no competent roofers in the neighbourhood who could re-do the beautiful Spanish-colonial-style roof. For two years in the dry season, the sun beat down inside that skeleton part of the house. In the rainy season, I needed an umbrella to get from the halls to the sitting room. Other patches of market gardening were also arbitrarily ploughed up, and Antonio Moreno confessed to me that Jaime had called him aside and given him an order that was to countermand all subsequent ones.

'He said, if I ever tell you to chop down the avocado groves, you are not to do it, do you understand? Today, I'm giving you the definitive order on that, no matter what else, I say, don't touch the avocados.'

I could see that Antonio was torn by disloyalty at having relayed this conversation. I supposed he wanted me to know that *el padrón* was not entirely sane. But I was living with him. I knew that, subconsciously I had known it for some time.

24

Many thousands of acres of the Hacienda Santa Rita were gentle hill slopes unused for anything. Beyond the crest, there was a wide valley, almost as fertile as the valley of the Momboy but used for nothing more than a few strips of subsistence crops by the families who lived on that side. Further down towards the plains, Ceibu cattle were farmed, but the *hacienda* was not suitable for cattle, it was too hot for European cattle and too cold for the Ceibu. Antonio Moreno kept a couple and used them for milk, eating the yearly calf, but ours was not cattle-farming land.

I had, since my arrival, been trying to broach the possibility of sheep, but sheep were unknown. Luis Daniel was enthusiastic about the idea of pioneering sheep on the *hacienda*. Joanna sent me a number of books on the subject, and Luis Daniel did some research to see where the stock could be found. He discovered that a gift of prize-winning sheep had been given by the Argentinian government to the Venezuelan government, who in their wisdom had had them flown to an experimental farming station above Merida, the capital of the high Andes. Several of the prize rams had instantly died of heart attacks in the high altitude. During the next few weeks, most of the flock had followed suit. Apparently there were no more than a handful left, and Luis Daniel, by pulling strings, secured a stud Corriedale and a stud Suffolk ram to start my own experimental project.

A derelict peasant's hut was restored, a pen built complete with a dipping trough and the two rams were driven to Santa Rita. Almost simultaneously, another cousin, who was a big cattle farmer, offered me a shipment of 400 Romney Marsh sheep. He had thought of introducing them on his own *hacienda*. I asked him what had made him change his mind and he shrugged and said, 'The Labastida'.

These sheep had been shipped, at great expense, from Australia, travelled half-way round the world and then been held to ransom at the customs in La Guaira. They were, he assured me, a present. His trucks would deliver them straight from the docks. His truck drivers were used to transporting cattle, they were not used to sheep. The animals had been crammed into far too tight a space and over a hundred of them died of suffocation *en route*. The rest arrived in an extremely sorry state, reeking of urine, covered in droppings and hardly able to stand up. Together with the Romney Marshes, 140 Red African sheep had been thrown in. They had coped far better with their journey and were the only ones to walk off the lorries unassisted, kicking their way free like red goats.

Antonio Moreno had picked the boy called El Mudo to shepherd them. On his first day, he lost two-thirds of them and we had to call out the entire workforce to get the wandering flock back. During the intervening month of convalescence, when the seasick sheep had been kept in their pens, El Mudo developed an affinity for sheep. Two more small boys were chosen to help, and the near hills of the *hacienda* were cropped by the grazing flock. We grew marrows to supplement their diet, bought a machine to grate them, bought mineral salt licks and vast quantities of vitamins which I injected them with once a week. They were dipped, vaccinated and fed, and gradually, they regained the semblance of a reasonable flock.

Most of the workforce found the smell of the sheep offensive and the idea of tending them demeaning. Unless there was a dire emergency, they refused point-blank to help with them in any way. They said, as they had about mending my roof, removing snakes from the house and taking vitamin supplements, 'We would do anything for you, Doña, but not *that*.'

The work devolved to me and the children. It was made easier by the biannual appearance of a roving Italian vet called Dr Bertoloni. Dr Bertoloni had lived in Venezuela for over forty years. He spent most of his time in Los Llanos on the Orinoco plain. Twice a year he made forays into the Andes. He had no family, and no home, no ties other than his work and no fixed address. He had heard in Valera that I was farming sheep and came up to investigate. He had a gentle reticence, a self-deprecatory manner and endless patience. He tended not only my dogs, cats, birds, cows, chickens, ducks and sheep, but also the dogs, rabbits, guinea pigs and pigs that the peasants brought down for him to see. He was the vet, and I his willing assistant. Together, we examined and treated the animals while he explained to me their various ailments. If any animal died on the *hacienda*, it was always kept for twenty-four hours for Dr Bertoloni, in case he chanced by. On the rare occasions when his visits coincided with a carcass he performed autopsies out in the shade of the orchard. He was painstaking in his work, and timed his visits by the amount of sick or injured animals he needed to see. Only after the last of his patients had been dealt with would he come inside for a cup of coffee. Then, on the old cathedral bench, with its carved back, he would conjure up the only memories of Europe he allowed himself to recall.

I never knew his first name, he said it hurt him to hear it, it was part of the past he had left behind him, 'If I let myself think of the past, I would find it hard to carry on. I would want to stop and have a family and a home again, and then what would become of all my *haciendas*? This is the life I have chosen. I am nobody. I am the travelling vet. I am Dr Bertoloni.'

'Don't you miss it, though? Don't you ever want to go back?' I asked him.

He closed his clear blue eyes and shook his head. 'I have no one to go back to, my family is dead.'

'I miss so many things here, sometimes. Don't you really miss anything?'

'The soft fruits,' he said, hardly pausing to think. He ran through a list of four or five, then stopped.

'And gooseberries?' I asked.

He nodded, smiling slowly as though savouring their tang.

'And greengages.'

'Blackcurrants.'

'Raspberries.'

'Apricots.'

'Blackberries.'

'Plums.'

We alternated through all the soft fruits unobtainable and unheard of in the tropics. After every visit, the communion of the soft fruits was repeated. He took a sensual pleasure in the litany and I fuelled his excitement, prolonging the lists for as long as I could to keep him there with me. The soft fruits brought back my childhood, lifting, temporarily, the responsibilities that usually sat like a millstone round my neck. Yet more than that, they brought me close to this man I had come to love.

He never shook hands because, he said, his hands spent half their time up the backside of a cow. Unprompted, he never spoke of anything other than his work, our conversations were of disease and death. His advice was about sulphur and pig's grease for mange, paraffin and milk for the sheep's bloat, tetramycin for eye infections, saline washes for infections and arnica for broken bones.

He never asked me about myself except to ask if I was lonely on the *hacienda* on my own. Dr Bertoloni had a sadness in his eyes that I found almost unbearable. I sensed that he didn't want me to be lonely, that he really cared. So I lied. And when I asked him if he was lonely, out on the plains, he told me that no one could feel lonely once they had been part of life, once they had loved and made contact and I knew that part of that too was lies. I thought of our lists of soft fruits as surrogate sex and each new name as a caress.

For weeks after he left, I fantasised wildly about Bertoloni, the man I had never touched even to shake hands with. I waited impatiently for the months to pass and for him to return. Once my excitement over his latest reappearance subsided, I chided myself for my absurd imaginings. Apart from the soft fruits, what evidence had I of any kind of reciprocity from this mysterious man who wouldn't even tell me his name? I clung to the only two straws I had: the soft fruits and the fact that every time he left me, there were tears in his sad blue eyes.

The *comadre* Matilde told me he couldn't be much of a vet

because vets were rich and Dr Bertoloni's Jeep was battered and his trousers threadbare. From the way he refused to charge anything to *la gente* for treating their animals, I knew that he wasn't in it for the money. He had a vocation. Matilde was not impressed.

'Didn't he charge Antonio Moreno when he treated his cow for mastitis?'

I shook my head; Matilde was shocked, 'But Antonio could afford it!'

I shrugged. Matilde pulled her rosary out of her black apron pocket and began muttering under her breath. Not to make money when you could, was wasteful, and Matilde hated waste.

When a Corriedale ewe was brought from Merida and introduced anthrax into my flock in the second year of its flourishing, Dr Bertoloni arrived and stayed for three days, working through the first two nights with me, injecting and nursing the creaking flock. Anthrax feels like crushed glass under the skin. In an autopsy, the anthrax-diseased tissue is bubbly. After forty hours of continuous work, it looked as though some of the infected sheep could be saved and we were both too exhausted to do any more. He took a shower in the sunken bathroom usually reserved for Matilde and the girls and then refused to sleep anywhere other than across the seat of his Jeep. He slept for four hours and then recommenced, injecting and bottle-feeding the dying sheep. At the end of the day, after eating his first proper meal, he told me that I knew the treatment now and he had to move on. Antonio and the workers burnt up the piles of dead sheep, filling the air with the acrid smell of burnt wool and meat. I lost nearly half my flock to anthrax, slipping back from 740 to the original 400 sheep. The hybrid Romney Marshes and Afrikaners were the strongest and survived the epidemic best.

Whenever the servants were all out of the house, which combination was rare and hard to achieve, I showered in the sunken bathroom where Dr Bertoloni had showered. The gruesome circumstances of our forty hours of toil faded quickly to a fond memory of our prolonged proximity, and the memory and taste of all soft fruits have retained, for me, an erotic quality charged permanently with a yearning, not for Europe, but for Venezuela, where they do not grow.

The only thing that travelled round the *hacienda* faster than news was infection. Whatever infection was going, Iseult would get it. She spent so much time on an insulin drip that I bought my own, complete with stand, and kept one room permanently equipped as a sick room. Ever since her first bout of amoebiasis, the entire house was sluiced daily with disinfectant. Her clothes and bedding were boiled and sterilised, as were her plates, cups and spoons. Amoebiasis, in its chronic form, was endemic on the *hacienda*. It killed when it was acute. When it wasn't her guts, it was her lungs and when it wasn't either, it was her throat. She lived in a chain of fevers, ice-packs, alcohol rubs and febrifuges. In another room, at the other end of the house, local children could stay and have their ailments treated, their wounds dressed, their fevers lowered and their parasites purged. Ever since the death of the green boy, the collective faith in the local witch-doctor had waned. With my supply of antibiotics, my vade-mecum on how to use them and my stock of aspirin, I no longer had to ask the children to come to me, they came by themselves, or, when too sick to walk, their mothers brought them.

Ramón Rivas, the builder, was the first to do so. His youngest child had bronchitis and a high fever. Having lost one son to the callous neglect of the hospital, he brought the two-year-old baby to me. The baby was naturally feverish and not actually as ill as he seemed (or Ramón and his wife thought). The treatment was working by the next day. Ramón hailed it as a miracle and showed his gratitude in every way he could (except mending my roof). After Ramón's baby, the precedent was set and Mary, Matilde and I ran a part-time cottage hospital. The only child to die there was a month-old baby with diphtheria whom I treated in the little house at the *trapiche* because of the risk of infection, and who was brought too late for the anti-diphtheria drip to save him. I know that had I stayed longer, I would inevitably have had more children die in my care. It was a contingency I dreaded.

There were always cases that I couldn't treat and took, from the beginning to the hospital. Snake bites, hands mangled by machinery, stab wounds, severe burns, internal injuries and any cuts needing more than superficial stitching. *La gente* hated going to the hospital and always tried to avoid it. I was often called out in the night to traipse through the *hacienda* in the dark to a hut where someone needed surgery and not my glorified first aid.

When Abigail, the most malicious gossip on the estate had her head cut open and one arm nearly severed with an axe, her sons called me out to stitch her up and needed a lot of convincing to believe that it was beyond my powers. Abigail was so unpopular, they thought I was siding with her would-be murderer when I refused to tackle the job. I once had a shouting match with a woman whose womb had prolapsed. She came to the Casa Grande late at night and insisted that I put it back for her. The more I told her I couldn't the more she wheedled that I had to try.

June

Torrential rains. I am so wet my hand sticks to the paper, hence the scrawl. I have been since six this morning attending to Flora who is giving birth – 3 still-born puppies, one more to go. And our newly bought cow, Daisy and her three-month-old calf, Molly, and trying to organise a stall for the latter who is not used to such rains as these. She is very pretty pure-bred Pardo Suizo – those grey-brown cows one sees all over France and Switzerland. Another thing to bring: cheap roll-up plastic macs. 1: ten-year-old size. 2: 3 medium sized. 3 Large for Matilde our fat cook. 1lb soya beans (dried) to sow here.

Book or pamphlet or if not available, copy me some recipes on how to make cheese.

Lots of love, Joanna, from Lizzie

Hacienda Santa Rita,
Mendoza Fría
June 1974

Dear Joanna,

How are you? I received another letter yesterday – thank you. All is well here. We are happy together. I am writing again.

The new agricultural laws are good but hitting us very hard. Neighbours are already selling their estates. We are thinking of market gardening on a large scale.

Iseult has a happy time roaming around the gardens, picking flowers and chasing ducks.

I shall meet your plane in Caracas, with or without Iseult. We shall spend an afternoon and night in Caracas and then go together by plane to Valera. We can see Caracas on the way back.

293

Medical Column

Please: find out what, if anything can be done about
'PAPERAS' MUMPS LUMPS in the neck. I believe it is a lack of
iodine. Is there any cure (other than operation) or treatment to stop its growth?

Please: what is the latest on PARKINSON'S DISEASE? A friend
of mine who has it has heard of a cure in USA or
England – pills, weird remedies, 'Miss Lourdes' to heal
the sick.

More comprehensive book on first aid would be very
useful for the house.

I have taken to playing chess.

Put the dogs' Pedigrees in the case you are bringing –
for God's sake don't forget them.

Remember that clothes are cheaply made up here if
you want to have dresses or shirts made up here, bring
material, or buy it here (it's not *very* crumby).

Iseult now has chronic tonsillitis. By the way, she has
gained no weight since February despite the fact she eats
well and takes quantities of vitamins and vit B complex.
No amoebae appear in tests. Do you think she still has
amoebiasis?

Joanna came out to Venezuela in the summer of 1974 for
two months. She and I and Iseult spent a few days at Playa
Azul, a Caribbean resort for the super-rich. Doña Antonieta,
my mother-in-law, had a sister, Maritza, who took me under
her wing. On request, she put her chauffeur-driven limousine
at my disposal when in Caracas, offered me the run of her
villa (complete with library) and lent us her apartment at
Playa Azul. If one ignored the barbed wire and concrete

boundaries on either side of its white beach, and the armed guards who patrolled them to keep mere humans away from the privileged élite, Playa Azul was a tropical paradise.

The rest of Joanna's stay was spent immersed in the *hacienda*. She loved the Casa Grande and its grounds and took an instant liking to Mary and the girls. Matilde was fascinated by her inability to speak Spanish, as were Alba and Lorena, who wanted to know if it was because she had been dropped on her head as a baby. Every time Joanna said anything and I translated it with a 'Doña Joanna says . . .', they looked at me askance and said, 'But how do you know that?'

'Because she just told me so.'

'But she didn't say anything, we heard her, she just makes noises.'

Despite the language barrier, she and Luis Daniel got on famously. Joanna had learnt enough Spanish to scrape by, but her accent meant that the girls understood absolutely nothing she said. Alba persisted with the head-drop theory.

Luis Daniel claimed that it was the peasants' revenge to drop all the rich babies they were minding on their heads, thus addling their brains and getting their own back for the disparity between the rich and the poor.

'Look around you,' he insisted. 'Look at Valera, at the Cañada.'

Once translated, Joanna began to worry for Iseult's brain and urged me not to let Alba, an undersized eight-year-old carry her grandchild around lest she too got dropped intentionally on her skull.

The two months went smoothly and were marred only near the end by a lapse and a forest fire. It had always been the way of the Indians to slash and burn to make clearings to plant corn. The habit seemed to be instinctive, because the workers did it all the time on the hills, regardless of the state of drought, wind or fire-breaks. As a result, vegetable plots were set alight and annually burnt down great swathes of the *hacienda.* The fires burnt themselves out in horseshoes of embers, leaving black scars in the green.

I took Joanna to my favourite rift in the valley where orange trees grew high and wild and bluebirds nested in their branches. We clambered through ferns so exotic they seemed to come from the Palm House at Kew. We took picnics into the hills and sat (on her gaberdine squares) in the pink-tasselled grass, admiring from above the canary yellow wigs of the Araguaney acacias in full flower. We gathered armfuls of wild flowers which withered in the hot sun of our walk back. We talked. She was happy that I was writing and I was happy that she was there. The presence of Luis Daniel, and the visits of Otto and José reassured her, as did Matilde's expert running of the house. She discussed coming out to live with me permanently, meanwhile, she promised to return for Christmas. She returned to London on 1 September.

Letter I
Hacienda Santa Rita
September 15th

Dear Joanna,

At last I write to you, tell you the saga of from then till now. A really bad flu in Caracas. Hardly able to work at all (all coming over like a news bulletin, but . . .) Then back here. Planning Iseult's and my trip to London and then (to continue my saga) J. turned savage. Then got incredibly jealous of everybody near me and then Ross was run over and killed and J. went right out of his mind.

Things were really desperate. Ravings and rantings and

terrible bursts of savageness, striking out verbally and physically.

Things went back to normal the day before yesterday.

We have planted about 30 more avocados in lanes since you were here.

I still have not machined the curtains, but I shall, now the storm is over.

My book has been definitely accepted by Juan Sanchez, head of publication of 'Monte Avila', but Otto did not have enough time to finish translations, so some Eng. Prof is going to finish. I don't even know him as yet, but I shall do soon.

We miss you a lot here.

I have already bought a pair of turkeys for Christmas and am looking out for a Christmas tree. All depends on how J. manages these next few months. If all is well, I shall go in Feb/March/April. I do not know as yet.

How was your flight?

Do write, I have heard nothing from you since you left. Poor Ross.

My love to everyone, especially my sisters and Jonah. Keep well, and happy, we shall see each other again soon.

   Lots of love,
     Lizzie

Joanna was very fond of Jaime. Although she often found his behaviour bizarre, I had managed to disguise from her his recurrent bouts of insanity. This was something I needed to do less after her visit, because one occurred before her eyes and illustrated the unhappy state of his mind.

The first lamb to be born on Santa Rita was a cross-bred Suffolk and Afrikaner. We called him Rudi, and because his mother rejected him, we had to rear him by hand. He had his father's woolly coat and his mother's red colouring. Rudi became the family pet. Matilde, in particular, who had thoroughly disapproved of the sheep, doted on Rudi. Between us we bottle-fed him eight times a day and he grew into a sweet, cuddly, pig-headedly stubborn pet. Jaime always preferred animals to people. He loved the dogs, and he loved Rudi. When he got too big to live in the courtyard any more, we kept him in a pen and tethered him out to graze on better grass, moving him every two hours to keep him out of the sun. During Joanna's visit, Jaime had, conveniently, developed a kind of narcolepsy and slept in a hammock on the veranda for most of the day. If he stirred, he took it upon himself to re-tether Rudi.

One day, while Joanna, Iseult and I were eating lunch in the dining room, Jaime called me from the orchard. There was something desperate in his voice, 'Veta, Veta, Veta, Veta!'

Thinking he had had an accident, I ran out. With the tethering rope he was choking Rudi to death; as he did so, he was calling me. When I reached him, he said, 'Don't let me kill him. I'm killing him. Please don't let me kill him.'

But he couldn't let go of the rope. It took Joanna's, Matilde's and my combined strength to get the strangled ram free. Within seconds of releasing him, Jaime had no recollection of what had occurred.

Joanna was as upset by the incident as by the fact that both Matilde and I had obviously seen similar outbursts before.

For a while after she left for London, it seemed all right to talk about his violence. As it grew more extreme, over the years, it seemed best to keep it secret. Madness, like chronic illness, palls on bystanders after a while. There is a complex psychological process involved in the partly self-dug trap of domestic violence. Tyranny requires the partial consent of the victim. The more Jaime's violence turned on me, the more I covered it up. There was no question of getting any kind of medical help: he refused to recognise that there was anything wrong with him. If something died, then he hadn't killed it. If someone was hurt, then he hadn't done it. *He* was sane, and *I* was the one who was mad. He reminded me of his cousin Rosario Terán who had been forcibly dragged into a mental home after a year in the stocks. He could do the same to me, if he chose, he told me. Wives were chattels in the Andes and wives were chattels to the Teráns.

24 Oct '74

How is winter this year? Here it is the same old thing. I have learnt to drive, also Kung Fu classes with the twins in Valera. Sugar prices are down again: 17 Bs (1.80) for 24 kilos. All other food prices soaring.

16th Nov '74

Dear Joanna,

Jaime is *fine* now, has been for more than a month. I have been unwell of late, the same pains as in Playa Azul, weakness in my arm. I am under Dr Ceballo, he seems to think it is muscular distrophy – I hope he's wrong. Next week I'm going to Caracas to see a neurologist and a traumatologist? because I feel rotten and more rotten thinking I may have such an unwholesome disease. I can hardly lift Iseult any more or open a jar with my right hand. It is my right arm that is worse. It might just be the result of a fall or something like that. My book, by the way, seems to be forgotten. When I get to Caracas I shall reorganise things.

Lots of love, Lizzie

Joanna couldn't come out for Christmas, so the two scraggy turkeys lived on in the poultry pen. Benito spent his Noche Buena unhinderedly drunk, and the Comadre and I made perfect *ayacas* which we then shared out for all the girls and herself to take home.

29th Dec, Caracas

Dearest Jo,

I feel a little better and am in good care here in Caracas. I commute weekly for my appointments, tests etc. So far, an abnormal EEG – not epilepsy. It seems to be a minor cerebral lesion which accounts for nauseas, dizziness, fainting etc. Send me a list of things you want because I have practically *no* memory at the moment, for above reasons.

My neck had been impacted by four centimetres, pressing the vertebrae down. It was stretched back. I returned to my normal height. The 'accident' to my neck, caused by a monumental blow to the top of my head, gave me an excuse to travel. After I recovered, I was careful not to be in a position to receive quite such damaging blows again. And life went on, turning on the wheel of the *trapiche*. All around us, the neighbouring sugar estates were going out of business. Sugar prices plummeted down. By 1975, of the fifteen sugar plantations that had been operating in the neighbourhood when I arrived, only three were left in production. There was an influx of dispossessed and unemployed estate workers who drifted into the slums of Valera and sometimes, further afield, to Caracas, where, they said in the shanty town of Valera, that the streets were paved with gold. So the massive shanty town of Caracas, with its cardboard and corrugated-iron *ranchitos*, swelled as well. Every time the rains came in Caracas, they washed these slums down into its valley, then, every year, the dispossessed workers built them up again.

I began to take in work translating to help make ends meet.

Hacienda Santa Rita
2 June 1975

Dear J,

What can I say on these days that only repeat themselves? No news but the old news. No, I am not depressed, just somehow not quite here. When are you coming? For how long? For good? The latter I hope.

I hope you do not decide that you could not bear 'those awful ranchitos'. Only the ostrich bears nothing but the weight of the sand . . . Please write lengthily and copiously about all and sundry but most of all about your dear self much missed here. Goodbye, love from Lizzie, Iseult, Jaime, Animals, Relations, Mary, Matilde and Alba

25

DURING THE RAINY season, the valley of the Momboy was the greenest valley I had ever known. Not only the hills and the terraces and the fields were green. The paths and ditches overgrew with rampant goose-grass and tangles of morning glory and an orange flowering bindweed that grew so fast and tied such knots that it seemed to possess supernatural powers. During the rains, the tin roofs of all the huts and the tiled roofs of all the houses were also green, slimed over with a kind of pondweed that thrived on their permanently wet surfaces until it was burnt off by the dry hot summer to come. And every object in and out of every house gathered a fine coating of mildew.

The mornings were misty. At five o'clock, I drank coffee with Antonio Moreno, Abrán and Matilde, wiping the mildew from the cups and spoons, from the lid of the damp sugar bowl in which hacked pieces of hard brown *papelón* oozed into the bottom like melting toffee. Then I wiped the mildew from the high boots I had taken to wearing as a protection against the snakes and another day began. We used to light the oven and open its door, keeping Iseult near its source of warmth, bundled up in woollens against the early morning cold. Newborn lambs were also brought in, wrapped in wool and placed on the shelf the open door made to resuscitate them if they were unlucky enough to be born on the chill winter mornings when the mist covered the valley and sat in pockets like low clouds on the hills. The sun rose over the crest of the range at ten-thirty, and steamed or baked the valley, depending on the time of the year.

Antonio Moreno's battered straw hat was green with mould, as was my own. The rainy season was interminably long, filled with the monotony of dripping water, like Chinese torture. The floor of the rooms where the roof was missing and the tiles of the corridor in front of it were also a slippery green. Mopped daily, they ignored the brown, pungent creosote used to clean them, and kept their natural burnt terracotta colour only for a matter of hours after the milky mixture had been swabbed across them. Then they reverted to slime, to green, to the repeated avowal of the rampant fertility of the foot-hills of the Andes. Things grew with indecent haste. When illness kept me away from the fields, weeds stole them, balancing up the young trunks, entwining with the tenacity of vines, choking and smothering young trees until all that was left of the new orchards was a billowing sea of green. It was the sheep and the avocados that suffered most during my absences. The sugar-cane and the market gardening were second nature to Antonio Moreno, the other two crops were new. Antonio José, though an excellent avocado grafter, pruner and planter, was easily disheartened. Once the weeds got past a certain point on any given patch (which they could do in a matter of days), he resigned himself to defeat, as though it was in his genes to accept that no man could battle against nature and win.

It was in 'winter' that death took its highest tithe on the

hacienda, culling the old and the very young and sending them with the hired tin chalices and the hired church candles to the burial plot in Mendoza Fría. A cart collapsed under its weight of picked avocados and a spoke impaled old Molinas, the man who lived in a shed next to the stables. He never recovered, and died shortly afterwards. The old goat-herd, Natividad, wheezed his way through his last season of rains, living on a quarter of a lung, wheezing in the damp air of the *hacienda* as though anxious to take it with him to his grave. Then Josefa, his graceful wife, followed him only days afterwards. A son of Abigail's was stabbed to death in a drunken brawl. La Ciega (the blind man who kept the biggest still, who was the richest man on the *hacienda* and lent money to all the other workers, keeping a tally on a notched stick and charging gossip as interest) lost a son run over on the road.

A generation of older Terán cousins died in rapid succession and their elaborate funerals became, for a while, the focus of all social life.

It seemed, in May, that everyone bloated on hot chocolate. May was the cruellest month on the *hacienda*. An unhealthy miasma, escorted in by flies, induced a general sickness known as La Mayera. Doctors could never diagnose precisely what the Mayera was. It seemed to be a combination of all the valley's ills. It took its toll.

The government continued to subsidise the imported white sugar, bringing the native sugar farmers to their knees. Even those who changed their factories or sent their cane to be processed at La Central, the main sugar plant beyond Valera, could make no profit. Foreign sugar was cheaper. Mile upon mile of cane-fields on neighbouring estates were left to revert to scrub. By 1977, Santa Rita was the last *trapiche* to be in use. For a few heady months, it sent the price of *panela* sugar back up. *Panela* had rarity value and lorries came to buy our output at the *trapiche* itself, eliminating the need to sell to the middle-man, forcing him to come to us to haggle on our terms.

From 1976 to 1977 there was drought. There had been minor droughts before, if the rains started late, the hillsides parched and the valley died back, clearing the cane-fields of their weeds of their own accord, crisping the entwining climbers as though with a blowtorch, leaving the noble cane to stand alone. The River Momboy dwindled regularly, and arcs of fire lit up the hills.

La Ciega and the other illicit distillers of rot-gut rum were often to blame for these fires. The natural charcoal from the burnt woods was the fuel they used to run their stills. When it ran short, they made their own, setting fire to a slope and then watching helplessly while it spread and engulfed the surrounding land.

Antonio Moreno set up a band of fire-fighters to beat and hack belts of land to deaden the fire when it reached them. The longer the dry season lasted, the worse were the fires. The beautiful landscape spiked by frangipani trees and shaded by ancient, spreading jacarandas was, intermittently, burnt to cinders. The fires increased at such a rate, that where once the rainy season had greened over the scars, now they stayed as grey, ashen testaments to the changing times.

With the drought, the *hacienda* was brought to the brink of ruin. It lasted for fifteen months. It took half the new avocado groves; it scorched the near grazing for the sheep, forcing El Mudo to take them further and further into the hinterland of the *hacienda*; it made the cane suffer, lowering the normally high sugar content of the Campo Brasil cane that had always thrived on the *hacienda*. We planted stronger, drought-resistant varieties like Cluston with a higher yield of sugar, we increased the irrigation ditches fed by the dwindling streams. We worked flat out and left no more than scratch marks in the parched soil. My garden died back once and for all to a handful of mature shrubs, the trees, the aromatic Malagueta and a trellis of climbing plants.

The *comadre* Matilde was convinced that the end was nigh, and carried out her chores nodding her head sagely with a grim smile holding her loose purple lips closed over the commentary of muttering that otherwise escaped them. This was the disaster she had prophesied. This was the calamity no one had believed in. She showed me, almost gloatingly, how the weevils had finally powdered our store of food. Molly, our second cow, who had never fully acclimatised, keeled over in the heat and died. Within minutes, Antonio Moreno and the men had chopped her into buckets and made off for the hills to feast on her meat. In the Casa Grande, we lived off lamb and avocados and the stewed pink-grey bananas so dear to Matilde's heart.

Jaime's sleeping sickness passed after nearly two years of almost constant slumber. He had risen to drive into town. It had been, in many ways, the calmest period of our marriage. When he awoke, it was with a vengeance. Luis Daniel announced that he would be moving prematurely into his unfinished house. He said, 'Look, you married the man and that's a cross you have to bear, but I didn't marry him and I have a weak heart, all the Teráns do, I can't be eating my *arepitas* and avocados when he bursts in like Count Dracula on one of his rampages. It does terrible things to my digestion. I'll have a heart attack if I have to live in such proximity to his rages. And then, you know, madness is contagious. If you live with it, it gets to you. You're dealing with a Terán here. The Teráns had Arturo Lino. He was a psychopath, he used to kill for fun. He decimated the valley of the Momboy at the turn of the century. He wiped out entire families. He murdered literally dozens of people until they finally had to lock him away. When the list of his crimes was read to him in the court, and I tell you, the list was long, the judge said, 'How do you plead: guilty, or not guilty?' Arturo Lino said, 'I am an eagle.' They locked him up in an asylum. *'That'*, Luis Daniel said, setting his mouth, 'is the kind of material we have in our genes.'

I had heard this story before. I was stunned more by Luis Daniel's leaving than by its repetition. Benito Mendoza had been the boy-servant of Don Arturo Lino towards the end. He had told me more than I needed to know about his master's lunacy. The presence of Luis Daniel made me feel safe. He imbued the household with a semblance of normality by the sheer force of his extraordinary character and his biting wit.

It was during the drought that two of the shepherd boys brought me down a present of a pair of harpy eaglets in a sack. They were so proud of their nest-robbing. They couldn't understand my anger at their desecration. Eagles were rare on the *hacienda*.

'But we brought them for you, Doña. They're a present.' I forced the boys to take them back with me and we scoured the hill where they said they had found them until nightfall sent us home. There was no sign of a nest. They bickered endlessly between themselves as to where exactly it had been. They offered to return at dawn the next day to try again. Meanwhile, I kept the eaglets in a small room and fed them minced raw meat which they shook out of their mouths indignantly. Each bird was the size of a harris hawk. Their talons and beaks, despite their relative youth, were vicious enough for me to have to use a leather glove to tend them.

No nest was found and the eaglets stayed. They began to eat regularly from my hand, to drink water and to take more interest in their surroundings. I moved them to a larger, lighter room, reconstructed a big nest of twigs for them and prayed that Dr Bertoloni would arrive to guide me in their rearing. It was five months, at least, since his last visit, so he was due daily. The eaglets grew at an alarming rate; they eyed me with continuous dislike, or so it seemed. I took to spending all the hours I could with them, coaxing and calming the ruffled outrage they never ceased to show. They were consistently suspicious. They began to walk around their room, exploring the terracotta floor, worrying twigs, and protesting noisily when they felt their food was late. They were tyrannical and I was their willing slave. They still had some of their fluffy baby plumage when they arrived, and this they shed for fine strong feathers. I took them out into the courtyard and tried to get them to move about, hoping to help them to fly. For a few days, they seemed excited by the change, but then they took to slinking under the hibiscus bush and huddling miserably there until I took them back to their room.

Much as I loved both the idea of the eagles and the eagles themselves, our relationship was utterly one-sided. They suffered me to hood and hold them, to stroke their fine plumage and to feed them by hand; beyond that, they showed a haughty indifference to my existence. Worse than this, they pined. They began to lose weight, I varied their diet, feeding them all the kinds of meat I could find, allowing Alba to indulge in her chicken-killing hobby, culling the ducks, the feather-brained guinea-fowl, rabbits, even guinea-pigs begged from Coromoto's stock.

'But they're for fevers,' she complained.

'The eagles have a fever,' I lied.

'But I don't know if that would be right, Doña, *qué dirán* if you feed one of my guinea-pigs to those things?'

In the end, she relented, I could wheedle virtually anything out of Coromoto just as she could from me; we were the pioneers, the earliest allies and she never lost her post as guide and mentor, although her advice was no longer needed or useful most of the time. The years were long but so was my memory, and her help in the early days outweighed any amount of subsequent sulkiness or racalcitrance. Her friendship with Mary had made her life happier by far, and between them, they bustled around the Niña Iseult as they called her, teaching her to ask my blessing with her hands folded in prayer and to curtsey to me in a quick bob as they did to their own parents. They taught her to call me Señora when I called her rather than Mama. They taught her to address her father as Don Jaime, which she did, bypassing entirely the use of the word Papa. On the rare occasions when Don Jaime surfaced and remembered his child, they knew to stick to her like lice if he took her out for a walk, lest he have one of his turns while with her. They had a natural tact. They knew how to cover up for their employer as well or better than me. They felt no embarrassment when they lied to his friends and family and swore he was away when he had actually locked himself in his rooms for days, weeks, and sometimes months at a time. They never mentioned the fact that he climbed in and out of his suite by means of a ladder through the window rather than by the marble staircase and the door. They never commented on his sudden rages or made use of the things he said in them to use against me. They put flowers with me on the graves that Benito dug for the animals which fell foul of his temper, and when other children asked what had happened to them or to any other injured member of the household, they insisted loyally that 'se cayó' they had fallen down. There was a lot of falling down in the Casa Grande.

The last two years of my time on Santa Rita were a time of retrenching, of drawing real and imaginary demarcation lines. Otto continued to visit once or twice a year. He didn't understand why Jaime lived locked in his upstairs apartments and refused to see him, who used to be his best friend. When their paths did cross, Jaime kept his silence and Otto let it pass, as a transitory phase. There were times when they talked, but these were few and far between. By the last two years, Jaime was marginally more aware of whatever was controlling his mind. He warned me that if anyone tried to penetrate his space, he would destroy them. Sometimes, when the house was empty, he sought me out and confided his plans to prune the family back to its one-time strength. Iseult and I and he himself were last on the list of limbs to be cut off the noble rootstock.

He had always been fascinated by the life and work of Napoleon Bonaparte. He read biographies of him avidly. He didn't, he said, want any help from doctors, he didn't need doctors, he needed time. I listened to his plans and when his mind wandered, he reverted to the man I knew again if we talked about the avocado pears and his and my plans for them. I felt sorry for him and afraid of him. I played out our unusual relationship by ear. On the few occasions that he wanted me, I was there: the keeper of a tenuous peace. If he left, I breathed more easily. When he returned, I was reminded of Jane Eyre.

It was a big house, big enough for someone to lock himself away in. Big enough to hide innumerable eccentricities. It was easier to keep the peace in the house than on the farm. The drought brought a general state of unease to the *hacienda*. There was change in the air. Antonio Moreno kept the threads of the workforce in his hand, but he held them there uneasily. Each time Jaime had one of his 'turns' in front of the men, it became harder to keep the *hacienda* running along the lines it had always run on before. Wages had doubled but so had the price of food. There were many bonuses but these were regulated by the pressure of neighbouring landlords, who claimed that Santa Rita was augmenting the general state of discontent. It was a valley of powerful overlords. Both Luis Daniel and Antonio Moreno warned me about overstepping the mark. It was a neighbourhood of vendettas. Workers who suffered 'accidents' in the avocado groves or around the Casa Grande were sometimes reluctant to cover them up. They too began to long for justice and revenge. Some heavy bribery was used to buy their silence. Several families were placated only by being set up in Mendoza or Valera with other work, housing and a handout. This mini exodus upset the fabric of Santa Rita, families who had lived in its hills for generations left gaps as obvious as the scars of the forest fires.

A domestic pattern evolved whereby when *el padrón* was in residence Mary and the girls were sent away. When he left, they returned. The house was full of doors into the grounds, and these Charlie Chaplinesque exits were easy to engineer. Notwithstanding, there were a few mishaps and a bout of general falling down. Given their age and vulnerability, their past loyalty and the deep affection I had for Mary, Alba and Lorena, it seemed only fair to let them go rather than make them bear the brunt of a situation that, ultimately, wasn't or shouldn't be their problem. It was a very sad parting for all concerned. Iseult was lost without them, and so was I.

Mary's widowed mother had found employment at Los

Pollos de Eladio at its new location outside Valera. She had found ways of sending brown paper bags of chicken necks and gizzards to her three daughters. They used to sit with Coromoto on the steps overlooking the road and eat trails of greasy intestines, necks and feet from the bag with their fingers, joined often by Goyo. They could make a bag last for hours. Although Iseult was five when she left the *hacienda*, she has no memory of it at all. She remembers no one and nothing but sitting on some steps and sucking parts of the chicken she now disdains to eat.

The drought laid waste the *hacienda*, which never fully recovered from its attack. As though to mark time to its dying, the big house grew steadily more desolate. Hope is a weed. It grows out of nowhere, it flourishes on the most barren places. I am, by nature, an optimist; some people say mindlessly so. There, on Santa Rita, I clung to hope, I spoonfed it, coaxed and cajoled it as I did my pets and sheep and trees. I built my house on its grains of rock, magnifying them. I found a way to see light in the dark tunnels of that desolation.

Joanna had been planning to move to Venezuela, to live with us in the Casa Grande. She had no real idea of what the state of play was with Jaime. He was strange, taciturn, and often distant on her continued visits. She grew used to his not being there. We were happiest on our own. I persuaded myself that between us we could carve out a decent life for ourselves and Iseult, keep the *hacienda* running and cure the loneliness and depression that we both suffered from with an ocean and a mountain range between us. Together, life would be better. She was very excited about leaving England and coming out. Sometimes it seemed in itself a madness, but I hadn't the heart to tell her so and hope took the upper hand.

Luis Daniel had said that mental illness was contagious. I

succumbed: on the one hand, I began to organise my tactical retreat both from the *hacienda* and from Venezuela; on the other, I made plans for my mother's definitive coming. I told myself that this was the only thing to do, Joanna herself had always taught me that in life one needed 'both belt and braces'.

The eaglets were in my amateur care for three months. When they began to pine, I wrote to London Zoo to ask for help. It must have been one of the many letters that went astray because no advice came and the young eagles became crippled in their legs. They hobbled and then flopped around in their room. They ate and lost weight, I felt their thin bones through their feathers in my hands. They became too listless even to want to swipe out at me. I could have tended them ungloved and been none the worse for it by the time Dr Bertoloni finally came.

The drought had hit the entire country. He told me that the state of Trujillo where I lived had got off lightly. Down on the Orinoco plain entire herds of cattle had died of thirst. Hundreds of rivers had dried and died probably never to return. The country was permanently damaged. The short-sighted policy of clearing trees from the banks of the rivers and streams was greatly to blame. He had thought of me often, he said, and wondered how I was faring, but the needs of his *haciendas* on Los Llanos had never been so great. I showed him the eagles and he told me that they had vitaminosis. I should have given them whole meat. The mince I fed them was killing them by slow starvation. They needed bones and brains, eyes and guts. They would always be crippled, they would never fly. They would probably die anyway. They were suffering, and I should put them down. As though to prove his point, the smaller of the pair died in his hands.

He said, 'No time for greengages, Lisaveta, even the soft fruits have withered on their stalks this year,' and left.

I buried the dead eagle under one of the avocado trees in the orchard outside the Casa Grande. We buried all our dead pets there, covering the soil with heavy stones to stop the vultures from digging them up. It took me two more days to pluck up the courage to kill the other eagle. It seemed like such a terrible thing to do. Antonio or Benito or any of the other workers would have dispatched it without a qualm, but the eagles had been mine. It was I who had reared them, loved and unintentionally hurt them, and I felt it had to be me who killed the last surviving one. It seemed like sacrilege to kill an eagle: like murder.

Despite my faith in Dr Bertoloni, I hoped for a miracle in the intervening days. I sent Abrán to Valera to buy me ether at the chemist's and on the last night I sat up with the sick bird, cradling it guiltily in my arms.

The easiest way to kill it was to shoot it in the head. I had a Smith & Wesson in my bedroom, a present from the twins, which I had used to dispatch injured sheep. There is something impersonal about a gun: it allows you to kill without contact. I have never been able to kill anything with my bare hands. I am squeamish to a degree. When animals are in agony and obviously dying, I can speed their death; I did many times on Santa Rita. But the Andes was a land of guns: the rich all carried them. I had seen how men were shot in bars, shot in Valera, in Mendoza, in the street. It was a way of killing that encouraged a lack of remorse, you didn't have to feel anything, you just pulled the trigger and the deed was done. It was, I decided, too cowardly a way to put down an eagle. The next simplest way was to poison it, but again I felt that I had already been poisoning it for too long. I had to bear the responsibility for its death, to kill it painlessly and in such a way that I would always remember what I had done. I had come too easily and too young into too much power and I had to teach myself not to misuse it.

This idea was very strong in my mind at the time. My transition from schoolgirl to Doña had been brought home to me by a trifling incident that I found disturbing. A few days before, a stranger had come to the high gates of the courtyard of the Casa Grande. He had called to me across the yard. In Spanish there are formal and informal modes of address, the 'thou' and the formal 'you'. In the rest of Venezuela the 'thou' form, 'tu', is used almost universally, but in the Andes the 'thou' is never used except to animals. I would never have dreamt of addressing one of the peasants with 'tu', nor they me. I never used the 'tu' to Jaime, nor he to me, nor had he ever, even in England. Children addressed their parents formally, parents addressed their children formally; there was a structure of dignified address, the cornerstone of which was the formal 'you'. Given the social structure of the *hacienda*, it was inconceivable that anyone would ever address me as 'thou'. All this was very important as a way of getting by, but not intrinsic to me because I wasn't Andean, I was English and in English the distinction, or lack of it, doesn't exist.

Notwithstanding, when this stranger had come to my gate and called me across in his Maracucho accent with a casual, 'Come here, thou', I had felt deeply offended, so offended that the blood rushed to my face in anger and a pride that was none of my business had gripped me. By the time I had strode across the yard, the anger had given way to surprise, not so much at the address and the stranger but at my own reaction to it.

I soaked a wad of cottonwool in the ether and prepared, tearfully, to kill the eagle. Coromoto couldn't understand what all the fuss was about. One of the birds was already dead, the other had twisted legs and was never going to fly, and anyway, it was only a bird. I held the impregnated wad over the eagle's beak, covering the breathing holes and clamping the beak shut with my gloved hand. Before I did this, it had been limp and weak. At the threat of death, it clung tenaciously to life, developed a strength superior to my own and refused to slip into the painless sleep I had planned for it. I got a pillow and tried to smother it. It fought back and no matter how long I forced the pillow over its face, it wouldn't give in. Coromoto, watching from the doorway, suggested I wring its neck. It didn't seem right to do so, and was probably unwringable. The eagle was big. It was frantic and determined to fight. Coromoto brought me a knife to slit its throat. I had braced myself to murder it, but not to carry the memory of its actual blood on my hands for the rest of my life. Its yellow eyes stared defiantly into mine. It seemed to say, 'I am an eagle'. I kept remembering Dr Bertoloni, he had said that the bird was doomed to die. I had tortured it for months, the least I could do was put it out of its misery. The passion it showed in its last minutes was more than it or its dead sister had shown in the three months of their sojourn. I took it to a barrel of rainwater that sat in the courtyard catching the rain from the guttering and forced it in, holding it underwater, by the back of its neck, pressing down while it struggled up. I have no idea how long this actually took, it seemed to take a very long time; the eaglet lived long after it should have been dead. Its strength almost broke my own as I held it down, the king of the forest, in a barrel of slime.

26

DURING THE YEAR of 1977 we held some disastrous *moliendas*. The price of sugar was the lowest it had ever been in my time and the sugar itself was darkened by the drought. We tried to hold out for better prices, but the cane was growing past its prime and the ensuing sugar would have been blacker and blacker and nearly useless. We had five *moliendas* in a row that either just broke even or ran at a loss. The *hacienda* Santa Rita had been growing sugar since the middle of the nineteenth century, before that it had been a coffee zone, but for nearly a hundred and fifty years it had been under sugar-cane. Nothing had ever seriously stopped its production in all that time before. Earthquakes, floods, droughts, fires, cholera and war had all failed to do what Carlos Andrés Perez's short-sighted sugar policy had done. Despite the low prices, the buyers still came to the *trapiche* with their lorries and bought whatever sugar we produced. The ignominy of having to sell at a loss had hit Antonio Moreno and the other workers hard in their pride. The lorry drivers had been disrespectful, and we had had no choice but to put up with it. The decision to cease sugar production had been taken, gradually and reluctantly, many months before, but the cane that had already been planted would have run to seed and been wasted had it not been crushed. Although we made no profit at the factory, the *moliendas* did, at least, pay the workers. There was enough cane left in the fields for one more, giant *molienda*.

We decided to take our revenge on the buyers and middlemen, cut the cane, make the sugar and then refuse to sell it to them. We had very little to lose by doing this and a lot to gain. It was a way of saving face, of rebelling against the market and of having, if only for a few sweet weeks, the upper hand. No one must know that this was what we were doing, to which end the workers didn't know either. Secrets are things you tell not keep on the *hacienda*.

When the sugar was ready, it was dark, as we had expected. The buyers gathered round in their trucks and lorries, hovering like vultures for the kill. They looked at the sugar, criticised it, and offered their by now usual derisory sums. We turned them down. Once or twice every day they came back, offering first a lower and then a better price. If the sugar isn't sold and moved on within a certain time, it begins to melt. This was pointed out to us. I left all the negotiations to Antonio, to allow him the pleasure of playing with the price vultures after all his decades of toil. Word spread up and down the road that we had sugar and wouldn't sell it. They threatened never to come back and buy sugar from us again, they called Antonio every name under the sun from stupid to criminal. They insisted on going over his head. I was called out: did I know that Antonio was refusing to sell the sugar?

'Antonio Moreno is in charge,' I told them. 'He is the *capataz*.' The charade dragged on and on. By a stroke of good fortune, a load of *panela* sugar was needed for some big still up at Timotes. They were offering good money for our by now melting stock. Antonio shook his head. They came back with a better offer for 144 kilos of it. Antonio came to the big house and checked if we were sure, if we shouldn't maybe take the money and run: 'I learnt to swallow my pride a long time ago, you can take the money if we need it.'

We held out. It wasn't a great sum to be lost or won, it was a great principle, a moment of power for Antonio, a moment of elation for the workers who now all knew what we were up to. I had been saving money from the avocados and the green beans, I had been doing translations for Otto and Luis Daniel. We could afford to let the sugar melt and trickle into the mill-race and then the river, which it did eventually, thick with a cargo of ants, streaking the Momboy with treacle, giving it back its last offering from the sugar-cane that had grown on its alluvial plains for so long.

Dearest Joanna,

Forgive this long letterless time. I have been unbeliev-ably busy: have just got over tropical leprosy, am bookkeeping for the whole estate, sugar, avocados and market gardening, raising six puppies, hand-rearing four lambs (i.e. bottle feeding them eight bottles a day each) keeping the house together.

I enclose photo of Iseult standing in the corridor in front of the kitchen, in the background is Charlie, a very young monkey that was given to me, its mother had been killed. He is very sweet and affectionate when it suits him but still rather savage. Four days ago he ate through the cord that he has attached round his waist and has climbed up my beautiful trellis full of flowering climbers and is playing havoc with their last six months' growth. He comes down to drink milk and takes food when offered but is too quick for one to catch him.

Later.

I have caught the monkey and put him on his perch again. I have been reading *The War of the Salamanders*. Do read it.

Tell me your news,

Love Lizzie

After the sugar came to an end, there was less to do on the *hacienda*. It was as though the sugar had held it together. Without its regular harvest *moliendas*, time was set adrift. The avocados were gathered once a year, the coffee was too, the market gardening kept only a handful of workers in full employment. A system of share-farming was devised. I spent my time with Iseult, with the sheep, with the dogs and with Matilde and Benito. Coromoto, my first and last ally, no longer came to the house. She waited for me at its gate and accompanied me wherever I went around the *hacienda* but she told me that she was no longer allowed in the Casa Grande. Someone had to be the scapegoat with the other girls gone, I had known for some time that I should have really sent Coromoto away. As it was, Antonio had taken the decision out of my hands.

Abrán was talking about giving notice, there was less work to do, less need for him, less chance of his making enough money to buy himself a car and keep it running (something he had set his heart on doing), and an ever-increasing chance that he would fall out seriously with his boss. I asked him to stay on for six months to 'see if things blew over'. He agreed, but I could see he must have thought me as much in orbit as my husband if I thought that anything other than disaster was going to blow over the Casa Grande. I sensed that when Abrán left, so would the *comadre* Matilde, and I had become very dependent on her. It was 1978. I had spent a year doing what seemed like very little other than sifting a monotonous routine through my hands.

I had written a great many short stories based on the tales of Benito Mendoza, *comadre* Matilde and Luis Daniel. I felt confident that despite my by then total lack of success at Monte Avila, the publishing house in Caracas which had agreed to publish me years before but done nothing, I would one day find a publisher. Meanwhile, Renato Rodriguez, the novelist, had translated some of them into Spanish. I spent all my evenings and much of the night typing them out on the old typewriter, keeping them safe and reading them. I had also honed down my poems to a collection, which I typed and retyped so many times it must have almost run to a full edition.

Without the sugar, I was less tied down by the *hacienda* and freer to travel. I spent several days with Ana Enriqueta Terán, the poet who was Luis Daniel's sister. She had not lived in the Andes for many years, but she had distilled some of its magic into her house on the Caribbean island of Margarita. She had a deep, throaty voice which she hushed dramatically when she talked. She used the words of her everyday life like spells. She described the past of the Momboy valley with a sense of awe. She had a love of poetry so great that there seemed to be no division between her life and her work. She encouraged me to write and to fight for my work. She described her life in Paris in the 1930s, in Buenos Aires in the 1940s, and in a little house by the sea called La Gaviota, where she had lived for many years. Her house was like a safe haven, a time-warped, misplaced version of what the Casa Grande would have been like without the violence and the changes that hung over it like a double-edged blade. She said, 'Listen to the River, listen to the Momboy. Don't just touch the earth, taste it.'

I was tempted to cry on Ana Enriqueta's shoulder, to confess my loneliness and fears to her. I was moved by her so much that the lump in my throat being near her brought me prevented me from speaking much at all. I never knew where to begin. I sensed that with her deep understanding of life she could have helped me and perhaps Jaime too. She had written, long ago,

> *La soledad me envia mensajeros de llanto,*
> *los recibo en los mares nocturnos de mi pecho . . .*
> *(Loneliness sends me messengers of weeping,*
> *I receive them in the night seas of my breast . . .)*

So she knew not only about *trapiches* and poetry, *la gente* and their magic, she knew about loneliness too. But she didn't know anything about Jaime's state of mind and I thought, if Luis Daniel who dotes on her and is close to her and who does know, hasn't seen fit to say anything, then neither will I.

When I went away from Santa Rita, I took to spending time with Luis Daniel's and Ana Enriqueta's other sister, La Bebella. In her house, I could relax entirely. Iseult and I spent many weeks, on and off in the villa she lived in on the hills above Caracas. It was there that I drew strength for my return trips to the bewildering cycle of toil and sabotage on the *hacienda*. By 1977 the years of kidney infections that had run almost unabated ever since my arrival had taken their toll and permanently damaged my kidneys. I had grown so used to the dull ache that I hardly noticed it any more, but the recurrent haemorrhages and accompanying fevers were finally breaking into my life not as the irritating heckler but as the capricious dictator. La Bebella took me in many times and nursed me back to health. Just stopping sometimes from the routine of the long days and the endless chores, was, in itself, a cure. Iseult loved staying at La Bebella's and so did Joanna when she came to visit. Physically, I knew, I still looked like a child despite my twenty-three years, but spiritually the *hacienda* had prematurely aged me.

I spent less and less time in Caracas itself and at El Chicken Bar. I found myself less and less able to equate the contrast of its Bohemian atmosphere with the grim realities of my estate. I was writing much more and feeling, therefore, less need to talk about what I was going to do, so the security of its raucous debates seemed less important. Also, being unable to drink any alcohol because of my kidneys, I lost pace with the crowd of drinkers. Friends I had made round its tables came out to Santa Rita to visit me there. 'El Chicken' made me think of my grandfather, who had been gassed in the First World War and had had to live, on doctors' orders, all his life in wide open spaces. I too seemed to need the wide open spaces. I needed to be in the purple hills of the estate, or in its enchanted rifts. I needed to stand in a place so quiet I could listen to the river speak. The most built-up areas I could tolerate in this state of galloping neurasthenia were roaming around the Casa Grande or the abandoned brick terraces of the disused *trapiche*.

Interleaved with the depression and the sense of decay, I think I enjoyed myself more in my last years on the plantation than I ever had before. I had time for myself, and my own space. In 1975 I moved from Iseult's bedroom to the old wooden wing of the house. I had spent most of my nights in Iseult's room from her babyhood, nominally to nurse her, but actually staying over when she was well. The nights I spent in the master bedroom were few and far between and not ones I was anxious to repeat. This regime had initially been imposed by Jaime as part of his 'A serious man doesn't touch his wife after she has forced him to have a platinum jaw' routine. But it actually suited me down to the ground. I didn't feel personally responsible for his own rigid grimace, but I did like to keep as much distance between us as was tactically possible.

In 1975, though, I moved officially into the wooden rooms, complete with study and balcony and a staircase that creaked, so it gave me warning of anyone lurking on its treads.

I had grown so used to my fifteen-hour days of things to do for *la gente*, the house and the estate, that I seemed to be deliciously idle when the sugar ceased.

The *compadre* who had helped with the green boy, Carlos Vethencourt, had fourteen sons and daughters. Four of these became my close friends and regular visitors to the *hacienda*. They came and helped me with whatever needed doing, enjoyed the freedom of the estate, taught me to dance the *paso doble* in the big sitting room with the marble floor and took me out to picnics on the edge of Lake Maracaibo at a place called Gibraltar.

Gibraltar was a revelation. I loved it on sight. It was originally a village of runaway slaves who hid there before their liberation in 1810 and then stayed. It was hidden from the rest of the world by great swathes of sugar-cane, grown in bulk to feed the Central Refinery. It opened out on to a white sandy beach. Behind the beach was a band of virgin rain forest in which their clearing had been made. The people of Gibraltar fished for food when they were hungry, or ate plantains, bananas and coconuts (which grew all around them wild and in natural abundance) when they couldn't be bothered. Their

entire lives were spent rocking in fibre hammocks and drinking rot-gut rum. The only work they did was to steal the cane
to make this rum and then distil it. They had lived like that,
cut off from the world since the time of their ancestors' escape.
The horrors of slavery seemed to be stamped on their sub-
conscious, because their freedom was spent in an idleness so
complete it had to be a reaction.

Because of their isolation, they had preserved many of their
African customs, the principal of which was their festival of the
Cimbanguele, an arcane rite that was performed every year.
Although they didn't work to earn a living, they worked hard
in their preparation for this festival of dance and rum. At the
Cimbanguele everyone in the village regardless of age, sex or
infirmity danced themselves into a trance. Someone in the
1930s had discovered Gibraltar and tried to convert it to
Catholicism. A small concrete church, no bigger than a truck,
had been built. In it nothing remained except for a peeling,
battered St Benito made out of plaster. St Benito was the
black saint with blue eyes beloved of Venezuelans. For hour
after hour and day after day the half-naked black community
of Gibraltar danced to the African rhythms of their drums. If
there had been drought in the previous year and the fruit for
their picking was scarce, then the statue of St Benito that was
jogged around by the dancers was thrown unceremoniously
into the sea. If it had rained and all was well, then the saint
was danced along the beach, back through the belt of forest
along their secret paths and back to the church which was one
in name only and in that it housed a saint.

In the 1950s the dictator, Perez Jimenez, had ordained that
Gibraltar should become a major inland port. An enormous
jetty was built out into the salt-water lake and a town was
planned on its shores. A hundred houses were built along

carefully gridded tarmac streets. Each house, in contrast to shacks of the village of Gibraltar, was properly roofed and each had a wide roof terrace on which one could lie and look at the stars. The floors were tiled, there were windows and floors and each bungalow had from four to eight rooms. After the dictatorship was ousted, but before the new town of Gibraltar had been given its finishing touches, the project was abandoned and the jungle claimed back the land that had been carved out of it. Most of the new town was swallowed up by the rampant forest and its undergrowth, but the last row of houses, the ones built, literally, on the edge of the sand, was only partially veiled by giant weeds and creepers.

Together with the Vethencourts, Abrán and a couple of workers borrowed from the *hacienda* to hack their way through the encroaching jungle, we freed three of these bungalows and used them to camp in, on our increasingly frequent visits to Gibraltar. The sea was warm and pale green, the beach was lined with palm trees, the sun shone all day and the beautiful rain forest displayed its green treasures and its wild orchids and its parrots, monkeys and snakes. Abrán would drop us off, complete with coconut oil for the sun and a hamper of food and a container of drinking water, and pick us up a couple of days later, to bump along the dust road tracks through Caja Seca and Mototán to Valera, Carmania and the *hacienda*.

Despite the poverty of the rough reed shacks with their roofs made out of layers of palm leaves, their sandy floors and lack of space, none of the barefoot villagers had ever moved, or wanted to move into the new town on the other side of the strip of jungle from their clearing, only 800 metres away. They beat a little track through the forest with their bare feet, fished with simple lines and nets made of lianas, caught more

fish than they could ever eat and asked for nothing more than
to be left in peace.

During all the time I spent in Gibraltar, I only really managed to make contact with a couple of children and a blind
woman called Alminda Rosa. We were sitting on the beach
feeling hot and hungry. The food we had brought had long
since run out and our day trip was proving more exhausting
than we had thought. Juan Carlos Vethencourt and two of his
sisters were nursing their sunburn, Mary was nursing Iseult's
and I was nursing mine. Somebody said, 'I wish we had some
chilli fritters.' Somebody else told them not to be daft on that
long, utterly deserted beach. Within minutes of this wish, a
very tall, very black woman, dressed in a multi-coloured skirt
down to her bare feet and a wrap-around top, came walking
towards us with a big cane-fibre basket on her head.

She was singing rather than calling out, 'Chilli fritters, chilli
fritters.'

Sure enough, hot from her stove were five tiny fritters. She
seemed to be coming straight towards us. We stopped talking
in our surprise and she came up and nearly tripped over our
legs. She was blind, her eyes the blue of streaked speedwells
from cataracts.

Alminda Rosa seemed as pleased to meet us as we were to
see her. She took us back to her shack, which was on its own
near the water's edge not far from where we were sitting,
though camouflaged by undergrowth. She said that every day
she made chilli fritters for her daughter with star apple and fish.

'They were her favourites, you know. I never know when
she's coming back, so I have them ready.'

Mary asked what everyone was thinking, how could she
afford to buy the oil for such a luxury in a place where
nobody worked and no money seemed to change hands?

Alminda Rosa sighed and smiled, 'I used to live like that too,' she said, 'but then my daughter upped and left with one of the builders. I know she'll be back any day now, but I don't know when, so I keep the fritters ready because she always liked them hot about this time when the sun is hottest. I make baskets out of the cane leaves and sometimes I give them to a fisherman who comes by here, he brings me oil and maize flour. That's the kind of girl I had; couldn't be doing with yucca and plantains in sea water like other folk, she was a fine girl, like a lady, and she wanted maize flour, like a lady too.'

'When were the builders here then?' I asked. She looked puzzled. 'The ones your daughter left with.'

'Oh,' she said, 'that's about a year ago now when they built the new town. Don't you worry, though, that girl will be coming right back, I know it.'

Her daughter had been gone for twenty-five years and never once returned, yet Alminda Rosa spent her days in happy preparation, slaying the fatted calf of guddled fish and singing to herself.

I read and wrote and thought at Gibraltar. I bathed in the tepid lake, but mostly I lay in the sun and lazed like a lizard that has just escaped its prey, basking while the gentle tide lapped in and out across the fine hot sand.

27

AFTER SIX MONTHS Abrán gave me his notice to quit as he had said he would. He had been offered a good job as a mechanic in Valera in which he saw a future for himself.

'The land is dying, Doña,' he said.

The land itself was actually recovering slowly from the drought and the fires, but the way of life of the old *haciendas* was dying and I knew it as well as he. He told me that soon Matilde would have to go too.

'My mother is old, Doña, too old for the things that happen in your house.'

This was the most direct mention of anything untoward happening at the Casa Grande. Antonio Moreno and Benito turned blind eyes and never spoke of anything beyond the things that happened on the *hacienda*. Again, I knew that he was right. As Luis Daniel had pointed out, it was I who had married the man, not anyone else. I wondered for how long I would be able to run the Casa Grande on my own. It didn't seem right to subject any new maids to its sporadic madness and it didn't seem safe.

I had one month of grace before Matilde departed, one

month to say goodbye to the Casa Grande before I moved back to the little house I had so disliked by the *trapiche*. It would be easier to run. It had far fewer exits and entrances. It had to be approached from the front. In it, I would be safer than I could be in the big house. Also if, as I felt becoming inevitable, I had to make my escape with Iseult, I would leave no staff behind me to bear the consequences of my flight.

During my last six months in Venezuela, I played with fire. Jaime was dangerously suicidal and had been for several years. When I say dangerously, it was because his plan, which he had shared with me now several times, was to take his wife and child with him and thus, he said, finish what General Polidoro Africano, the youngest general ever in the Venezuelan army, had started with the massacre of the family Terán.

The magnolia tree in the hill town of Escuque marked the safe return of Rodolfo Terán, the lone survivor of the bloody feud. The magnolia tree in our garden had died in the drought. Most of the other Teráns, Don Felipe Neri and all his clan, were from another branch of the family, but the main line was the main line and he was the decider of its destiny.

For me to stay was to court disaster, to leave was to lose the one place that had finally come to feel like home and to betray *la gente*. To stay meant a home to offer to my mother, financial security, and a life that I liked in a place I loved. To go was to live safely with a small child to support and nothing to feed her on but my mother's charity. Joanna desperately wanted to retire; after a long, hard-working life she was on the brink of doing so. I had promised to support her. How could I ask her to support me? And yet, what good would my many skills be in England? I was a sugar planter, a factory overseer, a grafter of avocado pears, a tropical market gardener, a stitcher of wounds, an expert lowerer of fevers and eliminator of parasites, what use would any of these things be in London? I was a writer, I had written a lot, but I had never published anything. I was a dreamer and a hoper of miracles, but never so unrealistic as to hope that I could support Iseult and myself from being published. I had failed to sit the last part of my A level exams at the crammers, I had no qualifications at all, not even enough to go to university and get some. What job, I wondered, would I be able to do after running the *hacienda*?

So, while Jaime hatched his plans, I hatched mine. I had to solve the problem of what to do with an estate full of peasant workers and their families, fourteen dogs, ducks, chickens, cats, geese, three cows and 480 sheep. The men who dug their way out of Colditz and escaped, carried the earth from their tunnel in their trouser legs and shook it out over the prison yard. Cows, sheep and people were less smuggleable. I had to dismantle the complex machinery I had spent the last six years setting up. Once again, everything pointed to moving back to the little house. There, I would have an excuse, at least, for giving away most of the livestock.

I lied and cheated systematically for many months to get out of Venezuela. Almost every step I took, towards the end, was part of a careful plan. Luis Daniel had been urging me to leave for years, but he had also warned me to be careful, since to do so was to risk my life. He cited three members of the family who had lost their lives trying. Another cousin of his same generation, whom I scarcely knew, and had never really liked, came by the Casa Grande every couple of months and when no one was listening, he said, 'Veta, don't even think of running away, you won't make it past the state boundary.'

When he first started saying this, I wasn't thinking of doing it. But once I did, I bore his advice in mind. I believed that if

I tried to tell Jaime that I was leaving him I wouldn't have survived to run out of the house, let alone reach the road and the state boundary. He was not someone I could talk to, he was not someone anyone could cross or defy. My running away was one thing, the mess I left behind me was another.

I had been ill for a long time, the state of my kidneys was serious enough to warrant my being sent out of the country for treatment abroad. I had been under treatment from various specialists in Valera, Merida and Caracas for years and none had been able to put a permanent stop to the recurrent haemorrhages that accompanied the many infections which lodged there. They had warned me that if my condition flared up again, I could die. My kidneys, which had caused me so much grief, were to be my passport to safety. It was only a matter of time.

Antonio Moreno said to me before I left the Casa Grande, 'Don't stay for us, Doña, we survived before you came and we'll survive after you leave us. How long do you think you'll survive the way things are heading? Go while you can. You can't save us, and we can't save you.'

I could have left at any time during any of my trips away from the *hacienda*, but I couldn't have taken Iseult with me. Iseult was Venezuelan; because she had been born out of England, she had been refused a British passport. By British law, she was entitled only to take the nationality of her father. In order to travel out of the state of Trujillo with her, I had to have a signed document from her father. In Venezuela women had no rights over their children. Without this document, I could not take her to Caracas, let alone abroad. If, as I once thought of doing, I procured false documents for her, Jaime would know immediately who had helped me to get them. To escape like that would have been not only to ask Otto to betray his one-time best friend, it was to leave a trail that led right back to Otto's own doorstep.

I would somehow have to get the documents legally from the Court of Minors and get Jaime to sign them. This, too, would take time and a small miracle to enable him to be approachable. If I was so ill I had to go abroad for treatment, it was logical to go to England and the National Health Service. If I were to go to England, the logical thing would be to take Iseult to see Joanna.

Meanwhile I kept hoping: maybe Jaime would change, maybe he would get well again, maybe get some treatment. Maybe I would be able to stay, turn the avocado plantation into a co-operative, and keep the *hacienda* going while moving it into the twentieth century. Maybe the violence would stop, the urge to die in a family pact would stop, the woodworm would stop dropping piles of fine powder on the floors, where they were chewing down the fabric of the Casa Grande. Maybe the distillers would stop setting fire to the hills.

The first avocado groves we had planted bore fruit and money began to pour in. Meanwhile, the trickle of families who left the estate began to swell to a tearful exodus. For people who had lived on the same land for as many generations as *la gente*, and who feared to even cross the road, let alone travel along it, moving was a desperate last resort. I tried in vain to persuade some of the families I knew best to stay. They no longer saw me as able to protect them. As some of them pointed out, I couldn't protect myself. They had borne all they could.

'What would happen to us, if anything happened to you, Doña?', one of them asked me.

I couldn't protect them from anybody's wrath, but I could protect them from being turned off. Doña Antonieta, my mother-in-law, had long been lobbying for a partition of the *hacienda*. She would never have consented to any of the land, however meagre a strip, being made over to the workers. However, if the *hacienda* were legally partitioned (as it should have been twenty years before under the terms of my father-in-law's will) then Doña Antonieta would no longer be a signatory to any subsequent subdivisions. If Antonio Moreno, Antonio José (now newly married), Ramón Rivas and the others all owned the land their huts were on, they could subsistence farm them with the market gardening we had perfected, plant avocados with the help of Antonio José, and no one could either turn them off or starve them out.

This plan was not mine. It was Jaime who had first broached it to me in England. Lawyers were brought in to expedite a partition in 1975, and by the end of 1978 the estate was officially divided. We had been paying out allowances to Doña Antonieta since the first *molienda* and she was not entirely happy at the idea of losing what would undoubtedly be a hefty revenue when the avocado groves grew into full production. To sweeten the pill, I threw in the Casa Grande as part of her share. In 1975 when she had first asked for it, I had refused. I seemed to be being suddenly generous, when in fact I was pursuing my own plan.

For the last two months before I left Venezuela, I lived in the little house by the *trapiche*. The pretty cottage that had been out of bounds when I first lived there, and which had been my late father-in-law's workshop, had been cleared out and whitewashed anew and it became my and Iseult's room. It had, in the style of a Tuscan farmhouse, a wide wooden balcony at one end, and here we slept.

The tension during the last months was almost unbearable. It had been at other times before, but I didn't know if it was because Jaime had somehow got hold of my elaborate plan to flee, or whether it was just the usual angst of his mind. I told no one of my plan, not even Joanna. I felt that in order to succeed, it had to be carried out in utmost secrecy. One word or one snippet of gossip, one clue left carelessly uncovered, and all would be lost.

The pressure to enact the family pact was also growing. I had to find excuses for not willingly laying down my own and my daughter's lives just yet, while still appearing to be enthusiastic about it for some date in the near future. When my excuses seemed lame or flat, Jaime would say, 'Maybe it's better if I just come in in the night with a shotgun, maybe it's simpler like that.'

Every night I went to bed wondering if tonight would be the night. I searched his pockets while he was out, and he searched mine. I learnt, among other things, that he had copied the key to my room. Every night I retired at the same time as Iseult, at seven o'clock, and locked us in. I stuffed pillows into our rumpled bed and then lifted her, sleeping, up into the loft, then followed her there. Under my pillow, safe from her hands, I kept my Smith & Wesson fully loaded. My aim wasn't very good, but it was adequate. If he came in and shot into our bed, I would have the advantage of a few seconds over him.

Despite all the momentary excitements and calamities on the *hacienda*, the overriding general pattern was that nothing happened. Days became weeks, weeks months and months years and it always seemed that nothing happened. Despite all the tension and the sleepless, apprehensive nights, nothing happened. Rather, nothing happened in my room, but the state of my kidneys deteriorated and the weekly analyses showed that despite the bombardment of antibiotics, the infection was getting worse. I looked suitably ill, the shadows under my eyes told everyone so. The doctor was urging me to go abroad and to hurry. It wouldn't do to have a kidney failure on the *hacienda*. It wouldn't do for anyone to say I had been neglected. 'Qué dirán, qué dirán?' Everyone was urging me to go, and I knew that when Jaime cruised round the town, people were stopping him to tell him too. 'Why didn't I go?' 'What was I waiting for?'

I wanted to take Iseult, it took time to get her papers in order to leave, the permits needed to enable me, her mother, to travel with her.

'Hurry it up,' they told him. 'If anything happens you don't want to be to blame. Qué dirán?'

I got the papers I needed a week before Christmas. The lead up to La Noche Buena was always a time of heavy drinking. Things were always worse when Jaime was drunk. After months of hardly noticing me, except to tell me of his pact (*our* supposed pact), he decided that we should do the Christmas rounds together and visit everyone. I feared the scenes that inevitably followed such visits, yet I feared more rocking the delicate balance of our raft. I talked avocados as I never had before. I knew so much more about them that I could keep his attention away from other sources of rage and paranoia as effectively as a sedative. I was ruthless in the use of his old cipher, as hard as the tropical greenheart wood which was the hardest wood of all, denser than iron and used for naval coffins. I wrote:

> *I could pull the trigger*
> *On your interest. I could hear*
> *Your voice and not the silence.*
> *I could feel you cared.*
> *So I would say, 'avocado'*
> *When my face ached,*
> *Or a dog died,*
> *Or a wheel broke on the cart*

The Hacienda

And a spoke stabbed old Molinas;
'Avocado' when the river spilled
Over our kitchen and the mud
Was worse than the flood and it
Left a dead pig in the hall.

When I had news for you,
I came to say,
'Avocado',
The one way to know that I
Was not alone was to say 'avocado',
And discuss the sheen on a Winslowson,
And compare the flesh of Trapp to Nellan.
Fear was a root fungus,
We could share at any time
By scraping mould from
The seeds. We could pare the tops,
Put them in the black bags,
Dig in their beds of compost.

I would save the best till last:
Savour the grafts.
Moist shield-buds for a death,
Tightened stem-bands for mourning;
Strops and blades.
We discussed crushed Fuerte leaves,
And the blighted scions of other stock.
The mating flowers were
A tribute to our cross-pollination.
A, b, a, b,
Row upon row,
I need you now:

Say, 'Avocado'.
I was your shadow
On the marble stair.
After ten years
You were still the same stranger,
But the orchard thrived.
When I needed you, you were
Never there. I didn't know
There was a code then. I learnt to say
'Avocado' later, and you cared.
So when my face ached,
Or a dog died,
Or a wheel broke on the cart
I had a way to touch your heart.

28

LA NOCHE BUENA took me all around the neighbourhood. We went to the *páramo* to greet a cousin in Timotes and drove back from its chill mists and the rich blue-greens of its strips of cabbages and its straggling oats to the brighter greens, already scorched at the edges, of Valera. We visited house after house and ate more than our fill of spiced *ayacas*. Because of all the outings, there was no time to even go through the motions of doing Christmas at home which was, in a way, a relief. How long could the avocado conversation sustain us if we were on our own? It was my seventh Venezuelan Christmas.

One year when Joanna had come out, I had fattened a turkey for a traditional English Christmas dinner. She brought the recipe with her. It said, 'Feed the turkey a glass of sherry and then make it run for ten minutes to loosen and tenderise the muscles.' It didn't say how Joanna, Benito and I were to make the turkey drink the sherry, nor how to make the drunken bird get back up on its feet.

Joanna didn't know I was going back. I needed her letters and messages to keep flowing. I needed it to look as though I were staying. She had never been able to lie. If I had told her, her letters back might have given me away. I was dreading having to tell her, when I arrived in London, that I had not only run away, but I would have to keep running. Mimita, one of the twins, had decided to come with me to London. She had no idea that I was not planning to return. I was supposed to go away for two months, and during those months I was safe. After that, I imagined, the problems would begin. Jaime had said that if I ever left him he would scour the earth to find me and wreak his revenge.

I had saved up enough money to support us for a year; after that I had no plans. I had transferred the pieces of land to the workers, giving Antonio a piece of the orchard to support him, he was eighty-six years old. I had found farms and homes for all the animals. I had saved the short stories and poems I wanted to keep and burnt all the rest, together with all my other papers, letters and my most personal things. I would, supposedly, be travelling light and coming back laden. That was the way, so I only had one suitcase for me and one for Iseult. To take any more would arouse suspicion.

The last three days on the *hacienda*, I spent alone with Iseult. Jaime didn't come home, which made it easier for me to make my farewells to the *gente*, although there was nothing easy about them, knowing, as I did, that I was not coming back. Every morning, Coromoto waited for me by the already crumbling Casa Grande, and we talked in its empty halls. I promised to write to her, although Antonio and Abrán had told me that no one would bother to keep or deliver letters to *la gente*. Mine only arrived because I was a lady, theirs never would. Some of the boys who had been pressganged away to the army must have written (there were scribes who wrote letters for people who couldn't read or write), but no word had ever come. Coromoto was fifteen, as sweet and as sulky as ever, and didn't know what to do with her life. She gave me a bracelet of *pepa de san pablo* seeds to ward off the evil eye. I gave her the gold chain that I always wore and that she had always coveted.

I spent my last night lying awake listening to the surrounding noises more intently than ever, on the alert for the turning of a copied key in my lock. I kept the Smith & Wesson close by my hand. Like so much else, I would be leaving it behind. I had worn it tucked into my waistband by day. The poor carried machetes, the rich carried guns. The gecko which shared my room scuffed along a rafter. *La gente* were afraid of geckos. They said they climbed inside virgin girls. They killed them on sight, beating them with brooms. I liked my gecko with its child-like hands and its long translucent fingers. It killed mosquitoes and dulled the incessant whirring that was a part of every night. A death's head moth was flapping somewhere in the room.

Outside the cicadas were tuning up the orchestra that never tuned. Frogs were croaking, the two remaining beagles were barking, the millrace trickled.

The bush of night-flowering jasmine that hugged the workshop filled the air with its cloying sweetness, blending with the scent of distant wild lilies that grew on the banks of the Momboy. Everything was overlaid by the ground smell of damp tropical soil, the rich smother of fertile earth laden with undergrowth. My books still had a waft of kerosene, and the floor of lingering creosote.

Cockroaches rustled across the floor and furniture. They sounded like rubbed silk, like hushed voices gossiping. A nightingale sang from within the bamboo glade. From somewhere in the abandoned *trapiche* a barn owl cried. I heard the river hurrying by: the Momboy that filled and emptied in a parody of life. It seemed to be whispering over its stones. I had listened to it many times, trying to decipher what it had to say. Now that I was going away, its babbling sounded clearer. It seemed to say, 'Qué dirán, qué dirán, qué dirán?'

Iseult and I left the *hacienda* on New Year's day of 1979.

The people of the Hacienda Santa Rita have been the greatest influence on my life and work. Although I have not returned, I know (filtered through a grapevine that straddles oceans) that everything has changed now. The Casa Grande has fallen down. The fields are overgrown, and everyone I knew has either died or moved away. They feared change so much that they feared the road that brought it. They feared that a time would come when no one would remember them any more. They feared it more than death. They never believed that the language I spoke with Joanna made any sense. By remembering them in it, and not in their own cristiano, I hope that I haven't betrayed the sense of life as distilled by them on the *hacienda*.